T0090053

The ULTIMATE Girls' Movie SURVIVAL GUIDE

What to Rent, Who to Watch, How to Deal

Andrea Sarvady

Illustrations by Jamie Bennett

SIMON SPOTLIGHT ENTERTAINMENT
New York · London · Toronto · Sydney

SIMON SPOTLIGHT ENTERTAINMENT
An imprint of Simon & Schuster
Children's Publishing Division
1230 Avenue of the Americas
New York, New York 10020

A Quirk Packaging Book
Design by Lynne Yeamans

Manufactured in the U.S.A.
First Edition 10 9 8 7 6 5 4 3 2 1

Library of Congress Cataloging-in-Publication Data

Sarvady, Andrea Cornell
 The ultimate girls' movie survival guide : what to rent, who to watch, how
to deal / by Andrea Sarvady ; illustrated by Jamie Bennett.— 1st ed.
     p. cm.
 Includes index.
 ISBN 978-0-6898-7373-7
 1. Young adult films—Catalogs. 2. Motion pictures for women—Catalogs.
3. Teenagers in motion pictures. I. Title.
PN1995.9.Y54S27 2004
791.43'75'0835—dc22
                              2004012240

WARNING
THE ULTIMATE GIRLS' MOVIE SURVIVAL GUIDE contains the ideas and opinions of its author alone (tragically misguided though they may appear to some of you), and is designed to provide useful, entertaining information about the featured movies. The PUBLISHER, AUTHOR, AND PACKAGER do not claim that the information contained herein is complete or accurate for your specific situation. It should by no means be considered a substitute for good judgment, skill, and common sense. In addition, neither the AUTHOR, PACKAGER, nor the PUBLISHER endorses or encourages any irresponsible (or any other) behaviors depicted in these films, and specifically disclaims responsibility for any liability, loss, damage, or injury allegedly arising from any information or suggestions in this book. We strongly refute any rumors you may have heard that a thorough reading of this guide will result in whiter teeth, shinier hair, or a date with a really cute movie star.

Please note that no amount of movie-watching, no matter how hot the leads or rockin' the soundtrack, will compensate for serious help if something is seriously wrong in your life. So when do we recommend that you get off your couch and go sit on one owned by some nice therapist? The general rule-of-thumb is if you are a danger to yourself (like, your mind or body), a danger to someone else (like, their mind or body), or if someone in your life is making you feel unsafe, it's go-time. If any of the above is true, call suicide prevention or your local mental health agency to find out where you can get confidential, affordable care. Now, of course, if things aren't that bad, just relax and enjoy the show. Do we have a deal?

Contents

Ultimate Girl Trailer

Ask some people their favorite movie and they kind of freeze up, don't they? Not because they don't have one; everyone has at least one. No, it's because they're afraid that it's TMI—Too Much Information. The movies we like, to some degree, give us away. Movies also tell us about ourselves. Stroll through a video store and you'll figure out what kind of mood you're in and what's on your mind. Had a rough day and need to vent? You find yourself picking up *Buffy the Vampire Slayer*. Need life to be what it should be, not what it is? You grab *Sixteen Candles*. For two hours you kick some vampires to the curb, or live in the kind of world where the cutest guy in school likes you just because you like him.

The Ultimate Girls' Movie Survival Guide takes a look at the movies that focus on the major challenges of adolescence: love complications, family strife, friends and enemies, body image angst, issues of goals and identity. You know, life while conscious. For those times when you're not sure what you're feeling—and don't we all have those days?—our mood controls will help you identify your current mood.

Friends can help when you've just got to talk. But sometimes all you want to do is pop in a video, curl up on the sofa, and watch people your own age dramatize what you're feeling. Sure, maybe their skin is much clearer than yours and they get paid to cry, but they're there for you. They get you to laugh or inspire you to try again or motivate you to change something. Maybe they just give you two hours of insight that you forget the minute the lights come up. So what? It's cheaper than therapy—and you can wear your bunny slippers.

So how did we pick the movies profiled here? We talked to a lot of teenagers and to former teens who remember the movies that got them through and helped them deal. You may consider some of the older films to be cheesy at first, but give them a chance. Just because somebody moonwalks and dresses like a Madonna wannabe doesn't mean she's totally brain dead. (Okay, maybe that's a bad example.) We also did a ton of research to find movies that you might never have found on your own: foreign films, movies about teens more geared for adults, and movies beyond the selection of your average local video store.

Given that we think all these movies are worth watching, we've given each an Ultimate Girl Rating, judging the films by how well they inspire you to action, empathize with what you're going through, divert you from your troubles, or comfort you with a screen teen whose life is possibly far worse than yours.

Lots of movies that teenage girls love have nothing to do with being a teenage girl, but we had to narrow the viewing field down to around a hundred films. To accomplish this, we invented some basic rules. With few exceptions, the movies we selected were released within the last twenty years, and generally center on girls coping with one thing or another. A few movies feature sensitive teenage boys, or people who are technically past adolescence but face similar issues.

Needless to say, a film guide intended for middle school girls and those off at college is going to include both *The Princess Diaries* and *Thirteen* within its pages. We trust you to read the description and see if the movie is right for you. To help with that decision, we've included all the MPAA ratings. Movies are often rated R for graphic sex or violence, of course, but if the rating is for other reasons, we've tried to let you know. However, we don't put a little artistic nudity or words that you probably hear everyday at school on the same plane as graphic violence—and maybe your folks don't either.

Now, we know how movie buffs are: opinionated, persnickety, prone to loving certain movies beyond reason. So be forewarned: there will be films you'll be amazed not to find in here. The film that changed your life was quite possibly left out of this collection. For this, we can only apologize in advance. We talked to as many teens as we could. We didn't have your phone number. Or maybe we called, and your mom lied about you not being home. She didn't want you telling us that your favorite movie is *Throw Momma from the Train*. For the most part, though, we think you'll be pleased. You'll be reminded of some old celluloid friends, and introduced to some new ones. You can take this book with you to the video store and everyone will think you're a film student working on a paper, and the cute video clerk will want to talk to you, or you'll get inspired to go to film school and make something better than anything written up in these pages. Opportunity abounds.

Anyway. We can't promise that a movie will fix whatever in your life needs fixing, but sometimes spending a couple of hours watching someone else try to deal is a welcome vacation from your own reality. It's not easy, this life. You're just trying to find your own voice, your own way, and everyone always has so much advice for you: "Just get over him." "Just focus on your studies." "Just get into a good college." "Just don't get into trouble." "Just be yourself."

We've got one more, if you can bear to hear it. "Life getting you down? Just press PLAY."

How to Use This Guide

We know what you're thinking. "I need instructions to program my TiVo, not to use a movie guide!" You're right. This isn't so much a guide to understanding the various categories as an explanation of what we were thinking when we created them. There's some variation within each entry, but listed below are a few categories you'll find within every review.

Mood Control: Sometimes you want a movie to echo your mood and sometimes you want it to lift you out of it. That's where the Mood Control comes in. It includes twelve buttons representing a variety of moods, from Ambitious to Heartbroken to Playful. If you find yourself experiencing the highlighted moods, then consider watching the recommended movie. It might sustain a positive mood (HOPEFUL), pull you out of a negative one (DEPRESSED), or just give you someone to relate to on the screen (ARTSY).

Ultimate Girl Rating: We've judged these movies more on their ability to inspire or empathize than for their brilliant cinematography or Oscar-worthy acting. Here's how the UG ratings add up:

🌸🌸🌸🌸🌸 An Ultimate Girl must-see.

🌸🌸🌸🌸 This movie rocks.

🌸🌸🌸 We're feelin' this film.

🌸🌸 You could do worse (you know you have!)

Birthplace: Is this a mainstream film or an independent, local or foreign born? We thought you'd want to know.

File Under: A snappy phrase that sums up the movie.

The Problem: What problem in your life might this film address?

The Reel Deal: We introduce the main players and kick-start the plot.

Line That Says It All: This is not necessarily the best line in the film; often it isn't, because those lines work best in context. It's just a bit of dialogue that captures the mood or theme of the story.

Girl to Watch, Guy to Watch: You can figure this one out.

Scene Worth the Rewind: Don't be mad if we didn't pick your favorite scene to share with other readers. We only had room for one!

Watch This One With: Who in your life might like this film?

Movie(s) with the Same Vibe: Here we've tried to suggest movies that are similar in mood or theme. ("Also Check Out" indicates a likeminded movie not written up in this guide.)

How It Helps: Explains how each movie addresses a problem you might have. We hope you'll find value in watching the selected movies, whether they give you hope, give you laughs, or just make you feel less alone in this crazy world.

Now—go watch some movies!

Feature Presentations

Adventures in Babysitting

1987 ULTIMATE GIRL RATING: 🍀 🍀 🍀 🍀

DIRECTOR: Chris Columbus
BIRTHPLACE: Mainstream Hollywood
FILE UNDER: Alice in Urbanland
RATED: PG-13

STARRING: Elisabeth Shue, Maia Brewton, Keith Coogan, Anthony Rapp, Calvin Levels, Vincent D'Onofrio, Penelope Ann Miller, George Newbern, John Ford Noonan, Lolita Davidovich

THE PROBLEM

Your life is incredibly boring. You feel like nothing ever happens to you. If these are supposedly such amazing years, why are you spending them in your sweats watching bad television? We could recommend a million cool activities to jumpstart your life. Better yet, stay in those sweats and watch the Night From Hell unfold in this charming, exciting, funny film. It may only solve the boredom issue for an hour and a half, but "Oh, the places you'll go!"

The Reel Deal: Chris (Elisabeth Shue) is eagerly awaiting a big night out in downtown Chicago with her boyfriend. When he calls and cancels, she reluctantly agrees to babysit for Brad and Sara Anderson (Keith Coogan and Maia Brewton) while their folks head into town for a big office party. Not long after the job begins, Chris gets a frantic call from her best friend, Brenda (Penelope Ann Miller), whose aborted attempt at running away has landed her in seedy circumstances. Chris, with kids in tow, borrows her mom's car to rescue Brenda. Things would have been just fine except—well, everything else that follows.

Suffice it to say that criminals are part of the mix, from low-level car thieves to mobsters, and that blues club jammin' and frat house hijinks make an appearance. You'll marvel at the film's ability to take a small detail from earlier in the movie and tie it into the ever-thickening plot.

Line That Says It All: "Don't mess with the babysitter!"

Girl to Watch: The main character, Chris, is played just right by Elisabeth Shue. Chris is a total babe, but she's also totally sure of herself and her values, and it shows in how she handles both the good guys and the bad guys—who switch places sometimes, just like they do in real life.

Guy to Watch: All the male actors are lots of fun, but when boyfriend Mike finally shows up, you'll go, "Wait! Isn't that that dude from *The West Wing* that my mom thinks is so hot but who reminds me of a nerdy social studies teacher?" His name is Bradley Whitford, and you would be right.

Scene Worth the Rewind: The restaurant confrontation. We love those, don't we?

Fashion to Catch: It's all so very '80s. The best fashion item has to be little Sara Anderson's Thor hat. Apparently, it's her dream to be (or at least to meet) the Norse god Thor. Can you say *quirky*?

Watch This One With: Your fellow babysitters.

Movies with the Same Vibe: THE PRINCESS BRIDE, SIXTEEN CANDLES, FERRIS BUELLER'S DAY OFF.

HOW THIS MOVIE HELPS

Sometimes you just want to watch a movie that will take you on a ride, and this one does the trick. Yet if you're looking for more than that, you might find it here too. Sure, Chris and her young cohorts are basically catastrophe-slayers in a fun film that keeps the calamities coming. Yet it's also a story about a girl who discovers that it's kind of okay when your world falls apart if, at the same time, you get to learn that there's pretty much nothing you can't handle.

American Graffiti

MOOD CONTROL

1	2	3
4	5	6
7	8	9
10	11	12

▶ Press PLAY if you're feeling:

1 Adventurous
2 Ambitious
3 Artsy
4 Cynical
5 DEPRESSED
6 HEARTBROKEN
7 Hopeful
8 Insecure
9 Misunderstood
10 OVERWHELMED
11 Playful
12 Weird

1973 | **ULTIMATE GIRL RATING:** 🍿🍿🍿

DIRECTOR: George Lucas
BIRTHPLACE:
Mainstream U.S.A.
FILE UNDER:
The Mother of All Teen Movies
RATED: PG

STARRING: Richard Dreyfuss, Ron Howard, Paul Le Mat, Charles Martin Smith, Cindy Williams, Candy Clark, Mackenzie Phillips, Wolfman Jack, Bo Hopkins, Harrison Ford

THE PROBLEM

Is there a reason why so many teen movies take place right after high school ends and the future begins? Sure there is. After spending four years with every minute of the day divided up into working on someone else's priorities (go to Algebra 2, study for the history test, take the garbage out, eat your lima beans), suddenly it's your turn to be cruise director of the big Life Ship. Easy, right? It should be. Yet with the future at your command, it suddenly becomes hard to do anything but hang out with your friends and put major decisions on the slow boat to China. Or maybe the decisions have already been made, but there's still plenty of raw fear mixed in with the relief. And why shouldn't there be? Just because you're finally allowed to run your own life doesn't make you a pro at it. At some point, you'll get off the barge, jump in the car and speed away to your bright and shiny future. Right now, though? Going around in circles never looked so good.

The Reel Deal: It's 1962 and a couple of teenagers are hanging out on their last night in their small California hometown, which they can't wait to leave. Steve (Ron Howard) and Curt (Richard Dreyfuss) are getting ready to go to college the next day. Steve's girlfriend, Laurie (Cindy Williams), is extremely upset about this: they've got one night to figure out what this means for their relationship. The two guys spend their last night cruisin' the strip, encountering other locals like John (Paul Le Mat), who still drives the boulevard in his cool 1932 Ford Deuce Coop and just can't leave adolescence behind; Carol (Mackenzie Phillips), a sassy thirteen-year-old who's out way past her bedtime; and Bob Falfa, (Harrison Ford) a hot-rod driver with a brooding presence. Presiding over this drama, spinning records and giving a raspy narrative, is the famous DJ Wolfman Jack. With its awesome rock-'n'-roll soundtrack and its all-star cast, AMERICAN GRAFFITI is one of the best—and most enjoyable—movies about coming-of-age in the '60s.

Line That Says It All: "Do you want to end up like John? You can't stay seventeen forever."

Girl to Watch: This seminal teen movie centers much more on the boys, but Cindy Williams feels real as an anxious girl wondering how Steve can just walk away from such a good thing.

Guy to Watch: Richard Dreyfuss is terrific as Curt; he really grabs your attention. It's fun to see Harrison Ford make the most of what is essentially a bit part. It isn't surprising that he was soon-after cast in a little movie called STAR WARS by the same director.

Scene Worth the Rewind: The ending is surprising and quite touching. You'll see.

Soundtrack Note: Tons of rockin' 1950s and early '60s hits in here, like "Why do Fools Fall in Love?" and "Teen Angel." No Elvis, though—the filmmakers couldn't afford the rights.

Watch This One With: Your retro-loving buddies.

Movies with the Same Vibe: FAST TIMES AT RIDGEMONT HIGH, CAN'T HARDLY WAIT. Also check out *Grease* (1978), a musical look at a similar time.

HOW THIS MOVIE HELPS

This movie makes you wonder how teens entertained themselves before the invention of cars. Did they cruise the prairie in their horse-drawn buggies? While not as girl-centered as most of the Ultimate Girl movies, AMERICAN GRAFFITI connects us to that confused part of ourselves that wants both to leave and to stay at the same time. What better metaphor is there for that dilemma than cruising the strip? It may look like a big waste of time and gas to the old folks, but lots of drama can unfold on that endless loop of asphalt.

Anywhere but Here

MOOD CONTROL

1 2 3
4 5 6
7 8 9
10 11 12

▶ Press PLAY
if you're feeling:

1   Adventurous
2   AMBITIOUS
3   Artsy
4   CYNICAL
5   Depressed
6   Heartbroken
7   Hopeful
8   Insecure
9   Misunderstood
10 OVERWHELMED
11 Playful
12 Weird

1999   **ULTIMATE GIRL RATING:** ♣ ♣ ♣

DIRECTOR: Wayne Wang
BIRTHPLACE: Mainstream Hollywood
FILE UNDER: Babysitting Mom
RATED: PG-13

STARRING: Susan Sarandon, Natalie Portman, Hart Bochner, Eileen Ryan, Ray Baker, John Diehl, Shawn Hatosy, Bonnie Bedelia

THE PROBLEM

Is your mom charismatic and full of life—maybe a little *too* full of life? It's not like you expect her to sit in a rocking chair and crochet while you're off having adventures. Still, it seems that while other moms are getting on with adulthood, your mother is experiencing a second adolescence. It's like she's your twin sister, except that she gets to make all the major decisions. How fair is that?

The Reel Deal: Adele August (Susan Sarandon) lives with her second husband and daughter (Natalie Portman) in a quiet Midwestern town. It's too quiet for Adele's liking, and she leaves her husband and home in one impulsive move, forcing her daughter, Ann, to relocate to Southern California with her. Adele is one of those moms who wears her clothes too tight and who constantly dreams of having a larger-than-life existence.

Meanwhile, the bills aren't getting paid, the parking tickets pile up, and Ann increasingly feels like she's living with an overgrown teen. (For instance, when her mother gets fired, her impulse is to go shopping.) Adele pushes Ann to pursue a show biz career, without even considering or noticing what kind of interests and dreams her bright daughter has. And she regularly wakes her daughter up in the middle of the night to babble on about a date. You get the picture. As a result, Ann becomes the kind of daughter who seems wise beyond her years, and who yearns for structure and responsibility. Adele looks for work and a man while continuing to dream of a movie career for her daughter, but Ann's plans are far more practical than that. She's determined to head for the East Coast to attend college—and to take care of herself for a change. ANYWHERE BUT HERE takes a tender look at a selfish mother and a selfless daughter who wish they had a soul connection as well as a blood tie.

Line That Says It All: "That summer I turned seventeen—and started planning my escape."

Girl to Watch: This movie focuses on the two lead actresses, and they both do an admirable job. Susan Sarandon works hard to give many dimensions to a woman we could easily write off as not worth our time. Natalie Portman is amazing as Ann. You know this girl, with all her confusion and silent rage. Maybe *you* are this girl.

Scene Worth the Rewind: The car sing-along. We don't know if the family that sings together stays together, but it's nice to see those two in harmony, if only for a song.

Fun Factoid: Rumor has it that Susan Sarandon didn't even want to make this film unless Natalie Portman could costar. You'll see why when you watch the movie.

Soundtrack Note: Not surprisingly, the soundtrack includes a great selection of female artists, from LeAnn Rimes to Lisa Loeb to Sarah McLachlan. We were particularly taken with k.d. lang's title track, "Anywhere but Here." She could sing the phone book and you'd be in awe before she got through the As.

Watch This One With: Your girlfriends who are also bustin' to bolt.

Movies with the Same Vibe: WHITE OLEANDER, GETTING TO KNOW YOU. Also check out *Tumbleweeds* (1999), another good film with a similar story—sensible daughter trying to put up with flighty mother—but it has more of an indie feel.

HOW THIS MOVIE HELPS

Ann is very smart to realize that her mother will write her story if Ann doesn't take charge of her own life. Sure, flamboyant moms have flashier clothes and louder voices, but many are capable of listening and learning too. You just have to speak up—and repeat things a lot. You can obsess all day about whether or not your mom wants what's best for you or what's best for her. You can waste your energy imagining what it would have been like to have a different kind of mom. But this takes up a lot of valuable time, time you could spend planning your own road trip to the future. Everyone has to take that trip at some point, and if you're not behind the wheel, you're probably going to hate the scenery.

Beautiful Thing

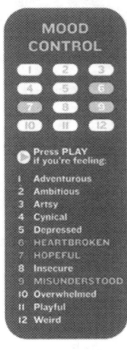
1996 ULTIMATE GIRL RATING: ♣ ♣ ♣ ♣

DIRECTOR: Hettie MacDonald
BIRTHPLACE: London
FILE UNDER: Coming-Out Fairytale
RATED: R

STARRING: Linda Henry, Meera Syal, Glen Berry, Martin Walsh, Steven M. Martin, Scott Neal, Tameka Empson, Andrew Fraser, Ben Daniels, John Savage, Julie Smith

THE PROBLEM

Would people accept you if they knew the truth? Would they still protect you, still treat you like part of the family? You look around and don't see much evidence that they would. You live in a world where there is an ideal that few can live up to, but that everyone is expected to follow. Can your family ever change their expectations of you? Whether you need to come out of the closet or just come out as yourself, it isn't easy. Maybe in a land far, far away this would be more tolerable. (And if that land was populated by cute British boys, so much the better.)

The Reel Deal: Jamie (Glen Berry) and Ste (Scott Neal) live next door to one another in a London housing project and have opposite problems. Jamie is an unpopular, unathletic boy who hides out from life with his caring mom, Sandra (Linda Henry). Ste is a jock who fits in fine at school but is brutalized at home by his father and brother. One night after Ste's dad beats him again in a drunken rage, Jamie's mom lets him hide out for the night with Jamie. Jamie has shot Ste looks before, but this time Ste looks back, and the boys tentatively begin an unexpected romance. Dealing with their emerging homosexuality, beginning a relationship, and keeping it from

Ste's abusive family would be plenty for one film. But this movie also takes on the problems of Sandra, who longs to open a pub and move out of the projects, and Leah, the young black woman next door whose love of Mama Cass makes her a particularly memorable cinematic character. "Beautiful thing" aptly describes both the love between the boys and this sweet and hopeful film.

Line That Says It All:
"Do you think I'm queer?"
"It doesn't matter what I think."

Girl to Watch: We loved the character of Leah (Tameka Empson).

Guy to Watch: Glen Berry and Scott Neal are both brilliant, as the Brits are wont to say.

How You Know It's a Movie: Some aspects of the coming-out process shown in this movie look more like how we wish it would go than how it usually does. But so what?

Watch This One With: Any friend who enjoys a nice romance. Being gay, British, or a boy is so not a requirement to adore this little film.

Movies with the Same Vibe: CIRCLE OF FRIENDS, THE INCREDIBLY TRUE ADVENTURES OF TWO GIRLS IN LOVE. Also check out *Edge of Seventeen* (1998), another movie about young gay love (more sex, less sweet).

HOW THIS MOVIE HELPS

Here's the weird thing about sexual attraction: it can sprout up anywhere, at any time, and it doesn't always fit into prescribed plans. Sometimes you don't get a choice. You do, however, get to choose whether or not to accept it, and in doing so, accept yourself. A movie about love blooming in a cold, hard place is comforting. It reminds us that intimacy exists everywhere and anywhere, and that love can transform a lousy housing project balcony into something that Juliet herself might stand on, expecting Romeo to dash up the fire escape any minute. BEAUTIFUL THING is a heartwarming film that shows people in rough circumstances trying to find a soft landing.

Before Sunrise

MOOD CONTROL

1	2	3
4	5	6
7	8	9
10	11	12

Press PLAY if you're feeling:

1. ADVENTUROUS
2. Ambitious
3. Artsy
4. Cynical
5. Depressed
6. Heartbroken
7. HOPEFUL
8. Insecure
9. Misunderstood
10. Overwhelmed
11. PLAYFUL
12. Weird

1995 ULTIMATE GIRL RATING: ♣ ♣ ♣ ♣ ♣

DIRECTOR: Richard Linklater
BIRTHPLACE: Indie America Takes a Vacation
FILE UNDER: Some Enchanted Evening
RATED: R

STARRING: Ethan Hawke, Julie Delpy

THE PROBLEM

Okay, so he was never your boyfriend, but you did spend a perfect day together; or carried on an amazing flirtation at the coffee shop; or had that one conversation at that party you'll remember forever because it was like the words flowed without effort, and when you looked at each other.... Where in your brain should you keep that magical mini-relationship? And for how long? Will you see him again, or is it all the more perfect because you won't?

The Reel Deal: Jesse (Ethan Hawke) is a scruffy young American heading home after bumming around Europe on vacation. Celine (Julie Delpy) is a French student returning to France, and her studies. While traveling from Budapest to Vienna, they spy one another through the crowds on the train. Jesse finagles a seat next to Celine, and they begin to talk. The talk flows freely and they are mutually intrigued. Jesse is suddenly struck by an impulse. He convinces Celine to agree to get off the train with him in Vienna, just so they can spend more time together. Surprising herself, Celine agrees, and they embark on a fourteen-hour relationship that seems to be filled with more honesty and romance than many people find in a lifetime. They walk around Vienna, experiencing life in that intense way you do when you've decided to let adventure show up, unannounced. Sure, there's some "will they or won't they?" sexual tension, but it's mostly just great talk about everything in life that matters most. Crazy stuff happens, too, the craziest thing of all being that two people can get to the heart of everything in just a few hours.

Girl to Watch: If you think all French girls are snooty and self-confident, think again. Julie Delpy. Julie Delpy is such a cool actor to watch, kind of like a young Meryl Streep. You'll be screaming, "Who *is* this girl?"

Guy to Watch: Ethan Hawke will so remind you of that guy in high school whose impulsivity and confusion are his most attractive features. It also helps if that guy looks like Ethan Hawke.

Line That Says It All: "If there's any kind of magic in this world, it must be in the attempt of understanding someone, sharing something. I know it's almost impossible to succeed, but...who cares, really? The answer must be in the attempt."

Watch This One With: A friend who is sleeping over or the dorm crew. There's so much fodder for conversation here.

Movies with the Same Vibe: GETTING TO KNOW YOU, FLIRTING. Also check out *Before Sunset* (2004), the new sequel, nine years in the making. We won't give away the plot, but we will tell you that director-writer Richard Linklater and his two leads holed up together writing and rewriting the script to make it feel true to what would have happened to Jesse and Celine. Collaborations like that show real respect for actors, don't you think?

HOW THIS MOVIE HELPS

This lovely, intelligent film brings home the fact that transitory connections can change our lives (or at least our travel plans). We like the fact that even though the two leads are definitely gorgeous, their initial attraction makes way pretty quickly to a deeper appreciation of one another's creativity, compassion, and honesty. No one's afraid to sound smart here, and when all the posing stops their connection will remind you of the best late-night conversations you've had in your life. If you've ever talked to someone who seemed like your soul mate moments into the conversation, you can relive that feeling with this cool film. Oh, and did we mention that it was romantic? So romantic that it will take your breath away—and send you packing for Vienna.

Bend It Like Beckham

MOOD CONTROL

1 2 3
4 5 6
7 8 9
10 11 12

▶ Press PLAY if you're feeling:

1 Adventurous
2 AMBITIOUS
3 Artsy
4 Cynical
5 DEPRESSED
6 Heartbroken
7 Hopeful
8 Insecure
9 Misunderstood
10 Overwhelmed
11 PLAYFUL
12 Weird

2002   ULTIMATE GIRL RATING: ♣ ♣ ♣ ♣ ♣

DIRECTOR: Gurinder Chadha
BIRTHPLACE: England
FILE UNDER:
Kicking Tradition
RATED: PG-13

STARRING: Parminder K. Nagra, Keira Knightley, Jonathan Rhys-Meyers, Anupam Kher, Archie Panjabi, Shaznay Lewis, Frank Harper, Juliet Stevenson, Shaheen Khan, Ameet Chana, Pooja Shah, Paven Virk

THE PROBLEM

There's something you love to do. You're even good at it, if you do say so yourself. People close to you think it's pretty weird, or inappropriate, or not important, so you have to fight for the right to do this thing that you love so much. Is it easy? No. Is it worth it? Only if you want to have a life worth living.

The Reel Deal: A spunky Indian girl (Parminder K. Nagra) is "Jess" to her soccer-playing guy pals when she kicks it something fierce in the parks of London. She's "Jesminder" at home, though, the dutiful daughter of orthodox Sikh parents who emigrated to England from Uganda. Her mother wants nothing more for Jess than to become an Indian domestic goddess and get engaged to a nice Indian boy, like her older sister, whose engagement dramas and details consume the family. Yet Jess is only crazy about one boy, the British soccer sensation David Beckham, only she doesn't want to marry him—she wants to *be* him. Her father doesn't mind the soccer playing quite as much, but the prejudice he faced in his own sports-playing past makes him view her dreams with grave concern. Yet Jess keeps on kicking, especially after a British girl, Jules

(Keira Knightley), spies her on the field and invites her to try out for a women's team. The coach is a feisty Irishman, Joe (Jonathan Rhys-Meyers), who takes to Jess as a player and a woman, and for a while it looks like Jess can have her ball and respect Indian traditions too. Naturally, complications ensue—on the field, at home, and between Jess and her new best friend. Nothing is easy, Jess learns, when you're trying to straddle two cultures and a little round ball.

Line That Says It All: "Anyone can cook aloo gobi, but who can bend a ball like Beckham?"

Girl to Watch: Parminder K. Nagra is tops. She's in almost every moment of the film, which is good, because you don't want to take your eyes off her.

Guy to Watch: Jonathan Rhys-Meyers makes Joe complicated yet likeable. A coach you'd want to go clubbing with? Now there's a team anyone would join....

Watch This One With: Your soccer team.

Movies with the Same Vibe: BLUE CRUSH, LOVE AND BASKETBALL, REAL WOMEN HAVE CURVES.

HOW THIS MOVIE HELPS

This movie rocks! Even people who hate soccer love this film. People who don't eat Indian food try it after seeing all the mouthwatering dishes in this movie. So many of the issues transcend one person's culture: trying to please your parents, trying not to like the one guy your best friend is crushing on, trying to grab your big moment before it's gone forever. It's one of those films where it doesn't matter whether or not you can see the end from far afield; you still wanna give a "whoo hoo!" when you get there. Why? Everyone has had stand-up-and-cheer moments in their own lives that passed them by. So see this movie and stand up and cheer for Jess. Just like you, she deserves to have the life she's dreamed of.

What do you look for in a role model? Or maybe that's the wrong question. We find that the real role models in our lives are people we stumble upon, not the people we think should inspire us. From a prostitute to a factory worker to an office assistant, movie heroines blow us away with their determination to succeed despite humble origins, uncaring employers, and "bad outfit" days. Here are a few hardcore heroines we've loved over the years:

Pretty Woman (1990)

Sophisticates roll their eyes at the sugarcoating that prostitution gets in this hit romantic comedy, but girls continue to embrace this story of a plucky woman (Julia Roberts) who refuses to let her circumstances determine her worth.

Erin Brockovitch (2000)

Julia Roberts snagged an Oscar with this role, a bright woman with a tough manner and too-tight clothes who pushes her way into a law office job and then becomes obsessed with a case involving families who've been destroyed because of corporate greed and neglect. Roberts is a blast to watch, and it's amazing to know that the heroine she plays is based on a real-life firebrand. In the category of "One Person Can Make a Difference," this film is Exhibit A.

Norma Rae (1979)

Sally Field won an Oscar for her portrayal of this Southern textile worker who was inspired to lobby for union representation at her factory. Soon her whole life becomes focused on getting her fellow workers to agree that only by banding together can they improve their difficult working conditions.

Silkwood (1983)

Meryl Streep plays a blue-collar worker in Oklahoma who was instrumental in exposing the flaws of her nuclear parts factory. It's a long movie, but worth watching for the good acting and the poignant story. As Meryl's close friend, a down-to-earth lesbian, Cher showed us in *Silkwood* that she could act—who knew?

Working Girl (1988)

Melanie Griffith stars in this light romantic comedy about a working-class secretary who attempts to outwit her rich and powerful associates with cleverness and hard work. Funny and romantic, *Working Girl* also tackles class warfare issues and the ways in which the decision to better yourself can be threatening to the people in your life who should be the most supportive. A real treat.

Blue Crush

MOOD CONTROL

1	2	3
4	5	6
7	8	9
10	11	12

▶ **Press PLAY** if you're feeling:

1 ADVENTUROUS
2 AMBITIOUS
3 Artsy
4 Cynical
5 Depressed
6 Heartbroken
7 Hopeful
8 INSECURE
9 Misunderstood
10 Overwhelmed
11 Playful
12 Weird

2002   **ULTIMATE GIRL RATING:** ♣ ♣ ♣

DIRECTOR: John Stockwell
BIRTHPLACE: Mainstream U.S.A.
FILE UNDER: Girls Just Wanna Make Waves
RATED: PG-13

STARRING: Kate Bosworth, Michelle Rodriquez, Matthew Davis, Sanoe Lake, Mika Boorem, Kala Alexander, Chris Taloa

THE PROBLEM   You've got one great passion in life, the thing that you do the best. Yet you're also a girl with a passion for that special someone. Sure, your friends give you a hard time for neglecting your dream, but how often does a great relationship come your way? It's not fair that you're expected to choose between the thing you love and the person you could love. That's too much pressure during what should be the greatest time of your life.

The Reel Deal: Anne Marie (Kate Bosworth), Eden (Michelle Rodriguez), and Lena (Sanoe Lake) live for surfing. The way they live, however, is far from glamorous. Unlike many sports-oriented movies that show athletes living fairly cushy lives, BLUE CRUSH shows the lengths to which these surfers will go to live their dream. The girls work as maids in a luxury hotel, live in a crummy apartment, and work hard to keep

Anne Marie's kid sister, Penny (Mika Boorem), in school and well cared for after her mom abandoned ship. It's a tough, working-class life, but it feels worth it every morning when the girls ride the waves before work. Anne Marie is the best surfer of the three, who stood a chance of winning a big surfing competition in Oahu a few years earlier. But she found herself trapped in a hold-down, the waves curling around her like a rope, and she very nearly drowned. Nervous about a replay of that terrifying day but anxious to prove herself, Anne Marie is busy preparing for another big contest when a guy comes along to throw her off balance. Matt Tollman (Matthew Davis) is one of a crew of pro football players staying at the hotel, and he and Anne Marie soon hit it off. Her friends are furious, thinking she might throw away her dreams of glory (and turning pro herself) for some hotshot athlete who is going to forget her as soon as he returns to the mainland. With problems flaring up at work and a relationship that may or may not be the real thing, Anne Marie almost forgets how important surfing is to her. Thirty-foot waves, however, have a way of reminding you where you are….

Line That Says It All: "What do I want? Oh my god, I want Penny to quit smoking and go to college. I want to be able to pay the phone, electric, and water bills in the same month. Also, I'd like a girl to be on the cover of a surf magazine. It would be cooler if that girl was me, but any girl will do."

Girl to Watch: Kate Bosworth's performance makes Anne Marie far more than just a cute surfer girl.

Guy to Watch: Matthew Davis' football player is only partly a superficial dude. We like the other part.

Scene Worth the Rewind: The surfing scenes are incredible. The ocean is practically a character in the movie. Lots of filming was done on and under the surface of the water, so you can almost feel what it must be like to tackle the pipe…or get tackled by it.

Soundtrack Note: A nice mix of tunes: Bob Marley for history, Lenny Kravitz for romance, Beenie Man, Playgroup, and Moby for the fun of it. Note that "Walk About" is written and performed by Sanoe Lake, who also plays Lena.

Watch This One With: All your friends who are dreaming of Hawaii. Have a tropical-themed party and feature BLUE CRUSH after you're done dancing on the sand. (Okay, so your back yard doesn't have any palm trees or sand. Where's your imagination?)

HOW THIS MOVIE HELPS

BLUE CRUSH is a fun surf film that plays it both ways—empowerment for the girls, hot girls for the guys. If you can live with that reality, you'll relate to the struggles of a girl who wants her life to feel the way it does when she's up on a board. People are always telling you that you need to have priorities in life, that focusing on one thing means giving up another. Anne Marie doesn't want the moon, just the right wave when it counts the most. Doesn't everybody?

Boys Don't Cry

MOOD CONTROL

1	2	3
4	5	6
7	8	9
10	11	12

▶ Press PLAY if you're feeling:

1 Adventurous
2 Ambitious
3 ARTSY
4 Cynical
5 Depressed
6 Heartbroken
7 Hopeful
8 Insecure
9 MISUNDERSTOOD
10 Overwhelmed
11 Playful
12 WEIRD

1999   ULTIMATE GIRL RATING: ♣ ♣ ♣

DIRECTOR: Kimberly Peirce
BIRTHPLACE: Indie U.S.A.
FILE UNDER: Gender Crime and Punishment
RATED: R

STARRING: Hilary Swank, Chloë Sevigny, Peter Sarsgaard, Brendan Sexton III, Alicia Goranson, Alison Folland, Jeanetta Arnette, Rob Campbell, Matt McGrath, Cheyenne Rushing

THE PROBLEM   You feel enormous constraints in what it means to be a girl or a guy. Labels, labels everywhere, and none of them seem to fit who you are, what you think, how you feel. This would be fine if people didn't seem to care so much. But we live in a world that demands that everyone check off just one of the little white boxes to fit in. Or maybe you fit in just fine, but feel guilty that the rules just naturally go your way. You don't want to be part of the problem. Maybe part of the solution is to watch this amazing, gut-wrenching film.

The Reel Deal: BOYS DON'T CRY is based on the true story of Brandon Teena, formerly Teena Brandon, a girl who lived happily as a guy for the last part of her short life in rural Nebraska. Teena (Hilary Swank) doesn't identify herself as either a lesbian or cross-dresser; she just thinks of herself as a guy, and dresses to look the part. The first half of the film shows how Brandon managed to charm women he encountered. Looking like a handsome, though somewhat effeminate, teenage guy with a genuinely tender side, Brandon would rack up dates until his ruse was discovered and he had to leave town.

Wandering into a bar in a new town, Brandon spies Lana Tisdel (Chloë Sevigny), who is out enjoying herself with girlfriends Candace (Alicia Gornason) and Kate (Alison Folland). Lana and Brandon fall in love, after which the story changes completely. There is no big, dramatic moment when Lana realizes that the boy of her dreams is actually a woman; instead, you get the sense that she somehow knew it all along. Lana's friends like Brandon, even her mother thinks he's great, but her ex-boyfriend John (Peter Sarsgaard) and his buddy Tom (Brendan Sexton III) aren't sure what to think of the guy. It's not giving anything away to say that when Brandon's secret is revealed, male rage leads to tragedy.

The rape and murder of Brandon Teena was a huge story when it broke in 1993, and it was the subject of a documentary and numerous lengthy magazine and newspaper articles. For this reason, no one expected BOYS DON'T CRY to make much of a splash, much less win Hilary Swank an Oscar for best actress. The best actress Oscar went to a girl playing a guy? That irony would surely have amused the late, unforgettable Brandon Teena, the subject of this powerful film.

Girl to Watch: See why Hilary Swank won the Oscar in this unique role.

Guys to Watch: Peter Sarsgaard and Brendan Sexton III do a remarkable job portraying regular good ole boys consumed by homophobia and rage.

Scene Worth the Rewind: When Brandon is forced to buy tampons at a convenience store. It's clear that it's such a painful chore.

Fun Factoid: To prepare for this role, Hilary Swank walked around town dressed like a man for a month. It paid off; her performance is amazingly convincing. In real life, she's a lovely actress married to the actor Chad Lowe. When she showed up at the Academy Awards looking like an elegant princess, many found it disconcerting.

Watch This One With: Friends who appreciate amazing films—and can handle both brutal rape scenes and less-than-happy endings.

Movies with the Same Vibe: RIVER'S EDGE.

HOW THIS MOVIE HELPS

Brandon Teena's story shows that many guys have a long way to go to learn how to make women feel appreciated and loved. His life was tragically cut short, but at least Brandon lived it with passion and purpose. Because it contains several brutal and disturbing scenes, BOYS DON'T CRY isn't for everyone. But this deeply moving film vividly portrays the consequences of intolerance and of society's desire to put everyone in neatly defined categories.

The Breakfast Club

MOOD CONTROL

1	2	3
4	5	6
7	8	9
10	11	12

▶ Press PLAY
if you're feeling:

1 Adventurous
2 Ambitious
3 Artsy
4 CYNICAL
5 Depressed
6 Heartbroken
7 Hopeful
8 INSECURE
9 Misunderstood
10 Overwhelmed
11 PLAYFUL
12 Weird

1985 | **ULTIMATE GIRL RATING:**

DIRECTOR: John Hughes
BIRTHPLACE: Mainstream Hollywood
FILE UNDER: Multipurpose Room
RATED: R (for language)

STARRING: Molly Ringwald, Emilio Estevez, Judd Nelson, Ally Sheedy, Anthony Michael Hall, Paul Gleason

THE PROBLEM So you hate cliques? Maybe you tell yourself, "I'm friends with lots of different people at school." Yeah, right. Sure, you can have conversations with people from different circles, but it's hard to really get to know anyone but your best buds. Why? Because everyone is watching you, or at least it seems that way. They expect you to sit in a certain spot in math class, go to the same parties, hang out with the same crowd day after day. It's almost as if you'd have to be held hostage with kids from your school's various social groups to really find out what they're like. That's sort of the premise of THE BREAKFAST CLUB, the fun of watching kids forced to get to know one another just to keep boredom at bay. What starts as a light amusement becomes much more, as the clichés drop away and everybody reveals their true selves. Sick of being labeled? Sick of being left out, or struggling under the pressure of being on center stage? Spend a Saturday at Shermer High School.

The Reel Deal: Five totally different high school kids, each representing a classic type—the jock (Emilio Estevez), the tough guy (Judd Nelson), the nerd (Anthony Michael Hall), the prom queen (Molly Ringwald), and the crazy girl (Ally Sheedy)—get Saturday detention for a variety of minor infractions. Stuck in one room for hours on end, they have nothing to do but torment one another and their moronic supervising teacher (Paul Gleason). At first, it looks like we're going to watch a whole movie about teenagers glaring at one another while waiting to return to their real lives. Then, just out of boredom, one of them gets everyone to talk. Pretty soon, they find it a relief to tell a group of strangers about not only why they're in detention, but how they feel about their families, their reputations at school, and who they secretly wish they could be. When their masks peel away, they find common bonds. Two of them even find each other's tongues.

Line That Says It All: "Um, I was just thinking...I mean, I know it's kind of a weird time, but I was just wondering, um, what is going to happen to us on Monday? When we're all together again? I mean, I consider you guys my friends. I'm not wrong, am I?"

Girl to Watch: Ally Sheedy. There's this whole thing with dandruff....

Guy to Watch: Judd Nelson. That earring was so dangerous in '85.

Fashion to Catch: Molly Ringwald's snazzy suede skirt. You might not wear that to all-day detention, but you're not the princess of Shermer High.

Eye-Rolling Time: Goofy bonding dance and last-minute makeover.

Watch This One With: This would be a fun slumber party movie. There's lots to discuss: which character did you relate to most? Who said the most honest thing? What do you think the future holds for this group?

Movies with the Same Vibe: PRETTY IN PINK, SAY ANYTHING, CAMP.

HOW THIS MOVIE HELPS

This teen classic is the perfect movie for those days when you despair of ever breaking free of the stranglehold that cliques have on your high school. How nice to think that prom queens, nerds, and tough guys just need more "alone time" in order to appreciate one another. Sure, it's a fantasy, but a useful one. It's very cathartic to watch a bunch of stereotypes emerge as real people that call one another on their crap. In reality, probably nothing short of brain surgery will change the clique mentality for good. But who wants brain surgery? It's painful and expensive. Watch this surprisingly touching movie instead.

Bring It On

MOOD CONTROL

I	2	3
4	5	6
7	8	9
10	II	12

▶ **Press PLAY if you're feeling:**

I Adventurous
2 AMBITIOUS
3 Artsy
4 Cynical
5 DEPRESSED
6 Heartbroken
7 Hopeful
8 Insecure
9 Misunderstood
10 Overwhelmed
II PLAYFUL
12 Weird

2000 ULTIMATE GIRL RATING: 🍿🍿🍿🍿🍿

DIRECTOR: Peyton Reed
BIRTHPLACE: Mainstream Hollywood
FILE UNDER: Pom-pom Pilot
RATED: PG-13

STARRING: Kirsten Dunst, Jesse Bradford, Eliza Dushku, Gabrielle Union, Clare Kramer

THE PROBLEM

You find yourself in charge of something, whether it's a club at school, student government, or a community action project. You thought you wanted to be the leader, but now you're not so sure. Aren't leaders supposed to be smart and confident and inspirational? You're not any of those things. You're just the one who cares the most. Can you fake it till you make it?

The Reel Deal: Torrance Shipman (Kirsten Dunst) is a perky, blonde cheerleader in a movie that initially looks like it's about the fun of being a perky, blonde cheerleader. Fortunately, it becomes a lot more than that. Through a tip from Missy (Eliza Dushku), the new "punk rebel" on the squad, Torrance discovers that the former squad leader has been heading down to East Compton and stealing cheers from a hotshot African-American team. Torrance is embarrassed and outraged by this deceit, and with Missy's help works to convince the other cheerleaders that they need to earn the next win on their own merits. On the way, she has several run-ins with the justifiably angry East Compton squad (its leader played by the always-worth-watching Gabrielle Union), faces difficulties with her college boyfriend, and develops an interesting new friendship with Missy's cheerleader-hating rocker brother, Cliff (Jesse Bradford). Issues of racism, economic injustice, and ethics flutter lightly through this engaging movie, not a small feat considering that it is, despite all the cleverness, a movie about cheerleaders. Shouldn't there be an Oscar for combining deep issues with skimpy skirts in a way that actually works?

Line That Says It All:
"Look on the bright side.
It's only cheerleading."
"I *am* only cheerleading."

Girl to Watch: Kirsten Dunst is impossible to resist.

Guy to Watch: Jesse Bradford, one of the cutest boys to ever pick up a guitar and write a sixty-second punk-rock love song: "You got me feelin' butterflies/ In your locker, I would hide…"

Scene Worth the Rewind: The romantic tooth-brushing scene (yeah, you read that right) and also the dance sequences at the end. If this movie set out to prove that cheerleading is a real sport, they proved it with this exhilarating ending.

Watch This One With: A group of friends. Afterward, split into two teams. Each team should pick a weird topic for the other team, such as eating grapefruit or driving through North Dakota. Now split up and try to develop cheers on the subject. See? Just like the kids in BRING IT ON, you don't need a winning football team. You don't need any sport at all. You just need to be committed to the cheer.

HOW THIS MOVIE HELPS

Okay, they're not going to show this light, teen comedy in leadership training camps anytime soon. Maybe they should, though. The mistakes Torrance makes are right out of the "Leadership Mishaps to Avoid" book (rush into a plan, don't trust yourself or your team, let everyone doubt you). And her evolution into a courageous and admired team leader should ignite a fire under anyone pushed to the head of the pack. After all, you become the head of something because you care the most, right? So, in the words of the East Compton captain, "Don't hold back. Bring it on!"

Buffy the Vampire Slayer

MOOD CONTROL

1	2	3
4	5	6
7	8	9
10	11	12

▶ Press PLAY
if you're feeling:

1 ADVENTUROUS
2 Ambitious
3 Artsy
4 Cynical
5 DEPRESSED
6 Heartbroken
7 Hopeful
8 Insecure
9 Misunderstood
10 OVERWHELMED
11 Playful
12 Weird

1992   ULTIMATE GIRL RATING: ♣ ♣

DIRECTOR: Fran Rubel Kuzui
BIRTHPLACE:
Mainstream Hollywood
FILE UNDER:
Barbie Fights the Undead
RATED: PG-13

STARRING: Kristy Swanson, Donald Sutherland, Paul Reubens, Rutger Hauer, Luke Perry, Michele Abrams, Hilary Swank, Paris Vaughan, David Arquette, Randall Batinkoff

THE PROBLEM

You're not filled with rage, just mildly annoyed at the world. Maybe you got a parking ticket, maybe your jeans are too tight, maybe your dad won't stop telling the story about how you couldn't remember who was president for, like, ten seconds. What you could use right about now is a movie with some good old-fashioned fight scenes, but nothing too heavy, of course. Ready to go tough, but with fluff? That's our Buffy!

The Reel Deal: The opening of the movie sets the tone. We see a centuries-old slayer and hear the solemn words, "Europe, the Dark Ages." Next, we cut to Buffy bouncing through the mall, and hear, "Los Angeles, the Lite Ages." Buffy Summers (Kirsty Swanson) is a cheerfully vacuous cheerleader with no great plans for her life beyond her next manicure appointment. But that all changes when she gets tagged by Merrick Jamison-Smythe (Donald Sutherland), who informs her that she's next in a long line of vampire slayers. A slayer-trainer himself, Merrick's job is to get her to put down her pom-poms and prepare for a great showdown with the vampire leader, Lothos

⏸ PRESS PAUSE: Scream Queens and Final Girls

We doubt you go to horror films so that you and your friends can enjoy deconstructing the feminist and anti-feminist archetypes over a biggie fries and a diet soda. "Huh?" Okay, never mind. The point is, horror films have come a long way since the days when every pretty horror film actress with a few minutes to herself was destined to become a pile of ribbons the next time the creepy music swelled. In recent years, a few tough-as-nails girls have managed to escape the carnage, and some of them even kill off the jerk whose twisted behavior makes up the bulk of the plot.

Author Carol Clover wrote about the "Final Girl" in her book *Men, Women and Chainsaw,* but you know the Final Girl from your nights at the movies. She's often the one who gets the biggest salary, and boy does she earn it, fending off attack after attack from some never-say-die serial killer, surrounded by the corpses of her friends. Talk about a bummer. You couldn't pay us! (Well, unless we get a personal chef and our own trailer).

The Ultimate Girl salutes the Final Girl, in all her wild-eyed, blood-drenched glory. She's resilient, resourceful, and really stupid if she ever spends a minute alone again. Here's our list of the Best Horror Scream Queens: *The Ultimate Girl* Final Four.

1 **NEVE CAMPBELL** as Sydney Prescott in *Scream* (1996): Okay, that's it. No more boyfriends.

2 **JAMIE LEE CURTIS** as Laurie Strode in *Halloween* (1978): She's young, brave, and unaware in this first Halloween film. Little does she know what a long, hard fight lays ahead.

3 **JODIE FOSTER** as Clarice Starling in *Silence of the Lambs* (1991): Clarice may wear bad shoes, but she is trained as a cop and has a high IQ to boot. And she needs every point of it when up against Hannibal Lecter—the madman of Mensa.

4 **SIGOURNEY WEAVER** as Ellen Ripley in *Alien* (1979): She's the GI Jane of the space wars. Ripley rocks!

(Rutger Hauer). At first, Buffy refuses to participate, but it's hard to argue with destiny, especially when the alternative is watching your town being taken over by the undead. Her friends are furious with the new Buffy, who is too busy learning to slay vampires to help with the prom. They get the point, big time, when vampires arrive en masse, unprepared for what a very determined cheerleader with a stake and some impressive gymnastics can accomplish.

Line That Says It All: "My secret weapon is PMS."

Girl to Watch: Kristy Swanson as Buffy. Don't think about the unbeatable Sarah Michelle Geller from the TV show, and you might enjoy her performance.

Guy to Watch: Luke Perry as Oliver Pike. He's cute, to be sure, but he doesn't have half of Buffy's guts.

Scene Worth the Rewind: The final showdown with Lothos, of course.

Fun Factoid: This film spawned the Buffy TV hit, of course, so why is it so different? Rumor has it that Joss Whedon's original script was way watered down. In the original version, Buffy burns down the school gym (you hear references to that in the TV show), but the makers of this movie decided to go for the fun of the spoof rather than spooking you too much. For some, it doesn't work at all. Others find it a great laugh at the end of a long day.

Watch This One With: Friends that thought *Scream* was too deep.

Movies with the Same Vibe: Also check out *Scream* (1996) (a witty teen horror film) and *Charlie's Angel's* (2000) the original beautiful butt-kick squad.

HOW THIS MOVIE HELPS

If you rent this video only because you love the show so much, you might be disappointed. All the slaying and humor is still there, but none of the interesting teen angst subplot that fuels the Buffy TV show. However, if your favorite part of the TV show is watching cute, underestimated girls kick some serious butt, you still might have yourself a good time. When this little film came out, adult women in the movies were starting to fight back, but teenage girls were still, for the most part, screaming until help came. Now the number of movies that feature girls who own the streets is significant, and this makes us happy. We're not saying fighting is a good thing, but when the undead come at your neck with a hungry look in their eyes, it's time to ruin the French manicure and make them sorry they were ever unborn.

Camp

MOOD CONTROL

1	2	3
4	5	6
7	8	9
10	11	12

▶ Press **PLAY** if you're feeling:

1 Adventurous
2 Ambitious
3 ARTSY
4 Cynical
5 Depressed
6 Heartbroken
7 HOPEFUL
8 Insecure
9 Misunderstood
10 Overwhelmed
11 Playful
12 WEIRD

2003 ULTIMATE GIRL RATING: ♣ ♣ ♣ ♣ ♣

DIRECTOR: Todd Graff
BIRTHPLACE:
Indie U.S.A.
FILE UNDER:
Fame Into the Woods
RATED: PG-13

STARRING: Daniel Letterle, Joanna Chilcoat, Robin de Jesus, Steven Cutts, Vince Rimoldi, Kahiry Bess, Tiffany Taylor, Sasha Allen, Anna Kendrick, Don Dixon, Stephen DiMenna

THE PROBLEM While most of the kids at your school are filling their ears with the trendiest music, you're filling your soul with ballads, musical numbers, classical music, jazz—basically music that's not likely to win you popularity points. Well, so what? You are who you are, you love what you love, and popularity is highly overrated. It's just that sometimes you wish you lived in a world where *your* passion was the fashion. Crazy for cabaret, stupid for Sondheim? Spend some time at Camp Ovation....

The Reel Deal: Camp Ovation, a short drive (but essentially light years away) from the footlights of Broadway, is a yearly gathering place for the self-described "geeks" of musical theater, the flamboyant girls and gay boys who make up countless high school productions. There are other kinds of kids in high school plays, too, of course, and one of those is Vlad (Daniel Letterle), an unbelievably handsome and charming straight boy who lands at Camp Ovation one summer because a cute girl got him interested in acting. Vlad's arrival at the camp has the effect of a giant meteor landing in the middle of a backyard barbeque. Staff and teens alike are amazed that such an Adonis—and a heterosexual at that—has graced them with his presence for the summer.

Scene Worth the Rewind: Michael's party. It shows the love these friends have for one another, and the unique atmosphere of this campy camp.

Watch This One With: Your friends from Drama or Chorus, or Band, your gay friends, your straight friends, your mom. We don't know about your Grandma though. How cool is she with the whole teen drag queen situation? Well, it's time she knew. Invite Grandma too.

Movies with the Same Vibe: CENTER STAGE, HAIRSPRAY, RUSHMORE. Also check out *Fame* (1980) and *The Object of My Affection* (1998).

In between all the romantic and friendship drama, everyone at camp finds solace on stage, where dazzling, funny, inventive musical numbers keep astonishing us with their wit and style. These kids, both innocent and jaded, prefer world-weary, gin-guzzling characters to the cute Southern accents and perky costumes of, say, *Oklahoma*. You might, too, after seeing this funny, poignant movie about the various parts we find ourselves playing in a world without a script.

Line That Says It All: "The thirty-foot rule means Michael stays thirty feet away until we find out whether he's straight or gay."

Girl to Watch: Joanna Chilcoat as Ellen. This is casting genius. You get the feeling that the second the cameras stop rolling, she simply changes her name back to Joanna and has the same life. She's that real, that accessible, that good.

HOW THIS MOVIE HELPS

CAMP may not be able to convince you that there's a growing movement out there for what you're into. It doesn't even try, which is why we love it so. Instead, the message is clear: you may be a geek, but so what? Go for it. Life is too short to spend time and energy trying to jam your weird, larger-than-life form into the cookie cutter. In CAMP, success is defined as the little moments when we hit the perfect note, get the part, are surprised by a kiss—those moments when, without changing a thing about ourselves, we belong.

Can't Hardly Wait

1998   **ULTIMATE GIRL RATING:** ♣ ♣

DIRECTOR: Harry Elfont and Deborah Kaplan
BIRTHPLACE: Mainstream Hollywood
FILE UNDER: Party Out-of-Bounds

RATED: PG-13
STARRING: Jennifer Love Hewitt, Ethan Embry, Charlie Korsmo, Lauren Ambrose, Peter Facinelli, Seth Green, Michelle Brookhurst

THE PROBLEM

Parties drive you insane. You get yourself all psyched up to look good, **say the right thing, catch the eye of that hot guy, seize every opportunity, not eat too many chips....That's a big to-do list for one little evening, and you usually come home dragging your purse behind you, wondering where the night went wrong. Is it too much to ask that a party change your life, just a little? CAN'T HARDLY WAIT doesn't seem to think so.**

The Reel Deal: The defining moment in Preston Meyers' (Ethan Embry) high school career came freshmen year, when Amanda Beckett (Jennifer Love Hewitt) walked into his homeroom and pulled out a strawberry Pop-Tart identical to the one he was eating. At that moment, Preston vowed to himself that she would become his girlfriend. Of course, he forgot to share that vow with Amanda. She went on to date obnoxious jock Mike Dexter (Peter Facinelli) for all four years of high school, until Mike eventually dumps her to pursue college girls, about whom he's been told some wild stories. Spying his big chance, Preston attends a huge, rowdy graduation bash with his good friend Denise (Lauren Ambrose) and a love letter to Amanda in tow. Denise has her own escapade when she becomes trapped in a bathroom with Kenny Fisher

(Seth Green), who seems really unclear about the fact that he's a white guy. Drinking, sexual exploits, revenge pranks, and ridiculous one-liners populate this crazy night, with Preston and Amanda's situation forming the sweet, sincere core.

Line That Says It All: "That is the most disgusting thing I have ever seen! What is wrong with you people?" (This could have been used in most scenes in this movie.)

Girl to Watch: Lauren Ambrose as the outcast, Denise. She's funny, she's smart, she seems more like someone you might know than all the other characters put together. You may remember her from the edgy HBO series *Six Feet Under*. Let's see a movie about the day after, starring her.

Guy to Watch: Ethan Embry as Preston. You're on his team.

Eye-Rolling Time: There are musical and cultural references that make no sense at a party taking place in the late '90s. And what's with the angel? But, whatever. It doesn't claim to be a documentary.

Scene Worth the Rewind: Denise and Kenny get locked in a bathroom, and work it out in a scene that ranges from hilarious to something else entirely.

Watch This One With: High school friends who joined you in skipping the huge, ridiculous graduation party.

Movies with the Same Vibe: FAST TIMES AT RIDGEMONT HIGH, SAY ANYTHING.

HOW THIS MOVIE HELPS

If you actually like big, raucous parties where anything can—and does—happen, this movie will make you nostalgic for your last big night out. If you hate that sort of thing, you can enjoy smirking at the outrageous behavior, the flagrant breaking of laws, and the truly unbelievable preponderance of idiots per square foot. CAN'T HARDLY WAIT does successfully capture the truly weird interactions that can transpire during the "last big fling."

Even better, trapped inside this silly, manic film is a nice story about taking romantic risks, despite the overwhelming odds against you. It seems crazy to think that a party could change your life. On the other hand, why not? Some people find inspiration in quiet art galleries, others in crowded living rooms filled with obnoxious acquaintances. So is this a party you'd be smart to attend? Heavens, no! Instead, how about watching it from afar, with a bowl of popcorn and your fellow graduates? It might not rock your world, but it will be fun.

Center Stage

MOOD
CONTROL

1	2	3
4	5	6
7	8	9
10	11	12

▶ Press PLAY
if you're feeling:

1 Adventurous
2 AMBITIOUS
3 Artsy
4 Cynical
5 Depressed
6 Heartbroken
7 HOPEFUL
8 Insecure
9 Misunderstood
10 OVERWHELMED
11 Playful
12 Weird

2000 **ULTIMATE GIRL RATING:** ♣ ♣ ♣ ♣

DIRECTOR: Nicholas Hytner
BIRTHPLACE:
Mainstream Hollywood
FILE UNDER:
The O.C. in Tights.
RATED: PG-13

STARRING: Amanda Schull,
Peter Gallagher, Debra Monk,
Zoe Saldana, Susan May
Pratt, Sascha Radetsky,
Shakiem Evans, Ethan Stiefel

THE PROBLEM   Maybe you're a dancer who dreams of being a star someday. Or a poet. Or an artist. Or an accountant. (Okay, scrap that last one.) The point is, what do you have to do to make your dream come true? Do you really want it bad enough?

The Reel Deal: CENTER STAGE takes us beyond backstage at the ballet. We go back to the dorms, where hungry young dancers spend a year trying to get into the ficticious American Ballet Company in New York City. There's tough-talking Eva, sweet Charlie, dramatic Eric, and little Miss Perfect, Maureen. In the center of it all is Jody (Amanda Schull), a pretty, hard-working dancer who just might not be good enough to make the cut. Still, Jody's spirits are buoyed by her kind classmates, and her growing attraction to handsome choreographer Cooper (Ethan Stiefel). Sharing her emotional roller coaster is the frosty Maureen (Susan May Pratt), a shoo-in for the company who is burdened by an obsessive stage mother and some hidden problems that are bigger than just faulty technique. We follow this pivotal year in all the dancers' lives, especially Jody's, watching her fall hard and learn that life's experiences, painful though they may be, can only add to the power of our performance.

Line That Says It All: "Cooper, you're an amazing dancer, and you're a great choreographer, but as a boyfriend…you kinda suck."

Girl to Watch: Amanda Schull is engaging as Jody and she's an amazing dancer. Not surprising, since she was plucked from the pro ranks to be in this movie. Keep an eye on Susan May Pratt as Maureen. At first she's just fun to hate, then she gets more interesting.

Guy to Watch: Another professional dancer, the gorgeous Ethan Stiefel as Cooper. You're not sure you'd trust him as far as you could throw him. Admit it, though—it'd be kind of fun to throw him.

Scene Worth the Rewind: There's a great moment when Jody, sick of the stifling atmosphere of brutal competition in the ballet school, ducks out to take a regular dance class at a scruffy studio in the heart of Manhattan. Watching her flip around the room with Broadway hoofers and other dancers of all stripes, you see the love of movement return to her weary eyes.

We also love the beginning montage of pair after pair of unbelievably scuffed-up ballet shoes, tossed away like tissues. If that doesn't sum up this wear-and-tear lifestyle, we don't know what does.

Watch This One With: Your bun-wearing, callous-rubbing, neck-stretching, ballet-crazed friends. But even if you don't know a plié from an arabesque, you can't help but enjoy the outsized drama of this group—and the terrific dance performances sprinkled throughout the film. You thought ballet was stuffy? Think again.

Movies with the Same Vibe: SAVE THE LAST DANCE, CAMP. Also check out *The Turning Point* (1977), an old-school near-classic about jealousy, friendship, and ballet. Dancers your mom's age coming to blows? Be there.

HOW THIS MOVIE HELPS

CENTER STAGE is filled with juicy romances, conniving peers, and hold-your-breath audition results. Yet, in the end, what you remember most isn't the melodrama, but the life of the dancer, filled with sweat, pain, and constant insecurity. If you're a dancer yourself, then you will understand the dedication—and ambition—that drives them. Or maybe you have your own form of obsessive self-torture that helps you relate to the Capezio crew in CENTER STAGE. If not, what are you doing lying around watching videos all day? Could you be a movie fanatic?

Circle of Friends

MOOD CONTROL

I	2	3
4	5	6
7	8	9
10	II	12

▶ Press PLAY if you're feeling:

1 Adventurous
2 Ambitious
3 Artsy
4 Cynical
5 DEPRESSED
6 Heartbroken
7 HOPEFUL
8 INSECURE
9 Misunderstood
10 Overwhelmed
11 Playful
12 Weird

1995 **ULTIMATE GIRL RATING:** ♣ ♣ ♣ ♣

DIRECTOR: Pat O'Connor
BIRTHPLACE: Ireland
FILE UNDER:
Dublin Fairy Tale
RATED: PG-13

STARRING: Chris O'Donnell,
Minnie Driver, Geraldine
O'Rawe, Saffron Burrows,
Alan Cumming, Colin Firth,
Aidan Gillen

THE PROBLEM

You fall for a perfect guy, the kind of hunk that everyone would like to date. Meanwhile, you're kind of plump with wild hair and a strong, quirky nature, the kind of girl who is not everyone's cup of tea. Maybe he'll look past your differences and fall for your inner soul. Maybe, maybe not, but this movie is a primer for how it can happen.

The Reel Deal: It's Dublin, Ireland, 1955, where it's still a novelty for college girls to admit that they're smart and ready to take on the world. Benny, Eve, and Nan are finding their way at Trinity College, where learning to protect your purity seems to be more important than excelling in your academic courses. The orphan Eve (Geraldine O'Rawe) comes to Trinity with best friend Benny (Minnie Driver), leaving behind her convent childhood but not her deep sense of loyalty and morality. Pretty Nan (Saffron Burrows) quickly tires of the college boys and sets her sights on older, sophisticated Simon Westward (Colin Firth). Benny's parents presume their plainer daughter would do well to marry the simpering Sean Walsh, the creepy manager of their haberdashery shop. But Benny is smitten with gorgeous Jack Foley (Chris O'Donnell), a rugby-playing Adonis who, after a slow start, finds himself returning her interest.

He's drawn to Benny's fire, her surety of who she is and what she wants, a rarity in a time when family pressure was twice what it is now. (Imagine that….) Benny and her friends experience a fair amount of heartbreak during their time at Trinity, but experience is what they're all after in this sweet and charming film.

Line That Says It All: "I know I may look like a rhinoceros, but I'm quite thin-skinned, really. Don't mess me about. I'll flatten you."

Girl to Watch: Minnie Driver, of course, in the role that put her on the map. Think of the Harvard glam girl she plays in GOOD WILL HUNTING as Benny's future self.

Guy to Watch: Chris O'Donnell as Jack. You really believe he'd pick Benny over a dozen magazine covergirls.

Scene Worth the Rewind: When Benny and Jack are first alone together, just talking. You see her appeal through his eyes.

Fun Factoid: This story is adapted from a novel by Maeve Binchy, a successful Irish writer who specializes in simple, romantic tales slightly out of this time and place. If that's your cup of tea, this author might be to your taste.

Watch This One With: Your mom would like this one. Are you overdue for some cinema bonding time?

Movies with the Same Vibe: REAL WOMEN HAVE CURVES, ROOM WITH A VIEW.

HOW THIS MOVIE HELPS

People are drawn to one another for a variety of reasons that most movies oriented toward younger people never show. Too often the logic is "I'm cute, you're cute, let's be cute together." We imagine that some people—cute people, in particular—buy into this cinematic reasoning, but if you're even the tiniest bit different it doesn't give you much hope for romance, does it? CIRCLE OF FRIENDS portrays life the way it really is sometimes; it shows that we can get the hot guy without getting some magically transforming makeover, but by being our own irresistible selves. If that seems totally implausible then check out all the couples you see at the mall or school. There are lots of ways to be attractive—and lots of guys who understand that. This is a great movie to watch with someone who loves you just the way you are—maybe someone from your own circle of friends.

Clueless

MOOD CONTROL

1	2	3
4	5	6
7	8	9
10	11	12

⏵ Press PLAY if you're feeling:

1 Adventurous
2 Ambitious
3 Artsy
4 Cynical
5 DEPRESSED
6 Heartbroken
7 Hopeful
8 Insecure
9 Misunderstood
10 OVERWHELMED
11 PLAYFUL
12 Weird

1995   ULTIMATE GIRL RATING: ♣ ♣ ♣ ♣

DIRECTOR: Amy Heckerling
BIRTHPLACE:
Mainstream Hollywood
FILE UNDER:
Hottie Knows Best
RATED: PG-13

STARRING: Alicia Silverstone,
Paul Rudd, Brittany Murphy,
Stacey Dash, Donald Faison,
Dan Hedaya, Breckin Meyer,
Justin Walker

THE PROBLEM

You have to admit it: you're sort of naturally talented at being able to see how people should conduct their lives. When people take your advice they look better, feel better, and life makes more sense. There are only two problems: sometimes they don't listen to you, and sometimes you don't listen to yourself. Bummer.

The Reel Deal: Cher Horowitz (Alicia Silverstone) is the chief creation in this witty comedy set in Beverly Hills, California. Rich and beautiful, Cher glides through high school with her best friend Dionne (Stacey Dash). More intriguing than yet another designer shopping spree is the prospect of sprucing up Tai Fraiser (Brittany Murphy), whose urban decay chic and penchant for skater boys strikes Cher and Dionne as a tragedy in the making.

Meanwhile, Cher's own impeccable plans for life run afoul of reality. The boy she has a crush on (Justin Walker) may or may not be into girls, and her own former stepbrother (Paul Rudd) is inspiring weird fits of jealousy and attraction in her. Without a pretense of being anything other than cotton-candy fun, CLUELESS shows how even a "surface queen" like Cher can find humility in love and meaning in doing real good for others.

Line That Says It All: CLUELESS is chock-full of wickedly funny lines. Typical dialogue: "Would you say I'm selfish?" "No, not to your face."

Girl to Watch: Alicia Silverstone seems born to play this creature.

Guy to Watch: You're rooting for sweet, smart Paul Rudd, but Justin Walker as Christian is a rat pack riot. Oh my God, Cher, put down that mascara wand and pick up your Gaydar!

Fashion to Catch: Take your pick— Cher's closet is the size of Texas.

Scene Worth the Rewind: Cher's discussion of Haiti. Hait-larious.

Watch This One With: Any friend who has a totally different look from you.

Movies with the Same Vibe: BRING IT ON.

HOW THIS MOVIE HELPS

CLUELESS is such featherweight fun it's amazing to think that it was based loosely on Jane Austen's novel *Emma*. (Austen's cooler than you thought, no?) Yet even this funny froth-fest has a good reminder about the perils of thinking you know what's best for anybody else. Mainly, it's just a funny, funny film mocking and celebrating life in the valet-parking zone.

Confessions of a Teenage Drama Queen

MOOD CONTROL

1 2 3
4 5 6
7 8 9
10 11 12

▶ Press PLAY if you're feeling:

1 Adventurous
2 AMBITIOUS
3 ARTSY
4 Cynical
5 Depressed
6 Heartbroken
7 HOPEFUL
8 Insecure
9 Misunderstood
10 Overwhelmed
11 Playful
12 Weird

2004 **ULTIMATE GIRL RATING:** ♣ ♣

DIRECTOR: Sara Sugarman
BIRTHPLACE:
Mainstream Hollywood
FILE UNDER: Run, Lola, Run
RATED: PG

STARRING: Lindsay Lohan, Adam Garcia, Glenne Headly, Alison Pill, Eli Marienthal, Carol Kane, Megan Fox

THE PROBLEM

You just can't help it—you're too fabulous for the world you live in. You don't dress or talk or act like the conformist robots in your soul-killing town. You're destined for bright lights and big cities, even though you're stuck in the dark in Smallsville. How do you get people to see your true potential? Is it enough just to see it yourself? You're already a star, but no one knows it. Will they ever?

The Reel Deal: Fresh from FREAKY FRIDAY, Lindsay Lohan plays Lola (her real name is Mary), a melodramatic teenager from Manhattan with a penchant for poetic language and clothes that say "I'm in theater." She is mortified when she has to move with her mother (Glenne Headly) and little sisters to a suburb in New Jersey, presumably for the good public schools.

"Good" is a relative term, however—Lola discovers that her new high school is filled with rich brats who seem to make a full-time job out of destroying anyone who doesn't meet their standards. Their leader is the supremely snot-nosed Carla Santini (Megan Fox), who can't believe that Lola just might win the lead in the school play. Backing Lola are new friends Sam (Eli Marienthal) and

Ella (Alison Pill), a shy, mousy girl who shares Lola's love for the band Siddhartha. Lola's plan to triumph in the school play, meet the rock star of her dreams, and put the evil Carla in her place plays out in a series of colorful events that fit together like a crazy quilt. You'll grow dizzy keeping up with Lola's journey, but you might have fun too.

Line That Says It All: "Your parents encourage you to follow your hopes and dreams. Then they move you to New Jersey."

Girl to Watch: Lindsay Lohan and Megan Fox both get into their rivalry roles. Yet we loved Alison Pill as Ella. For once, the best friend role gets elevated to a true three-dimensional character, a person in her own right, not just a cheering section for the heroine. There's a scene where Ella's really disappointed in Lola, and she's crying, and it's not just a chance to clarify Lola's problems. The camera stays on Ella for a long time, giving her the scene and, for the moment, the film. How often does that happen to a movie second banana?

Guy to Watch: Adam Garcia as Stuart, the self-involved rocker who finally notices that he's forgotten how to be a person.

How You Know It's a Movie: School plays usually look more like Broadway productions. The over-the-top displays in this movie are no exception.

Scene Worth the Rewind: Revenge doesn't come when you expect it to in this fast-paced film, but it comes soon enough. And when it does, it's sweet.

Fun Factoid: Hilary Duff was originally offered the part of Lola. And Miss Baggoli is such a queen of frump that you'd hardly know she's played by the lovely actress Carol Kane.

Watch This One With: Your own Drama Queen self!

Movies with the Same Vibe: WHAT A GIRL WANTS, WIN A DATE WITH TAD HAMILTON, MEAN GIRLS.

HOW THIS MOVIE HELPS

If you're just entering the teen scene and you're scared of the Carla Santini's of the world, we don't blame you. Every school has somebody who seems to grab power through intimidation. We like the fact that when Lola first arrives at the school, she actually has an opportunity to get in with the pretty, popular crowd. It's a good thing that Lola was fortunate enough to meet Ella first, and smart enough to recognize that a friend who has your back and will call you on your stuff is worth her weight in Doritos. Lola is a little flaky, but her deep-down values are so solid that they give her star quality before she ever steps foot on the stage.

Crazy/Beautiful

MOOD CONTROL

1	2	3
4	5	6
7	8	9
10	11	12

▶ Press **PLAY** if you're feeling:

1 Adventurous
2 Ambitious
3 Artsy
4 Cynical
5 Depressed
6 Heartbroken
7 HOPEFUL
8 INSECURE
9 Misunderstood
10 OVERWHELMED
11 Playful
12 Weird

2001 ULTIMATE GIRL RATING: ♣ ♣ ♣ ♣

DIRECTOR: John Stockwell
BIRTHPLACE: Mainstream Hollywood
FILE UNDER: Warning—Bad Girl Ahead
RATED: PG-13

STARRING: Kirsten Dunst, Jay Hernandez, Bruce Davison, Herman Osorio, Miguel Castro, Tommy de la Cruz, Rolando Molina, Soledad St. Hilaire, Lucinda Jenney, Taryn Manning

THE PROBLEM

You're drawn to somebody that everyone else has abandoned years ago. What is it about her? Sure, your friend does bad things, but not because they're bad. In fact, you see some pretty amazing stuff in your troubled pal. Why does she hide that side of herself from the world? Everyone says that people like this will bring you right down with them. Sometimes, when you get scared, you wonder if they're right.

The Reel Deal: Nicole Oakley (Kirsten Dunst) and Carlos Nunez (Jay Hernandez) go to the same top high school, but they have very different attitudes about being there. For Nicole, the daughter of a wealthy congressman, a terrific school in a great town is an assumed privilege. Carlos, on the other hand, travels two hours each way to attend this school in the hopes that top marks here will help him get into the prestigious Naval Academy in Annapolis, Maryland. Nicole parties as hard as Carlos studies, but sparks fly when they meet, and they soon become a couple. Nicole is delighted to have such a handsome hunk for a boyfriend, but Carlos' feelings are more mixed: he loves Nicole but fears that her wild ways could destroy everything he's

worked for. Her father, Tom (Bruce Davison), shares this concern. In a refreshing twist on an old scenario, the rich father warns the barrio boy away from his daughter, not for her sake, but for his. He can't quite give up on his daughter altogether, but he comes close, seeing in her the same self-destructive tendencies that led to his first wife's suicide years earlier. Now he's remarried and Nicole's stepmother, Courtney (Lucinda Jenney), would just as soon fuss over her baby and not have to deal with the headache that is Nicole. Carlos is a great guy, but will he chuck his whole future to fit in with the love of his life? Will she stay that great love if she can't get her act together? When a movie is this romantic, you cross your fingers.

Line That Says It All: "You don't care about what people think, and when I'm with you, I don't care about what people think."

Girl to Watch: Kirsten Dunst as Nicole. When is that girl not lit up from within? It's fun to see her in such a no-holds-barred role. Kirsten, you're blinding us!

Guy to Watch: Jay Hernandez as Carlos. Not just cute, Herdandez is also a nuanced actor.

Fun Factoid: When the film was being rated there was a huge outcry about its portrayal of drugs and irresponsible sex in a teen movie. So they cut out the scenes that showed kids partaking and just hinted at the situation in order to get that coveted PG-13 rating. Those connected to the film complained that the movie became a cautionary tale that couldn't show any of the things they wanted to caution kids against. Kind of a good point, isn't it? Oh well. Use your imagination. Then use your common sense. Fair enough?

Watch This One With: Your craziest friends. That's probably most of them, isn't it?

Movies with the Same Vibe: THIRTEEN; ROMEO + JULIET; GIRL, INTERRUPTED.

HOW THIS MOVIE HELPS

If you don't know a Nicole, you must go to a pretty quiet high school. Girls like this character can be a blast to be around, but they can infect other people who might want a little more out of life than the next good party. In rooting for Nicole and Carlos, you root for anyone who wants their love to help someone get their act together. You root for love to eliminate all the barriers between two people too. That's a lot to put on love, but love puts a lot on us, doesn't it?

Crouching Tiger, Hidden Dragon

MOOD CONTROL

1 2 3
4 5 6
7 8 9
10 11 12

Press PLAY if you're feeling:

1 ADVENTUROUS
2 Ambitious
3 ARTSY
4 Cynical
5 Depressed
6 Heartbroken
7 Hopeful
8 Insecure
9 Misunderstood
10 OVERWHELMED
11 Playful
12 Weird

2000 ULTIMATE GIRL RATING: ♣♣♣♣

DIRECTOR: Ang Lee
BIRTHPLACE: East/West
FILE UNDER: Woman Warrior
RATED: PG-13

STARRING: Yun-Fat Chow, Michelle Yeoh, Chen Chang, Ziyi Zhang

THE PROBLEM You think that maybe you were born in the wrong time. You love tales of knights and daring, great quests and insurmountable challenges, but these tales seldom feature a girl as the warrior to be reckoned with. If you're tired of seeing women portrayed as damsels in distress, maybe it's time to go east. In this film, the damsels do the dueling.

The Reel Deal: Li Mu Bai (Yun-Fat Chow) is a warrior who is torn between his love for his warrior soul mate, Yu Shu Lien (Michelle Yeoh), and his desire to avenge the death of his master. Yu Shu loves him too, yet they have much work to do before they can be together. "Green Destiny," the magical jade sword that once belonged to Li Mu Bai's master, has recently been sold to a wealthy man. When it is stolen, the two warriors, together with the man's young daughter, Jen Yu (Ziyi Zhang), become enmeshed in a journey of vengeance that also involves the bonds of family, duty, and love. CROUCHING TIGER, HIDDEN DRAGON is definitely a martial arts movie—incredible, acrobatic swordplay makes up much of the film—yet it is so much more than that. It brilliantly captures both romantic love and the romance of living the life of a renegade.

"I would rather be a ghost drifting by your side as a condemned soul than enter heaven without you. Because of your love...I will never be a lonely spirit."

Three amazing women will captivate you. Michelle Yeoh is a famous martial arts expert, but the Jade Fox and the governor's pampered daughter will also dazzle you with their amazing swordplay.

Everyone in Western films talks themselves to death, especially about their feelings, yet look how much Yun-Fat Chow can say about his love for Yu Shu Lien with just a glance.

The swordfight that takes place atop a forest of swaying trees will take your breath away. You'll be even more impressed when you learn that this isn't all done with special effects. Wires are attached to the actor's bodies and removed through special effects in the editing room, but those are real people jumping from building to building and balancing in the treetops. What's more, almost no stunt doubles were used. If you guessed correctly that the CROUCHING TIGER cast had to be in top physical condition for this movie, reward yourself with a power bar.

Ang Lee is an incredibly versatile filmmaker whose projects are vastly different from one another. But one thing his films have in common is that they feature strong female characters who comfortably dominate the action, or at least hold their own. Other Ang Lee films you might like are *The Ice Storm* (1997), a dark, poignant drama about drifting adults and their kids lost in '70s suburbia, and *Sense and Sensibility* (1995), a beautifully realized version of the Jane Austen novel. You see what we mean about his range?

Your little brother. Finally, you can force him to watch a film with you that you'll both love.

GIRLFIGHT, THE PRINCESS BRIDE.

HOW THIS MOVIE HELPS

CROUCHING TIGER, HIDDEN DRAGON can't teach you how to defy gravity with swordplay that is so beguiling you almost forget who you're rooting for (you have to go to movie fight school to learn that), but it can give you an evening of drama, mystery, and romance. Besides, how often do you get to watch a movie that's a great love story and also shows women warriors kicking butt? Not nearly often enough, we think.

Dazed and Confused

MOOD CONTROL

1	2	3
4	5	6
7	8	9
10	11	12

▶ **Press PLAY if you're feeling:**

1 Adventurous
2 Ambitious
3 ARTSY
4 Cynical
5 DEPRESSED
6 Heartbroken
7 Hopeful
8 Insecure
9 Misunderstood
10 OVERWHELMED
11 Playful
12 Weird

1993 **ULTIMATE GIRL RATING:** ♣ ♣ ♣

DIRECTOR: Richard Linklater
BIRTHPLACE: Indie U.S.A.
FILE UNDER: Slacker Heaven, Slacker Hell
RATED: R

STARRING: Jason London, Wiley Wiggins, Sasha Jenson, Rory Cochrane, Shawn Andrews, Adam Goldberg, Anthony Rapp, Michelle Burke, Marissa Ribisi, Matthew McConaughey, Joey Lauren Adams, Cole Hauser, Ben Affleck, Milla Jovovich

THE PROBLEM

You barely start high school and people want to know where you're applying to college. You barely figure that out and people want to know what you're going to major in. You throw out a few ideas in that direction and people wonder what graduate schools you'll be looking at. Is it just us, or does it seem that teenagers are expected to have adult goals before they even learn how to drive a car? Sometimes you wonder if there's anyone else out there who's just biding their time, without a plan in sight.

The Reel Deal: Filmmaker Richard Linklater of Austin, Texas, sets his story in 1976, on the last day of school, when masses of teenagers mill about wondering about the future, getting into trouble, and just hanging out. There's a football jock named Randall "Pink" Floyd (Jason London) who hangs with just about everybody: jocks, druggies, and those in-between. The incoming freshmen are excited about their upcoming adventure at school, but hardly looking forward to the sadistic paddling ritual that awaits them. We meet characters looking for love, looking for a way out, looking for the answers to life, and engaging in hilarious random conversations. DAZED AND CONFUSED is filled with these bizarre soliloquies and pet theories that are a staple of Linklater's films. Little bits of plot hang all over this film like tinsel on a tree, but mainly it's character-driven, and these Texas teens are, indeed, characters.

Line That Says It All: "If I ever say these were the best years of my life, remind me to kill myself."

Girl to Watch: Marissa Ribisi is compelling as a girl who is slowly starting to realize that there must be more to life than her little corner of Austin.

Guy to Watch: Matthew McConaughey made an early mark with this character, a type we all know and pity: the high school guy who just can't make it outside of high school.

Fun Factoid: These days everyone associates the '70s with the disco craze, but plenty of kids were into rock-'n'-roll and hated the whole dance scene. DAZED AND CONFUSED focuses on the latter group, with details that anyone who was a teenager at that time will tell you are spot-on accurate.

Watch This One With: Your "Least Likely to Succeed" buds.

Movies with the Same Vibe: AMERICAN GRAFFITI, FAST TIMES AT RIDGEMONT HIGH, CAN'T HARDLY WAIT. Also check out *Almost Famous* (2000), in which an innocent high school journalist enters the world of an aspiring rock god, and Linklater's other films, particularly *Slackers* (2002), which shows the kids of *D and C* all grown up. (Well, not really grown up at all. But they are older.)

HOW THIS MOVIE HELPS

DAZED AND CONFUSED shows a bunch of fairly aimless kids who possess varying degrees of cynicism and hope for their future as they approach or leave high school. But they are pretty typical teens, and will probably grow up to be the same upright citizens who now harass you into doing your algebra. The adults in your life may try to convince you that your generation is particularly apathetic, but that's been the universal complaint of parents for more than a century. It's human nature to downplay your own youthful indiscretions when you're focused on raising the next generation of algebra-pushers. So try this: hunt around for an old photograph of your mom and dad. If they ever looked liked the kids in DAZED AND CONFUSED, chances are you'll find one of them wearing a "Disco Sucks" T-shirt. If not, ask them just what they *were* doing in the summer of '76?

Dirty Dancing

MOOD CONTROL

1	2	3
4	5	6
7	8	9
10	11	12

▶ Press PLAY if you're feeling:

1 ADVENTUROUS
2 Ambitious
3 Artsy
4 Cynical
5 Depressed
6 Heartbroken
7 HOPEFUL
8 INSECURE
9 Misunderstood
10 Overwhelmed
11 Playful
12 Weird

1987 ULTIMATE GIRL RATING: 🍿🍿🍿🍿🍿

DIRECTOR: Emile Ardolino
BIRTHPLACE: Mainstream Hollywood
FILE UNDER: Baby Grows Up
RATED: PG-13

STARRING: Jennifer Grey, Patrick Swayze, Jerry Orbach, Cynthia Rhodes, Jack Weston, Jane Brucker, Kelly Bishop, Lonny Price, Charles Coles, Wayne Knight

THE PROBLEM

There's this weird thing that happens when we start to like guys. Some of the guys we like remind us of our brothers or our neighbors, the kind of boys who would fit right in at any family gathering. Sometimes, though, we're drawn to that other kind of guy, the one who stands on the outside, not even trying to get in. We're the ones looking out, wondering if the world of our families and peers just might not be that great after all. For some strange reason, you drool over the guy you wouldn't dream of bringing home to meet the folks. Not that he'd ever notice you. Or would he? It just might be time to have the time of your life.

The Reel Deal: Frances Houseman, a.k.a. "Baby" (Jennifer Grey), is spending the summer of 1963 at a cheesy family resort with the rest of her pampered kin. She soon learns that there are two types of help at Kellerman's: the Ivy League college waiters she's encouraged to socialize with and the working class entertainers who must endure the guests who both desire and disdain them. Baby's sister is having a fine time jumping into all the activities and hanging out with the other mostly annoying guests.

Yet socially conscious Baby immediately prefers the world of the dancers. Fraternizing with the guests isn't really allowed at Kellerman's, but Baby, irresistibly drawn to a staff party, more or less forces her way into the lives of the resort's entertainers. Handsome Johnny Castle (Patrick Swayze) is wary of Baby at first, but soon requires her help when his dance partner discovers she's pregnant. Baby finds herself learning how to dance so she can be a substitute dance partner for Johnny in an upcoming contest. Johnny finds himself having second thoughts about a girl he originally dismissed as a spoiled rich kid just out for some fun. It looks like Baby and Johnny are starting to fall in love, but a series of misunderstandings and false assumptions threaten to keep them apart forever. This movie might as well be called "The Great Awakening," for Baby learns about courage, character, and more than one kind of dirty dancing.

Line That Says It All: "Me! I'm scared of everything. I'm scared of what I saw, of what I did, of who I am, and most of all I'm scared of walking out of this room and never feeling the rest of my whole life the way I feel when I'm with you."

Guy to Watch: Patrick Swayze. Especially when he's dancing. Also check out the actor playing Baby's father (Jerry Orbach). If you've ever watched an episode of "Law and Order" you've seen him as the crotchety Lt. Briscoe, cracking jokes and catching bad guys.

Girl to Watch: Jennifer Grey. Finally, a heroine who looks like a normal girl, not a model in a costume!

Fashion to Catch: All the early '60s looks are fun, but we'll go with Patrick, shirtless.

Eye-Rolling Time: The '80s power-pop ballads. Wasn't this supposed to take place in 1963?

Watch This One With: Friends who enjoy films about doing away with the snob system, reclaiming your sexuality, memories of a simpler time (that wasn't actually so simple), and most of all dancing in the dark with hot guys.

Movies with the Same Vibe: HONEY, FOOTLOOSE. Also check out *Dirty Dancing: Havana Nights* (2004). This recent "sequel" is a totally different story, but offers some fun moves as well.

HOW THIS MOVIE HELPS

This movie spawned a nation of happy, dancing "Babys"—and why not? In addition to its other charms, DIRTY DANCING taught a nation of young girls that their sexuality is nothing to be ashamed of (or maybe Johnny Castle taught them that). The point is, maybe the sexy tough guy of your dreams is really a man of integrity—integrity that just happens to look better without a shirt on. For years, men have fantasized about finding beauty and brains in one attractive package. Isn't it our turn?

Dogtown and Z-Boys

2001 **ULTIMATE GIRL RATING:** ♣ ♣ ♣

DIRECTOR: Stacy Peralta
BIRTHPLACE: Sidewalks of L.A.
FILE UNDER: He Was a Skater Boy
RATED: PG-13

STARRING: Stacy Peralta, Sean Penn, Jay Adams, Tony Alva, Jeff Ament, Bob Biniak, Paul Constantineau, Skip Engblom, Tony Friedkin, Glen Friedman, Tony Hawk, Jeff Ho, Shogo Kubo, Joe Leahy, Peggy Oki

THE PROBLEM

If you're into skateboarding, this is a great documentary about a sport that is still misunderstood. The general consensus of skating among the non-skaters is, "You'll break your neck on that thing!" Yet skaters know what it's like to fly with nothing but gravity pressing you to your wheels, ready to drop fifteen feet onto solid concrete and head back up the wall again. Even if you're not a skater yourself, you may like the culture and the kids drawn to the sport. Surrounded by skeptics? They need to meet the Zs.

The Reel Deal: Maybe you've seen them and didn't know it: a bunch of guys in their forties, some married with kids, talking about how it was "back in the day." You'd probably be surprised to learn that these guys were once a bunch of bored teenagers who together reinvented skating, and helped take other sports to new heights with their daring inventiveness. Dogtown is a coastal neighborhood between Santa Monica and Venice, California. A posh enclave today, it was a gritty hood back in the '70s, a hangout for druggies, hippies, and surf bums: kids who surfed in the morning and switched

Documentaries can be so cool. No, please, don't look at us like that. We're not talking about the videos of pyramids and pilgrims that help you catch up on your sleep in class. We're talking reality shows before there was reality TV. We're talking filmmakers who captured rare, amazing worlds on celluloid, giving us an inside look at secret lives and untold stories. See? No filmstrips, no tests, and any learning will be totally accidental.

Check out these hot docs....

Hoop Dreams (1994)

An intimate look at the lives of two inner-city basketball players as they work to keep their dreams alive. This movie has so many twists and turns you can hardly believe it's not fiction. Terrific.

Paris Is Burning (1990)

Explores the New York subculture of drag balls, where young black and hispanic gay men don a multitude of ordinary and extraordinary costumes in a fierce competition. Makes you think: one man's daily uniform is another man's "drag." A funny, touching film.

Spellbound (2002)

It's about a spelling bee, and you'll be on the edge of your seat. Seriously. It's I-N-S-P-I-R-E-D.

Madonna: Truth or Dare (1991)

You don't have to be a Madonna obsessive to enjoy this quirky, backstage look at our bi-continental queen diva. Even though it's a Madonna-approved product, the film offers up some interesting insight into the Material Girl.

Bowling for Columbine (2002)

They say "Guns don't kill people, people kill people." In this funny, infuriating unabashedly political film, perennially pissed off filmmaker Michael Moore (ROGER AND ME, FAHRENHEIT 9/11), gives a pretty convincing argument for the idea that guns kinda have something to do with it (not to mention the media circus that springs up after every tragic shooting). And the movie does touch on some Columbine-related issues, adding to the powerful message.

to skateboarding in the afternoon, thinking of it as a form of roller-skating (back before sleek in-lines ruled the day). One summer, when California was experiencing one of its perennial droughts, swimming pools in the area were drained. A group of adventurous skaters who called themselves the Zephyr Team, or Z-Boys, decided to try to "surf" up and down the empty pools. The Z-Boys kept pushing the boundaries of gravity until at last they were airborne, paving the way for the extreme skateboard moves we see today.

Line That Says It All: "Nobody was doing what we were doing."

Girl to Watch: One girl, Peggy Oki, was a " Z-Boy" as well, and her brief appearance adds another dimension to the film.

Guy to Watch: Actually, Boy to Hear is more like it. Sean Penn makes a great narrator for this unique film. He actually grew up near Dogtown and felt a personal connection to the Z-Boys and the making of this film.

Scene Worth the Rewind: If you're a skater, you won't be able to get enough of the great moves. Even if you're not a skater, you'll marvel at the elegance of this sport. No guts, no glory—and no helmets. It's amazing that most of the Z-Boys are still standing. The scene of the first big skateboard competition that the Zs entered as a team really gives you a feel for just how radical this group was. You see all these old-school skaters perched like cranes on their boards, then the Zs come out and do their thing, slipping and sliding, ripping around turns like they plan to shred the concrete for a salad.

Soundtrack Note: Skaters were, historically, rockers, and this movie has the soundtrack to prove it. Classic Aerosmith, Alice Cooper, the Allman Brothers, Black Sabbath, and Blue Oyster Cult—we're talkin' a total '70s freak fest. A little Herb Alpert cuts through the noise with his horn-centered jazz pop, and we can always stand to hear David Bowie's "Rebel Rebel."

Movies with the Same Vibe: BLUE CRUSH. Also check out documentaries in general (they're such a great way to learn about a world that may be new to you).

HOW THIS MOVIE HELPS

The people in your life who need you to look to the future may not understand how important skating is to who you are and what you love to do with your days. DOGTOWN AND Z-BOYS won't necessarily change that, but it can show you that guys who lived for skating years ago still value it hugely and want to share their tales of adventure and discovery with the world. The world wants to hear it too—DOGTOWN did well both with the critics and in the theaters. We look forward to more skating films. Let's see more girls on the boards in the next one.

Donnie Darko

MOOD CONTROL

1 2 3
4 5 6
7 8 9
10 11 12

▶ Press PLAY
if you're feeling:

1   Adventurous
2   Ambitious
3   ARTSY
4   Cynical
5   Depressed
6   Heartbroken
7   Hopeful
8   Insecure
9   MISUNDERSTOOD
10 Overwhelmed
11 Playful
12 WEIRD

2001 ULTIMATE GIRL RATING: 🍿🍿🍿

DIRECTOR: Richard Kelly
BIRTHPLACE:
The Parallel Universe
FILE UNDER:
Science Fiction Suburbia
RATED: R

STARRING: Jake Gyllenhaal,
Holmes Osborne, Mary
McDonnell, Jena Malone, Drew
Barrymore, Katherine Ross

THE PROBLEM

Okay, maybe you don't have a giant, malevolent bunny ordering you around. (If you do, please go get some professional help.) Yet life can make you crazy, and sometimes you wonder if you really have gone nuts. But are you crackers just because you spend a lot of time wondering about the meaning of life? And what about time and space? Are we really here, after all? Is the future really off in the future, or is it running on a parallel track? If it's crazy to wax philosophical about our very existence, then why do we do it so often? Maybe a giant bunny-wizard really *is* running the show....

The Reel Deal: Donnie Darko (Jake Gyllenhaal) is a bright, congenial, somewhat sardonic teenager who has, we soon learn, some "issues." Under hypnosis, he reveals to his psychiatrist (Katherine Ross) that he has a nocturnal visitor who takes him on sleepwalking trips around the neighborhood.

During one such outing, a jet engine crashes into Donnie's bedroom and would have killed him had he not been out roaming the streets. Soon, Donnie's whole life becomes like an episode of *Smallville*—only creepier and more cryptic. His English teacher (Drew Barrymore) is sympathetic, but other teachers have a problem with Donnie, and his parents get called into school. Even worse, his nocturnal visitor, a sort of rabbit-wizard creature, tells him that the end of the world is near. Yet there's still time for a charming romance between Donnie and Gretchen (Jena Malone), who gets him as well as anyone can. The ending of DONNIE DARKO will probably leave you scratching your head in confusion, but in a good way: it's fun to try to interpret the random moves of the universe, especially a universe as intriguing as this one.

Line That Says It All:
"You're weird."
"Sorry."
"No, that was a compliment."

Girl to Watch: We like Donnie's girlfriend, Jena Malone, but all the women in this movie are pretty three-dimensional and interesting.

Guy to Watch: Jake Gyllenhaal. He seems so normal, sometimes. Then…

Scene Worth the Rewind: The ending. It's like one of those hidden-picture paintings—not everyone sees the same thing, which gives you plenty to debate with your friends. (For even more Darko to discuss, be sure to see the Director's Cut version.)

Fun Factoid: This movie takes place over twenty-eight days, and that's exactly how long it took to film it, start to finish.

Soundtrack Note: DONNIE DARKO takes place in the mid-'80s and is filled with the jangle-pop, new-wave hits of that era. Echo and the Bunnymen, Duran Duran, and The Church all provide subtext to Donnie Darko's darkening world.

Watch This One With: Your friends who love to analyze and debate; this movie pretty much requires it. Don't like movies that are a bit weird? Save your money, honey.

Movies with the Same Vibe: HAROLD AND MAUDE. Also check out good movies with mysterious endings, like *2001: A Space Odyssey* (1968) or *Jacob's Ladder* (1990).

HOW THIS MOVIE HELPS

A perfectly crafted film chock-full of honest teen angst, DONNIE DARKO also contains wacky ideas that feel sort of like junior high science fiction efforts. We don't think this is a bad thing. Remember when you were little and thought the Easter Bunny and Santa Claus were married? That was pretty weird too. Besides, it's nice sometimes to puzzle over something besides a question on a history test. Too often these days movies want to wrap things up in nice little bundles so you don't have to think at all. That can be pleasant, but those movies tend to slip down the brain drain the minute you stop the tape. DONNIE DARKO stays with you, like a fever dream, and you'll turn it over and over in your mind, perplexed and invigorated.

Double Happiness

MOOD CONTROL

1	2	3
4	5	6
7	8	9
10	11	12

▶ **Press PLAY** if you're feeling:

1 Adventurous
2 AMBITIOUS
3 ARTSY
4 Cynical
5 Depressed
6 HEARTBROKEN
7 Hopeful
8 Insecure
9 Misunderstood
10 Overwhelmed
11 Playful
12 Weird

1994 | **ULTIMATE GIRL RATING:** ♣ ♣ ♣

DIRECTOR: Mina Shum
BIRTHPLACE: Canada
FILE UNDER:
East Meets West Test
RATED: PG-13

STARRING: Sandra Oh, Alanna Ong, Greg Chen, Stephen Chang, Callum Rennie

THE PROBLEM

You feel like the only way to live the life you want is to pretend to be living the life that your parents want for you. You look like a good girl but secretly get what you want. Everybody's happy. At least that's the theory. But how can you really be yourself when you're living with people who haven't even met the real girl? Happiness? A dream. So what's double happiness?

The Reel Deal: Jade (Sandra Oh) isn't a teen, but she sure lives like one. Stuck in Vancouver, Canada, with her Hong Kong–born parents, her life is swiftly becoming one big lie. All her folks want is for her to meet a nice Chinese-Canadian boy and settle down. She wants so much more. She wants to stay out until dawn, with boys her parents would never approve of, but even more than that, she wants to be an actress. Jade slips out to auditions where few casting directors know what to do with a Chinese actress. Her parents don't know what to do with her either, and force her on a blind date with a proper Chinese suitor. Of course, he turns out to be gay, forced into this charade to please his own traditional parents. Can Jade tell her parents the truth? No, she comes up with something "worse": he made her split the dinner check. Funny scenes like this remind us that, wherever we're from, it's hard to be yourself when you live in a world that doesn't welcome difference. When Jade falls in love, she has to make a choice between hidden happiness or double-the-fun by living a life she can lead in public.

Line That Says It All: "I wondered why we couldn't be the Brady Bunch. Of course, they don't need subtitles."

Girl to Watch: Sandra Oh as Jade. You can see her on TV and in the movies, and this film shows why she should be an even bigger star.

Guy to Watch: Callum Rennie as Mark. He sure seems worth the trouble.

Scene Worth the Rewind: Jade's auditions. They remind us how much people seem to want to stick to the stereotypes.

Fun Factoid: Writer and director Mina Shum wanted to make this film since she was eighteen, when she was ready to move out of the house but had no one to encourage her. She made this film to inspire others in the same position.

Game to Play: "Starring Me, Myself, and I." This movie is based on writer and director Mina Shum's life. What would the movie of your life be like? Pick a title then decide who would play your family and friends. Add an adventure and pick a famous screen villain, or a romance and pick a hot costar. Write it up in your journal for fun, or play it at the next girls gathering. Remember: make it larger than life—it's your movie!

Watch This One With: Your Asian girlfriends. Where are all *your* films? As the director herself once said "Give me a color I can identify with."

Movies with the Same Vibe: REAL WOMEN HAVE CURVES, BEND IT LIKE BECKHAM, I'M THE ONE THAT I WANT.

HOW THIS MOVIE HELPS

Nothing comes easy for Jade, but she makes things so much harder on herself. You watch her live two lives and grow increasingly exhausted by the effort it takes. It's generous to try to please everyone in your life, but films like this show why that strategy never works. Who do you know that's leading a double life? How much energy goes into keeping the secret, how much stress? Do you really think it's worth it? Sure, it's second nature to tell the folks only what they want to hear. It's a hard trap to escape, and it's inspiring to watch Jade finally try to blend her two worlds into one. You don't have to be a Chinese-Canadian aspiring actress to find DOUBLE HAPPINESS pretty relevant to your own struggle. How do you stay out of trouble yet still be true to yourself? It isn't easy. Sometimes you simply have no choice but to decide what kind of trouble is worth the effort.

Drumline

MOOD CONTROL

① ② ③
④ ⑤ ⑥
⑦ ⑧ ⑨
⑩ ⑪ ⑫

Press PLAY
if you're feeling:

1 Adventurous
2 AMBITIOUS
3 Artsy
4 CYNICAL
5 Depressed
6 Heartbroken
7 Hopeful
8 Insecure
9 Misunderstood
10 Overwhelmed
11 PLAYFUL
12 Weird

2002 **ULTIMATE GIRL RATING:** 🍀🍀🍀

DIRECTOR: Charles Stone III
BIRTHPLACE: Mainstream Hollywood
FILE UNDER: I'm with the Band
RATED: PG-13

STARRING: Nick Cannon, Zoe Saldana, Orlando Jones, Leonord Roberts, GQ, Jason Weaver, Earl Poitier

THE PROBLEM

You'd love to be part of some of the great activities at school, if only it didn't require being a team player. What's with this obsession about teamwork these days? Why can't the best person just stand out from the crowd?

The Reel Deal: Cocky-yet-talented Devon (Nick Cannon) has been recruited from the streets of New York to join the drumline of a prestigious Southern marching band. For some hip-hop generation kids, band wouldn't be cool, but for Devon it's a free ride through college and a way to play percussion all he wants. He got his talent from his jazz-loving dad, but was raised solely by his proud mother. Devon arrives at fictional Atlanta A & T University ready to show his bandmates a move or two. However, he soon learns that being the best isn't the smooth ride he thought it would be. He upstages his section leader, Sean (Leonard Roberts), winning himself a serious enemy. Dr. Aaron Lee (Orlando Jones) tries to play the wise, older mentor to Devon, but finds it rough going. Devon doesn't understand the reasons behind some of the rules, and won't follow directions he can't agree with. Soon, Devon is out of the band, and out of favor with the beautiful, classy Laila (Zoe Saldana), who he had worked so hard to charm. At some point Devon realizes that all the teamwork stuff can actually be creative, and considers joining forces with unlikely people to bring the band up to snuff.

Line That Says It All: "They don't tell you about all this when they recruit you."

Guy to Watch: Nick Cannon as Devon is quite a player. Don't be a player-hater.

Girl to Watch: From her roles in BRING IT ON to *Pirates of the Caribbean* (2003), Zoe Saldana adds her own special spark to every character she plays.

Scene Worth the Rewind: Right before Devon heads south, he drops by the subway booth where his absentee father works. He introduces himself, then spouts a litany of his accomplishments, all the things he's managed to do without a father. Then he walks away. It's a cathartic scene, especially for any kid who has wanted to say to a "disappearing-act" parent, "I made it, no thanks to you."

Fun Factoid: The final marching band competition scene was shot in a huge stadium in Atlanta. One of the bands participating, a group from Morris Brown College, has a real hotshot marching band and allowed themselves to be portrayed as the villains in this story. What good sports.

Watch This One With: Band people, either to cheer it on or to complain about the facts the moviemakers got wrong. Either approach can be a good time. Yet you certainly don't have to be in a band, or even love marching music, to enjoy this coming-of-age film.

Movies with the Same Vibe: FINDING FORRESTER, OUR SONG.

HOW THIS MOVIE HELPS

DRUMLINE isn't saying that we should all follow each other over a cliff or anything, but it does point out in a fun, entertaining way that sometimes one person needs to think for others in order for the whole group to succeed. Devon is not portrayed as a complete jerk, and there are characters in the film who think he should just do his own thing, since he's the best. Yet when he works with other people, when he makes more thoughtful choices, he becomes really good at the things that will make a big difference in his life off the field. Have Devon's trouble sharing the limelight? Get in line.

Edward Scissorhands

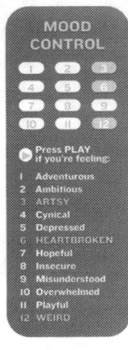

MOOD CONTROL

1	2	3
4	5	6
7	8	9
10	11	12

▶ Press PLAY if you're feeling:

1 Adventurous
2 Ambitious
3 ARTSY
4 Cynical
5 Depressed
6 HEARTBROKEN
7 Hopeful
8 Insecure
9 Misunderstood
10 Overwhelmed
11 Playful
12 WEIRD

1990 **ULTIMATE GIRL RATING:** ♣ ♣ ♣

DIRECTOR: Tim Burton
BIRTHPLACE: Mainstream Hollywood with an Edge
FILE UNDER: Fractured Fairy Tale
RATED: PG-13

STARRING: Johnny Depp, Winona Ryder, Dianne Wiest, Anthony Michael Hall, Kathy Baker, Robert Oliveri, Conchata Ferrell, Caroline Aaron, Dick Anthony Williams, O-Lan Jones, Vincent Price

THE PROBLEM You feel so out of place in the world, and sometimes it seems that the most you can get is sympathy. Is it wrong to want more? What you'd really like is genuine friendship and understanding, maybe even—gasp!—love.

The Reel Deal: This odd and oddly moving parable tells the story of a scientist high on a hill who creates a nearly human boy, Edward (Johnny Depp), but dies before he can exchange his temporary hands—pairs of monstrous scissors—for real ones. A kindhearted Avon lady (Dianne Wiest) visits the boy and soon welcomes him into her home. At first the town is suspicious of this strange creature, but he wins them over with his awkward charm and his way with scissors. Soon everyone is getting fabulous haircuts from Edward, and the neighbors' bushes are expertly snipped into exotic topiary sculptures. Sadly, a backlash against the exotic boy looms—does anyone ever rise in popularity quickly without suffering the dreaded backlash? Edward Scissorhands is no exception, and not even the budding romance with the Avon lady's daughter, Kim (Winona Ryder), can prevent Edward from having to face some tough confrontations.

Line That Says It All: "Forget about holding her hand, man. Think about the damage he could do to other places."

Girl to Watch: Winona Ryder is lovely as the kind and confused Kim. It's funny to see her as a popular blonde, yet she brings her "outsider" touch to this role too.

Guy to Watch: Johnny Depp can play the strangest people with utter believability. Is this a case of typecasting?

Scene Worth the Rewind: There are many moving moments. Simply watching Edward turn ho-hum suburban shrubs into elegant garden topiary is the most fun. The whole movie looks amazing. Director Tim Burton is all about fantastical stories that unfold in otherworldly settings. He's one of those guys that your film geek friends can't stop talking about—and you'll see why.

Soundtrack Note: When you hear a musical score that is both classic and contemporary, one that sweeps you up in a tidal wave of emotion, chances are you're listening to the amazing work of Danny Elfman. Elfman's magical style works beautifully with Burton's films, and this score is one of his best—haunting, poignant, and ethereal by turns, like the music of dreams.

Watch This One With: Those film geek friends, or maybe the Avon lady.

Movies with the Same Vibe: DONNIE DARKO, MOULIN ROUGE! Also check out *Beetlejuice* (1988), an earlier Tim Burton film.

HOW THIS MOVIE HELPS

Seeing Edward Scissorhands try to fit in may make you feel like your load ain't so heavy. At the very least, Burton's wild fairy tale is a gripping Frankenstein for the modern age. It's a refreshing film for people who never tire of stories about alienation and prejudice, but who like to see these heavy topics packaged in interesting new ways. Sometimes when you're having trouble with peers or family, when even your closest allies think you're a bit of a freak, you'd rather get your catharsis from a dark fairy tale than some too-close-to-the-bone young adult novel that just succeeds in making you feel like a bigger outcast than before. There's a time to get real, and a time to go weird, and Burton's films are made for that time. When you watch EDWARD SCISSORHANDS, keep in mind that it was made more than a decade ago; now it's a little more common to see films that take place in an alternate universe. I think we can guess that Tim Burton must have felt like a bit of an outcast himself back in the day, but he sure is handy behind the camera. Do you suppose Edward helped in the cutting room?

Election

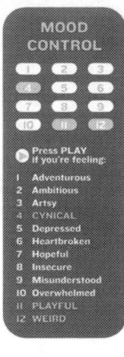

MOOD CONTROL

1 2 3
4 5 6
7 8 9
10 11 12

▶ Press PLAY
if you're feeling:

I Adventurous
2 Ambitious
3 Artsy
4 CYNICAL
5 Depressed
6 Heartbroken
7 Hopeful
8 Insecure
9 Misunderstood
10 Overwhelmed
II PLAYFUL
12 WEIRD

1999 ULTIMATE GIRL RATING: ♣ ♣ ♣

DIRECTOR: Alexander Payne
BIRTHPLACE:
Mainstream Hollywood
(with an Indie Heart)
FILE UNDER: Student
Government—Exposed!
RATED: R

STARRING: Matthew
Broderick, Reese
Witherspoon, Jessica
Campbell, Chris Klein,
Phil Reeves, Molly Hagan,
Delaney Driscoll, Mark
Harelik, Colleen Camp

THE PROBLEM

We generally think of the most popular kids running for student council. Yet in every school, there's that one kid who, if we really stop to think about it, we don't really like at all—but they always seem to win everything anyway. It's almost as if the sheer force of their ambition brainwashes us into thinking that they should get the job. Can a force actually brainwash you? If that force emanates from Tracy Enid Flick, you bet it can.

The Reel Deal: James "Jim" McAllister (Matthew Broderick) is an award-winning teacher at a good high school in a normal Midwestern town (Omaha, Nebraska, to be exact) with a nice wife and a job he enjoys. It's startling to discover early in ELECTION that he has an archnemesis, and even stranger to learn that his enemy is a perky, overachieving student named Tracy Flick (Reese Witherspoon). Tracy's bulldozer-with-beauty energy and her spirited attitude annoy him, but why? We soon learn that his animosity is of the personal sort: Tracy's scandalous affair with his best friend, Dave (Mark Harelik), led Dave to lose both his job and his marriage. As the election for student body president looms, McAllister becomes obsessed with finding a candidate who can beat the formidable Miss Flick, who naturally assumes that her victory is in the bag. He enlists dopey, endearing Paul Metzler (Chris Klein) to run, much to Tracy's fury. Paul is the perfect choice: a good-natured jock who is as kind as he is cute, who's popular because he actually deserves to be. As the campaign heats up, McAllister's obsession takes on a life of its own. Soon he's self-destructing in every area of his life. Did we mention that this is a comedy?

Line That Says It All: "Who cares about this stupid election?…The only person it matters to is the one who gets elected."

Girl to Watch: It's fun to see Reese Witherspoon in a twisted incarnation of her LEGALLY BLONDE role—sort of like Elle's evil little sister. Many people think this is Reese at her best.

Guy to Watch: Matthew Broderick is pitch-perfect as a teacher who spins out of control.

Scene Worth the Rewind: The student government speeches are like nothing you've ever heard. A fantasy come true for anyone who's ever experienced "school assembly torture." Wouldn't it be great if at least one candidate got up there and said something honest about high school politics? They might not win the election, but they'd be sure to win the popular vote.

Fun Factoid: Director Alexander Payne moved the story to Omaha, Nebraska, because he's from there and liked the idea of setting a movie in his hometown. He has now made three films set in Omaha. Can you say obsession?

Watch This One With: The entire student council. Just kidding.

Movies with the Same Vibe: PUMP UP THE VOLUME, HEATHERS.

HOW THIS MOVIE HELPS

Although ELECTION is one of those movies that's more *about* teens than *for* teens, lots of kids enjoy its irreverence toward student government and the supposed power privileges that go along with it. Don't even think of renting this movie if you hate mean-spirited comedies or despise the apathetic crowd at high school that likes to sit around and make fun of all the activities. On the other hand, if you enjoy black comedies (even if the subject is teens themselves), you might get a kick out of this. Like HEATHERS, ELECTION peeks underneath the surface of the poseurs to see what's really going on in the hearts of the future leaders of America. This makes it the perfect movie for anyone who's had to deal with that annoying peer who parents all think is *wonderful*.

Empire Records

1995

ULTIMATE GIRL RATING:

MOOD CONTROL

1	2	3
4	5	6
7	8	9
10	11	12

▶ Press PLAY if you're feeling:

1 Adventurous
2 Ambitious
3 ARTSY
4 CYNICAL
5 Depressed
6 Heartbroken
7 Hopeful
8 Insecure
9 Misunderstood
10 Overwhelmed
11 Playful
12 WEIRD

DIRECTOR: Allan Moyle
BIRTHPLACE: Mainstream Hollywood, Indie Feel
FILE UNDER: Can't Stop the Music
RATED: PG-13

STARRING: Anthony LaPaglia, Debi Mazar, Liv Tyler, Maxwell Caulfield, Rory Cochrane, Johnny Whitworth, Robin Tunney, Renée Zellweger, Ethan Randall Embry, Ben Bode

THE PROBLEM

You have a job that blows. Maybe you have to wear a stupid uniform, maybe the boss is a total jerk, maybe you have to sell a product you don't believe in. What can you do? You need the money to buy the things you love. Too bad your job can't be the thing you love, right?

The Reel Deal: Empire Records is the real thing: an independent store where the clerks are insanely passionate about music, and there's literally dancing in the aisles when a great tune is cranked up on the speakers. A lovable assortment of slackers is "managed" by Joe (Anthony LaPaglia), a baby-boomer softie who is desperately trying to buy the store from big bossman Mitchell (Ben Bode) before he sells out to the dreaded chain store, Music Tower. When one of his oldest employees, Lucas (Rory Cochrane), gambles the night's proceeds away in a misguided attempt to triple the revenue, Joe tries to keep the truth from Mitchell, all while spending the day catching shoplifters and preparing for the big in-store appearance of Rex Manning (Maxwell Caulfield), an '80s has-been with a cold eye toward his cult following. (Know your music? Think Billy Idol crossed with Englebert Humperdink. Rex is hilarious.) Plenty of other dramas

abound. Will Cory (Liv Tyler) go off to Harvard or, even worse, run off with Rex Manning before A.J. (Johnny Whitworth) can tell her how he feels about her? Will the resident depressive take a razor to something more critical than her hair? Is there more to Renée Zellweger's character than her nickname, Turbo Slut? Will anyone stop dancing in the aisles long enough to wait on a customer? With this soundtrack, not likely.

Line That Says It All: "I guess nobody really has it all together. Maybe I should welcome you to the neighborhood or something."

Girl to Watch: Renée Zellweger. You can see her star power right here, right now.

Guy to Watch: A.J. has a floppy-haired sweetness, but some might prefer Lucas.

Scene Worth the Rewind: The scene on the rooftop. You know it's coming, but it's gratifying nonetheless.

Party Game: "Whenever They Dance, You Dance." This one needs no explanation.

Soundtrack Note: As you can imagine, in a movie like this, music functions like another character in the film. Rock of all eras and genres streams through the movie, everything from Billy Idol to Gin Blossoms to GWAR to AC/DC to the Cranberries. It's all good, and it fits each scene just right.

Watch This One With: Any friend who has more CDs than strands of hair on his head.

Movies with the Same Vibe: PUMP UP THE VOLUME, DAZED AND CONFUSED, HEATHERS.

HOW THIS MOVIE HELPS

Lots of critics were sort of hard on this film for its jumpy vibe, but kids who saw it were generally fond of the Empire crew, and rooted for everybody to get out of their jams and on with their lives. A workplace with this much caring—not to mention this much fun—will be good to recall when you have to go back to flipping burgers or answering phones. Better yet, leave those plastic franchises behind and look at the little shops in your hometown. Anybody dancing in the aisles? Ask for an application.

● PRESS PAUSE: Music Scene Movies

Five-star soundtracks abound in recent movies, and we've mentioned them throughout the book. Yet there's also some great movies about the music world, whether the subject is a bunch of kids getting together to create a new beat, some scrappy Dubliners putting together a band, or a dead-on satire about inflated "I-Am-a-Rock-God" egos. Here are a few worth checking out.

Krush Groove (1985)

A lively look at rap through the time-honored tradition of the musical. Fun performances and a can't-be-beat soundtrack.

Purple Rain (1984)

A thinly veiled biography of Prince that he claims is in not a thinly veiled biography of Prince. Either way, if you like Prince (or movies about people sort of like Prince, or thinly veiled biographies in general) you might enjoy this clever, fantasy-fueled take on the struggles endured by the true artist.

8 Mile (2002)

If you haven't yet caught this Eminem production, you might be surprised to discover some decent filmmaking and some genuine heart at its center.

The Commitments (1991)

Audiences adored this funny Brit/Irish film about a group of blue-collar folks trying to put together a decent cover band. A funny, delightful film.

High Fidelity (2000)

What if the kids in EMPIRE RECORDS never moved on to other pursuits? They'd be like the smart-yet-motley record store crew in this crisp, romantic comedy that declares music is easier than love, and often more satisfying.

The Rose (1979)

Sometimes you need a tearjerker, and this is a good one, featuring Bette Midler in a thinly disguised (here we go again) bio of the great-yet-tortured '60s singer Janis Joplin. You'll find yourself wanting to tell her "Drugs: Just Say No, Janis." She sure could belt it out, though.

Almost Famous (2001)

Patrick Fugit as the young journalist is adorable in this '70s nostalgia piece, but Kate Hudson will capture your heart playing a groupie with almost too much sense to lose her heart to the band.

Also check out *Beat Street* (rap), *Grace of My Heart* ('60s singer-songwriter), *The Fighting Temptations* (gospel), *Coal Miner's Daughter* (country)

Ever After

MOOD CONTROL

1 2 3
4 5 6
7 8 9
10 11 12

▶ Press PLAY
if you're feeling:

1   ADVENTUROUS
2   Ambitious
3   Artsy
4   Cynical
5   Depressed
6   HEARTBROKEN
7   HOPEFUL
8   Insecure
9   Misunderstood
10 Overwhelmed
11 Playful
12 Weird

1998	ULTIMATE GIRL RATING: 🐾 🐾 🐾 🐾

DIRECTOR: Andy Tennant
BIRTHPLACE: Barrymore Castle
FILE UNDER: Fairy Tale for the New World
RATED: PG-13

STARRING: Drew Barrymore, Anjelica Huston, Dougray Scott, Patrick Godfrey, Megan Dodds, Melanie Lynskey, Timothy West, Judy Parfitt

THE PROBLEM You want your life to be like a Cinderella story, but you know it's never going to happen. Oh sure, you figure that some day you'll have lots of adventures and maybe even love someone who loves you back. But does happily-ever-after ever really happen without a lot of complications? Every couple you know who fell in love at first sight and had it stick became unstuck in three weeks or less. Somebody should take one of those classic fairy tales and give it a spin through the reality cycle. Well, guess what? Somebody did.

The Reel Deal: Cinderella is given a cool makeover in this terrific film. Here she's called Danielle (Drew Barrymore), but the story's the same: the untimely death of her father casts her into the cruel hands of her stepmother (played to perfection by Anjelica Huston). Stepmommy dearest treats Danielle horribly, but more out of concern for her own daughters' welfare than because she thinks Danielle deserves it. There are two stepsisters, of course, and one, Jacqueline (Melanie Lynskey), lives up to the cardboard-cutout witch stereotype of the original story. The other one, Marguerite (Megan Dodds), is actually pretty decent. After accidentally bopping the prince on the head with an apple, Danielle pretends to be a countess (to help out a friend in trouble); his royal

The moment when Danielle and Prince Henry first meet. Right from the start, the stereotypes slip away.

Ball gowns that almost make you wish you lived in sixteenth-century France. Then you remember, the arranged marriages, no plumbing…No thank you.

Your younger sister and her friends. Babysitting was never more worthwhile.

THE PRINCESS BRIDE, NEVER BEEN KISSED.

highness, who is, of course, handsome, falls in love with her. Prince Henry of France (Dougray Scott) fancies Danielle as much for her intelligence and spunk as for her lovely appearance. (Remember, it's a fairy tale). Danielle spends the rest of the movie trying to escape her uncharmed life while still keeping the prince and helping the working class. Once you see Leonardo da Vinci (Patrick Godfrey) helping her out, you know she'll succeed—since when did one of his plans ever fail?

Line That Says It All: "And though Cinderella and her prince did live happily ever after, the point, gentlemen, is that they lived."

Girl to Watch: Drew, as always. The Barrymores are a famous acting family, and that girl is such a Barrymore.

Guy to Watch: Prince Henry (Dougray Scott) is a dreamboat.

HOW THIS MOVIE HELPS

Maybe the Cinderella story always annoyed you a little, even as you held your breath and hoped she'd get out of that palace before midnight. For one thing, what did the Prince see in her besides beauty and teeny, tiny feet? A fairy tale about a foot fetish? That's just weird. In EVER AFTER, you see what really attracts the prince to this sassy maiden, and it's not just her way with a slipper. The Cinderella in this story is interested in changing her world, and the prince loves her for it. Makes you feel better about your own big feet—or your big plans for life that involve more than making a grand entrance at the ball.

Fast Times at Ridgemont High

1982 ULTIMATE GIRL RATING: ♣ ♣ ♣

DIRECTOR: Amy Heckerling
BIRTHPLACE:
Mainstream Hollywood
FILE UNDER:
Raunchy but Real
RATED: R

STARRING: Sean Penn,
Jennifer Jason Leigh, Judge
Reinhold, Robert Romanus,
Brian Backer, Phoebe Cates,
Ray Walston

MOOD CONTROL

1	2	3
4	5	6
7	8	9
10	11	12

► Press PLAY
if you're feeling:

1 Adventurous
2 Ambitious
3 Artsy
4 Cynical
5 DEPRESSED
6 HEARTBROKEN
7 Hopeful
8 Insecure
9 Misunderstood
10 OVERWHELMED
11 Playful
12 Weird

THE PROBLEM

Just when you think you've got a handle on what people expect of you and on how to get by in life, things change. You've finally found a way to move through high school without too much angst, then angst finds you, hides in your locker, and jumps out like some weak imitation of Chuckie. Not many movies focus on navigating the rocky shores of reputation and personal growth in high school. This one does, and in the guise of a slightly raunchy sex comedy. Huh? Ah, just watch—if your little sister isn't around.

The Reel Deal: In this sometimes serious, mostly funny slice of high school life—based on writer Cameron Crowe's year spent as a twenty-two-year-old high school "student"—we follow a handful of teens going through the typical realities of life and love. What isn't typical is the way they're portrayed; clichés are eschewed in favor of fully realized, completely believable characters. The "slut" is actually a pretty decent girl, the "good girl" winds up being pretty wild, a "sleazy" guy atones for his past behavior, and so forth. Although the movie has a ton of plots and no one star, girls will probably be most interested in the trials of Stacy Hamilton (Jennifer Jason Leigh), a sweet, fairly innocent girl who decides to explore her sexuality and gets in way over her head. Despite Stacy's realization that sex without love isn't worth much, it definitely doesn't feel like your mom wrote this movie. Stacy and her best friend, Linda (Phoebe Cates), talk about sex in a frank way that's common for girls today, but was fairly provocative twenty years ago. In addition to Stacy's gripping tale, there's plenty of comic relief: from Stacy's pompous brother, Brad (Judge Reinhold), and his senior-year slide to the antics of amiable stoner Jeff Spicoli (Sean Penn), whose scenes with stern history teacher Mr. Hand (Ray Walston) are comic gold.

Line That Says It All: "Now, this is the most important thing, Rat. When it comes down to making out, whenever possible, put on side one of *Led Zeppelin IV*."

Girl to Watch: Jennifer Jason Leigh as Stacy. Her portrayal of what it's like to try to understand your sexual power is so honest that it's scary. There's a great scene where she's got a really nice guy in her room and she just doesn't know what to do with him, and he just doesn't know what to do with her. It's one of those great, awkward, geeky date moments.

Guy to Watch: You live for every shot of Sean Penn's Jeff Spicoli. This is your brain on drugs—a terrible idea for life, a hilarious

idea for a film character. See Jeff. See Jeff try to think. See Jeff get a pizza delivered to him in history class.

Fashion to Catch: During Brad's tumble down the social ladder he trades in his tolerable fast-food restaurant uniform for a truly lame ensemble. How lame? Pirate lame.

Movies with the Same Vibe: AMERICAN GRAFFITI, CAN'T HARDLY WAIT.

HOW THIS MOVIE HELPS

When FAST TIMES came out, the movie studio hated it, and was shocked at how well it did. The sex helped sell it, of course, but kids also really responded to the mix of cool and nowhere-near-cool characters, the wonderful one-liners, and all the great plot twists. It's a fine movie to watch just for laughs, but Stacy's journey makes it more than just a girls-and-gags comedy. You can really relate to her confusion about how to attract guys—and her almost-too-late realization that the only surefire way to get power in high school is to be yourself. We know that, you know that, but nobody gets there without a few bruises. Times were fast back in 1982, and they're even faster in this millennium. Take a break, order a pizza, learn about Cuba, rent this movie.

Ferris Bueller's Day Off

MOOD CONTROL

1	2	3
4	5	6
7	8	9
10	11	12

▶ Press PLAY
if you're feeling:

1 ADVENTUROUS
2 Ambitious
3 Artsy
4 Cynical
5 Depressed
6 Heartbroken
7 HOPEFUL
8 Insecure
9 Misunderstood
10 Overwhelmed
11 PLAYFUL
12 Weird

1986 | **ULTIMATE GIRL RATING:** ♣ ♣ ♣ ♣

DIRECTOR: John Hughes
BIRTHPLACE:
Mainstream Hollywood
FILE UNDER:
Everday Superhero
RATED: PG-13

STARRING: Matthew Broderick, Alan Ruck, Mia Sara, Jeffrey Jones, Jennifer Grey, Cindy Pickett, Lyman Ward, Edie McClurg, Charlie Sheen, Ben Stein

THE PROBLEM

You are so overprogrammed that your calendar has its own calendar. Work, sports, school, family obligations, clubs, friends—it's too much. There's no aspect of your life led in low gear, and sometimes that's okay. Most of the time, though, you're in a permanent state of stress. Wouldn't you just love to have one day when everything went right, when you were filled with such confidence and bravado that nothing could get to you for long? That's the everyday life of Ferris Bueller.

The Reel Deal: Ferris Bueller (Matthew Broderick) is the kind of kid who seems to glide through life, sliding out of trouble so smoothly that even his enemies find themselves impressed. One day he goes to elaborate lengths to feign sickness, just so he can have a day off from high school. He involves his best friend, Cameron (Alan Ruck), convincing him to borrow his dad's beloved Ferrari for a joy ride into the city of Chicago. He springs his girlfriend, Sloane (Mia Sara), by convincing the school that there's been a death in her family. On the surface, FERRIS BUELLER'S DAY OFF is a fun adventure that asks the question: can a popular, self-confident kid who gets everything he wants get some more things he wants? Not such a gripping dilemma, is it? Where this movie gets a little more complex is in its hero's efforts to rid his friend Cameron of paralyzing fear and crushingly low self-esteem. Cameron has a real problem: a father who cares more for his beloved car than his own son. Ferris attempts in one day to convince Cameron that life can't be spent trying to live up to other people's expectations of you. Meanwhile, principal Ed Rooney (Jeffrey Jones) smells a rat, and spends most of his day trying to catch a perfectly healthy Ferris in the act. Outsmarting the principal may be the oldest plot device in the book, but it stays fresh throughout this hilarious film.

Line That Says It All: "Only the weak get pinched. The bold survive."

Girl to Watch: Mia Sara. Hughes could have just cast a babe who seemed eternally shocked and giggly at Ferris' behavior. Instead, we have Mia Sara, who comes across as beautiful, smart, kind, level-headed—as dynamic in her own way as her wacky boyfriend.

Guy to Watch: It's obvious that Matthew Broderick enjoyed his role and he's pretty irresistible, but Alan Ruck's sweet, sad Cameron is just as compelling, in a different way.

Fun Factoid: Love was in the air during this filming. The acting duo playing Ferris'

parents later married, and at the time Broderick was engaged to Jennifer Grey, who plays his sister. Try not to think too hard about that one.

Scene Worth the Rewind: There's a parade. There's Ferris. That's all we have to say.

Watch This One With: Yourself, on a sick day.

Movies with the Same Vibe: WHAT A GIRL WANTS.

HOW THIS MOVIE HELPS

When Ferris takes the day off, so do we. This movie is like a vacation for your brain. You start to buy into Ferris' philosophy and wonder: why *do* I get so upset by life? Why do I let other peoples' opinions affect me so much? Or maybe you don't think any of that. Maybe you just enjoy the cat-and-mouse game and the big-city adventure. We don't recommend cutting school (your parents made us write that), but why not take a weekend off from your usual madcap routine and just leave the house with your girls and no real plans? You'll see the world differently when the destination is fun instead of some place you have to get to before your coach turns into a pumpkin. Chill out, Cinderella, and have a ball.

True love comes and true love goes. (It's horrible that it goes, but if it didn't, there wouldn't be many movies, would there?) Our **girlfriends, however,** see us through the worst of times. Journals and sympathetic family members are great, but there's something about a friend with the right words or just a hug that gives a glimmer of hope when things fall apart. Of course, not all friendships are created equal. If we're smart, we hang with people who bring out our best selves. They're thoughtful, they're good-natured, and they love us for who we are (yet won't let us get away with bad, self-defeating behavior).

In our favorite teen movies, we see both friends we'd love to have and friends that remind us of those moments in horror films when we want to scream at the screen, "Don't go in the woods, you idiot!" *The Ultimate Girl* loves to give awards, even to those who don't deserve them. Here *are* the friendship awards, for the ties that bind (and sometimes choke) us.

Friendship out of Circumstance: THE BREAKFAST CLUB

Most Unconventional Friends: CAMP and HAROLD AND MAUDE

Most Controlling Friend, Fun Division: CLUELESS

Most Controlling Friend, Un-Fun Division: HEATHERS

Most Willing to Overlook Differences: EDWARD SCISSORHANDS

Coolest Friends: EMPIRE RECORDS

Most Inspiring Friend: FERRIS BUELLER'S DAY OFF and FOOTLOOSE

Most Obviously in Love with You Friend:
GET OVER IT, LUCAS, SOME KIND OF WONDERFUL, and many more

Most Subtle Deterioration of a Friendship: GHOST WORLD

Most Toxic Friend, Grand Champion Division: THIRTEEN

Friends in Most Realistic Tough Circumstances: GIRLS TOWN and OUR SONG

Biggest Slacker Friends: REALITY BITES and DAZED AND CONFUSED

Hollowest Friendships: RIVER'S EDGE

Most Melodramatic Friendships: ST. ELMO'S FIRE and CENTER STAGE

Best Friend We'd Like to Have:
Alison Pill in CONFESSIONS OF A TEENAGE DRAMA QUEEN

Finding Forrester

2000   **ULTIMATE GIRL RATING:**

DIRECTOR: Gus Van Sant
BIRTHPLACE: Mainstream Hollywood
FILE UNDER: Ghost Writer
RATED: PG-13

STARRING: Sean Connery, Rob Brown, F. Murray Abraham, Anna Paquin, Busta Rhymes, April Grace

THE PROBLEM

Mentoring is a big thing these days, but what exactly is a mentor, anyway? If someone just shows up in your life and announces, "I'm your mentor," does that mean they have all the answers and you should want to grow up to be just like them? Sometimes, maybe, but not necessarily. The best mentors seem to come out of the blue. They might even be totally different from us. Maybe there's things about them we don't even like. Is it worth putting up with the differences to get the knowledge? Only you know for sure.

The Reel Deal: When we first meet him, Jamal Wallace (Rob Brown) seems like a typical big city kid. He loves to shoot hoops and hang out with his friends; doing schoolwork isn't really his thing. Yet there's another side to Jamal. He thinks it's fun to read classic literature: the works of the writers Chekhov and Kafka and the philosopher Kierkegaard can be found on his bookshelf. His grades are mediocre, so he surprises everyone by getting a really high score on an aptitude test. That earns him a full scholarship to a fancy New York City prep school, where his combination of brains and basketball talent thrills the administration. One night he's hanging out with his friends, shooting hoops, and they get to talking about the weird old guy who watches the street from his window but is seldom seen leaving his apartment. Rumors abound about this old white guy, and Jamal breaks into his apartment on a dare. He is astonished to find a place filled with wonderful books, and discovers that he is in the apartment of William Forrester (Sean Connery), a man who became famous years ago for a single, terrific novel. When the old man comes home suddenly, Jamal runs off, leaving his backpack. He later finds it outside the door and discovers that the man has marked up his journal with corrections and comments. Jamal shocks Forrester by returning soon after to ask if he'll teach him how to be a writer. FINDING FORRESTER tracks their unique and ever-deepening friendship, and demonstrates that the best mentor relationships go both ways.

Line That Says It All: "Family isn't always what you are born with. Sometimes it's the people you find and sometimes it's the people who find you."

Girl to Watch: Anna Paquin has a nice, small role as the headmaster's daughter who has a special place in her heart for Jamal, and he for her.

Guy to Watch: Sean Connery jumps with both feet into every role he plays. Newcomer Rob Brown ensures that Jamal Wallace is a complex character, not just a Hollywood creation.

Scene Worth the Rewind: Jamal and Forrester go to an empty Yankee Stadium and talk. We finally learn what happened to the great writer all those years ago.

Watch This One With: Your friends who like to write, or like to watch cute guys play basketball. We're not picky here.

Movies with the Same Vibe: GOOD WILL HUNTING, STAND AND DELIVER, DRUMLINE. Also check out *Dead Poets Society* (1989), starring Robin Williams.

HOW THIS MOVIE HELPS

Not everyone is lucky enough to break into the apartment of the person that will change their life. (We don't recommend trying that route). But thinking outside the box just might get you to that person quicker than sitting around hoping someone notices your genius and exposes you to the world. FINDING FORRESTER inspires us to think of people who might want to help us get to wherever we want to go. We can't just think in terms of nice people we see all the time. Some of the best mentors are people we'd never hang out with otherwise. Such people become our intimates because we share a common passion. When looking longingly at a far-off goal, it's nice to talk to somebody who has already walked down that road. They can't carry us there, but they can give us a compass and point out the obstacles to avoid. And who knows, maybe they get something out of the deal as well.

Flashdance

MOOD CONTROL

1	2	3
4	5	6
7	8	9
10	11	12

▶ Press **PLAY** if you're feeling:

1 Adventurous
2 AMBITIOUS
3 ARTSY
4 Cynical
5 Depressed
6 Heartbroken
7 HOPEFUL
8 Insecure
9 Misunderstood
10 Overwhelmed
11 Playful
12 Weird

1983 **ULTIMATE GIRL RATING:**

DIRECTOR: Adrian Lyne
BIRTHPLACE: Mainstream U.S.A.
FILE UNDER: MTV Makes a Movie
RATED: R

STARRING: Jennifer Beals, Michael Nouri, Lilia Skala, Sunny Johnson, Kyle T. Heffner, Lee Ving

THE PROBLEM You understand why reality TV continues to be so popular—it's the reality we're all hoping for, that someone will pull us out of our mundane lives and turn us into stars, or rich people, or the kind of girls who have adventures every day. Yet we know, deep down, that contestants must return to their "real" reality scratching their heads, wondering why the magic stardust had to wear off. We know that the only lasting dreams are the ones powered by our own grit and vision, not some producer's idea of how to grab ratings. Still, we love the miracles that happen on the screen to the tune of a hit song. For pure infectious fantasy, you can turn to the decade when MTV first ruled the airwaves and taught us that even movies can look like one big, splashy video. Reality? Hardly. Really popular? You got that right.

The Reel Deal: Had she been born into another family, Alex Owens (Jennifer Beals) would have been a dance major at some cool arts college. As it is, her blue-collar upbringing has her welding by day and working at a club as a dancer by night. Alex and her fellow hoofers love to dance, and they concoct elaborate routines that involve more atmospheric smoke and costume changes than the booty display these hard-drinking workers would probably prefer. You would think these two disparate activities would keep her busy enough, but after all this is done, she retreats to her unfinished loft and practices dancing for hours. Her real dream, it seems, is to be accepted into a prestigious ballet academy. Alex isn't looking for love, but stumbles into it, attracting the attention of wealthy townie Nick Hurley (Michael Nouri), who turns out to be her boss. As the romance between Alex and Nick heats up, she grows concerned that he'll use connections to snag her a spot in the dance academy. As much as she's tired of struggling and watching her friends work too hard for too little, Alex only wants the brass ring if she can earn it herself.

Girl to Watch: Jennifer Beals as Alex. She was dissed for not doing her own dancing, but she sure did her own acting, and was just right for this part.

Guy to Watch: Michael Nouri is a little too good to be true as the rich, handsome, devoted boyfriend—not that there's anything wrong with that.

Scene Worth the Rewind: Alex's elegant dinner out with Nick turns both humorous and sexy when his frosty ex drops by the table to annoy him.

Fashion to Catch: Jennifer's torn sweatshirt-and-leggings look started a sweatshirt craze. Soon girls everywhere were taking scissors to their own sweats.

Soundtrack Note: The soundtrack was mostly forgettable pop, but Irene Cara's heartfelt rendition of the theme song, "Flashdance…What a Feeling," won the singer an Oscar.

Watch This One With: Your mom (she'll no doubt remember this movie) and your friends who love to dance.

Movies with the Same Vibe: CENTER STAGE, DIRTY DANCING. Also check out *Fame* (1980).

HOW THIS MOVIE HELPS

FLASHDANCE won't change your life; it won't even change your day. Yet when you feel like being inspired by a feeling rather than a concrete call to action, you could do worse than take a look at this stand-up-and-cheer, music-drenched flick. Don't worry if you can't imitate the incredibly acrobatic dancing—neither could the movie's star, and she still had her day in the sun. They say life is an audition—just keep showing up and you're bound to snag a decent part.

Flirting

MOOD CONTROL

1	2	3
4	5	6
7	8	9
10	11	12

▶ Press PLAY if you're feeling:

1 Adventurous
2 Ambitious
3 ARTSY
4 Cynical
5 DEPRESSED
6 Heartbroken
7 Hopeful
8 INSECURE
9 Misunderstood
10 Overwhelmed
11 Playful
12 Weird

1991 — ULTIMATE GIRL RATING: ♣ ♣ ♣ ♣

DIRECTOR: John Duigan
BIRTHPLACE: Australia
FILE UNDER: Sweet Love Story Down Under
UNRATED

STARRING: Noah Taylor, Thandie Newton, Nicole Kidman, Bartholomew Rose, Felix Nobis, Josh Picker, Kiri Paramore, Marc Gray

THE PROBLEM

Turns out that time and place matter when it seems that they shouldn't matter at all. When you meet the right person, time should stop, and events in the outside world should have nothing to do with how things progress between the two of you. That's one of the challenges of being a teenager—they tell you to act like an adult, but your life isn't really your own, is it?

The Reel Deal: Danny Embling (played by Noah Taylor, who originated this character in *The Year My Voice Broke*) is a bright, witty stutterer, the kind of guy who would get the bejesus kicked out of him if he was away at a boys boarding school. Unfortunately, he is, and life isn't easy for this iconoclastic, slightly rebellious kid attending private school in the early '60s. Things pick up for him when an event at the nearby girls school brings him to the attention of Thandiwe (Thandie Newton), a cute, bright girl with a British mother, an African father, and an eye for a boy who dislikes the rules as much as she does. FLIRTING is not heavily plotted, but shows us Thandiwe and Danny's boarding school lives, together and apart. Nicola (Nicole Kidman) is a confident upperclassman who is assigned to keep an eye on Thandiwe, but winds up giving her some advice the administration would hardly appreciate. Needless to say, interracial dating raised quite a few eyebrows back then, and Danny

and Thandiwe are affected by their
differences. Yet a bigger difference is in their
levels of maturity. FLIRTING accurately
depicts a certain kind of teen romance seldom
seen in movies—a rather sophisticated girl
guiding and protecting her awkward, less
mature boyfriend. That kind of relationship
sound familiar? (You know who you are). As
the romance between Thandiwe and Danny
heats up, so do events back in Africa, and
politics threaten to get in the way of a
wonderful relationship.

Line That Says It All:

"I'm here for anthropological reasons."
"Huh?"
"Football. It's a form of mating ritual. That's
why you're here, isn't it?"

HOW THIS MOVIE HELPS

It's nice to see two people pick each
other out of a crowd because of a
shared worldview. By setting the story
in 1963, we see things in Thandiwe
and Danny's relationship that
wouldn't be as big a deal today. (Well,
depending upon where you live, and
who you live with....) Yet some things
about romance are universal. You
never know where you'll meet your
true love, and you never know what
the future has in store for you. All you
can do is take the romantic risks that
these two did—it sure makes for a
charming movie.

Fly Away Home

MOOD CONTROL

1	2	3
4	5	6
7	8	9
10	11	12

▶ Press PLAY if you're feeling:

1 Adventurous
2 AMBITIOUS
3 ARTSY
4 Cynical
5 Depressed
6 Heartbroken
7 HOPEFUL
8 Insecure
9 Misunderstood
10 Overwhelmed
11 Playful
12 Weird

1996 **ULTIMATE GIRL RATING:** ♣ ♣ ♣ ♣

DIRECTOR: Carroll Ballard
BIRTHPLACE: North America. Way North.
FILE UNDER: If Girls Could Fly
RATED: PG

STARRING: Anna Paquin, Jeff Daniels, Dana Delany, Terry Kinney

THE PROBLEM Whenever your whole life changes, people are so sympathetic—for about ten minutes. Then they really want you to get on with things. Lost someone you loved? They say just love the one you're with. Well, it isn't that simple, is it? You can't choose who you love and how you grow to love them. Sometimes a flock of geese can help. Well, at least in this adorable film.

The Reel Deal: Thirteen-year-old Amy (Anna Paquin) sees her world turn upside down when her mother suddenly dies in a car accident. All at once, she's forced to leave New Zealand for Canada and a father (Jeff Daniels) who she barely knows. Trust and communication between them is rough, yet they forge a bond when they adopt some goose eggs found in a soon-to-be developed woods. In no time at all, little goslings are parading around the house, which is fine with Amy's eccentric father. You would think that might be enough to warm her heart, but Amy reserves all her affection for the growing geese, who soon decide that Amy must be their mama. The problem is, the geese need to migrate south for the winter, and they learn that from their parents. Instead of consoling Amy while handing the geese over to wildlife authorities, Amy's dad gets a crazy idea. Since he's an inventor by trade, he builds an ultralight aircraft so he and Amy can fly south. The plan is that the birds will follow them to their summer home. Doesn't that make all *your* dad's harebrained schemes seem normal in comparison?

Line That Says It All: "Broken promises are the worst. Better not to promise anything."

Girl to Watch: Anna Paquin is great, such a normal girl. (Well, except for the whole "flying through the air with a flock geese following her" bit.)

Guy to Watch: Jeff Daniels is great as her nutty hippie dad.

Geese to Watch: The geese were all superb in their roles.

Scene Worth the Rewind: So you're in your Baltimore office, having a meeting, and suddenly this little girl flies by in a sort of bicycle-like airplane, accompanied by a flock of geese. Uh, can we take a coffee break now?

Watch This One With: Your animal-loving friends. The cinematography of the geese is spectacular!

Movies with the Same Vibe: LITTLE WOMEN, NOT ONE LESS, WHALE RIDER. Also check out *The Black Stallion* (1979).

HOW THIS MOVIE HELPS

It takes a long time to love again when you've suffered a loss like Amy's. Yet a dad as committed to your dream as you are can really shorten the process. Sometimes you feel guilty after a loss, as if it's wrong to get on with life. What fills the void at a time like that? Anna's father understands her need to give love to vulnerable creatures that need her as much as she needs them. We cheer for the birds, we cheer for the family as well—fractured and fragile, but surviving in its new, heroic formation.

Footloose

MOOD CONTROL

1	2	3
4	5	6
7	8	9
10	11	12

▶ Press PLAY if you're feeling:

1 Adventurous
2 Ambitious
3 Artsy
4 Cynical
5 DEPRESSED
6 Heartbroken
7 Hopeful
8 Insecure
9 MISUNDERSTOOD
10 Overwhelmed
11 PLAYFUL
12 Weird

1984 ULTIMATE GIRL RATING: 🍿🍿🍿

DIRECTOR: Herbert Ross
BIRTHPLACE: Mainstream Hollywood
FILE UNDER: Your Mama Don't Dance and Your Daddy Don't Rock-'n'-Roll
RATED: PG

STARRING: Kevin Bacon, Lori Singer, John Lithgow, Dianne Wiest, Chris Penn, Sarah Jessica Parker, John Laughlin, Frances Lee McCain

THE PROBLEM

There's a huge gap between you and your parents. They seem so uptight all the time, worried about your every move. Were they ever young? Did they ever want to let loose a little? Maybe even a lot? They're causing you to want to outsmart them at every turn. You get to have your own life, but at what cost? What you'd really like would probably surprise them and seems impossible: to be able to talk to them.

The Reel Deal: Ren McCormick (Kevin Bacon) is forced to leave the big city and move to the small town of Beaumont with his mother (Frances Lee McCain). A music-loving New Waver, he is disgusted to learn that dances have been outlawed in the town. As he tries to find out why this is true, he meets a lot of resistance, even from his new schoolmates, who think he looks like a city-boy freak. Willard Hewitt (Chris Penn) befriends him, and together they try to get the other teens interested in fighting the town's straight-laced rules. In trying to get the law changed, he comes up against a formidable opponent: Reverend Shaw Moore (John Lithgow). Moore's daughter Ariel (Lori Singer) is wildly angry at her father for his rigid stance, and their tempestuous relationship is the true heart of this otherwise lightweight musical. But it's Ren's story, for the most part, and we cheer him on as he gets the country kids to cut loose in a style far more wholesome than the vices they turned to without music. Yet despite the "rebel with a cause" cliché and imaginary evil (dancing? c'mon), FOOTLOOSE still manages to display some depth of character, as Ren learns that joining them just might be the best way to beat them.

Line That Says It All:

"Don't you know how long it takes for evil to spread?"

"How long? About as long as it takes for compassion to die?"

Girl to Watch: Lori Singer as Ariel. Her scenes with Ren and her dad hit just right.

Guy to Watch: Kevin Bacon is so perfect as Ren that it took him years to shake his *Footloose* image.

Eye-Rolling Time: The Kenny Loggins soundtrack that plays as backdrop for the town's rock rebellion is pretty tame stuff. Now we can see how dancing to The Darkness might have ruffled a few feathers.

Watch This One With: Friends who like musicals. Lots of people liked this movie. In fact, there was a Broadway show based on the film.

Movies with the Same Vibe: DIRTY DANCING, SAVE THE LAST DANCE.

HOW THIS MOVIE HELPS

Although the movie focuses on rebel Ren, the father/daughter dynamic in this film will remind lots of girls of their own struggles with Dad. The movie does a nice job of showing that Ariel isn't just a bad girl, and Dad isn't the typical teen-movie moron parent. When we learn just why the town hardened its heart against dancing, we realize it's a story centered on emotional pain rather than prudish fear. It's easy to make a teen movie where the adults are just ogres, and this one starts out that way, but where it goes from there is a whole lot more interesting. The family dance: more challenging than a town dance any day of the week.

Freaky Friday

MOOD CONTROL

I	2	3
4	5	6
7	8	9
I0	II	I2

▶ Press PLAY
if you're feeling:

I   ADVENTUROUS
2   Ambitious
3   Artsy
4   Cynical
5   Depressed
6   Heartbroken
7   Hopeful
8   Insecure
9   MISUNDERSTOOD
I0 Overwhelmed
II PLAYFUL
I2 Weird

2003 **ULTIMATE GIRL RATING:** ♣ ♣ ♣ ♣

DIRECTOR: Mark S. Waters
BIRTHPLACE:
Mainstream Hollywood
FILE UNDER: Worst
Nightmare, Sci-Fi Division
RATED: PG

STARRING: Jamie Lee Curtis,
Lindsay Lohan, Mark Harmon,
Harold Gould, Chad Michael
Murray, Stephen Tobolowsky,
Christina Vidal, Ryan
Malgarini, Haley Hudson

THE PROBLEM If your parents could just live in your shoes for one day, maybe they'd get a clue about how hard it is to be a teenager today. Maybe they'd see how unfair things are, how much adults talk down to kids, and how the demands on people your age far exceed any realistic possibilities. And if you had to live in their shoes for one day? Ugh. Maybe that's taking this whole empathy thing a little too far.

The Reel Deal: We meet the Coleman family during a whirlwind period in their lives. Tess Coleman (Jamie Lee Curtis) is trying to run a busy psychology practice, promote her new book, and get married all in the same week. Her daughter, Anna (Lindsay Lohan), is suffering the slings and arrows of high school, dealing with a teacher and an ex-best friend who are out to get her, a crush on an older guy, Jake (Chad Michael Murray), and a garage band that desperately wants out of the garage. Underneath Anna's punk-chick cool exterior is some real fragility about getting a step-dad (Mark Harmon) just two years after losing her real dad. The stress of the week gets to both Tess and Anna at a tense family dinner in a Chinese restaurant. In real life, they'd probably just throw egg

rolls at each other, but since this is a movie, the proprietress, who senses their mutual animosity, puts them under an ancient spell that causes them to wake up the next day in one another's bodies. Tess and Anna are forced to live each other's lives until they can figure out how to break the spell and become themselves again. Fun scenes include watching Anna give her a mother a far more youthful look and Tess taking over Anna's high school experience, bewildering peers and teachers alike with language that sounds straight out of *The Soccer Mom Handbook*. When Jake gets interested in Tess (who only looks like Anna) and Ryan starts to wonder what's happening to Anna (who only looks like Tess), it really hits you how hard it is to understand what someone else is going through, even if you do walk in their shoes, eat their lunch, and date their boyfriend.

Line That Says It All: "It's easy to be you. I'll just suck the fun out of everything!"

Girl to Watch: Take your pick—Lohan and Curtis are both great teenage girls.

Guy to Watch: Chad Michael Murray as Jake is girl-worshipped, mom-approved.

Fun Factoid: Your mom had her own FREAKY FRIDAY. The original movie was made in 1977, starring Barbara Harris and then-teen star Jodie Foster.

Fashion to Catch: Anna's DIY punkette style is fun and flattering. How many movie set stylists do you think contributed to that just-thrown-together look?

Soundtrack Note: There's quite a mix of tunes in this film, from Joey Ramone (the Ramones are the godfathers of American Fun Punk) to the Donnas to Lindsay Lohan herself. Lohan's "Ultimate" is Hilary Duff-ish, but what's wrong with that? This isn't a horror movie. We also got a kick out of Simple Plan's version of "Happy Together," a song even your grandma would recognize. Play it for her, will you? She'll feel *so* young.

Eye-Rolling Time: We can see Asian girls not loving the stereotype of the wise Chinese lady with her fortune-cookie dialogue and "ancient Chinese secret" magic spells. If you can overlook that bit of silliness, though, it's a really entertaining tale.

Movies with the Same Vibe: ADVENTURES IN BABYSITTING, THE LIZZIE MCGUIRE MOVIE, THE PRINCESS DIARIES, 13 GOING ON 30.

HOW THIS MOVIE HELPS

It's really hard for mothers and daughters to imagine living in each other's shoes. For one thing, the size and style are all wrong. Trading places for real would be brutal, but a few minutes contemplating what it would be like to have to deal with her stuff might be doable. So give it a shot. It might even bring a ceasefire to the turf wars, at least for a day. Rent this movie and offer mom a seat on the couch. At least you'll laugh together.

Gas Food Lodging

MOOD CONTROL

1 2 3
4 5 6
7 8 9
10 11 12

Press PLAY if you're feeling:

1   Adventurous
2   Ambitious
3   ARTSY
4   CYNICAL
5   Depressed
6   Heartbroken
7   Hopeful
8   INSECURE
9   Misunderstood
10 Overwhelmed
11 Playful
12 Weird

1992   ULTIMATE GIRL RATING:

DIRECTED: Allison Anders
BIRTHPLACE: Indie U.S.A.
FILE UNDER:
Trailerpark Dreaming
RATED: R

STARRING: Brooke Adams, Ione Skye, Fairuza Balk, James Brolin, Robert Knepper, David Lansbury, Jacob Vargas, Donovan Leitch, Chris Mulkey

THE PROBLEM

Do you want to go along or do you want to rebel? It's pretty hard to make up your mind when you have a sibling who seems to take up all the air in the room. Whether you like it or not, you're relegated to the role of "the good kid," if only because you're not a source of anxiety 24/7. Most of the time that's pretty cool, but once in a while you'd appreciate being the focus of attention, without having to start a screaming match to get it.

The Reel Deal: Shade (Fairuza Balk) lives in a trailer park with her mom, Nora (Brooke Adams), and her sister, Trudi (Ione Skye). Life hasn't been easy since Shade's dad (James Brolin) left, ostensibly never to return. Nora works at a truck stop; Trudi works at sleeping with all the boys at school while trying to figure out how to get out of Laramie, New Mexico. Shade is the good girl who spends her days trying to keep her family together and losing herself in the romantic exploits of Elvia Rivero, a Mexican cinema goddess whose movies always seem to be playing at the local theater. While Trudi continues to use guys for escape, Shade thinks finding her mom a boyfriend will make life better for all of them. She finally stops focusing on others long enough to meet Javier (Jacob Vargas), a guy with enough kindness to make her reconsider real life over the cinematic kind. Reconciling her situation with the glamorous sheen of the movies is a struggle that runs throughout GAS FOOD LODGING, a terrific film about negotiating your way through a life that you didn't choose and isn't perfect—but it's yours.

Line That Says It All: "Can I interest you in some cable television, ma'am?"

Girl to Watch: All three women are terrific in these roles, the kind of nuanced, fully developed characters all actresses love to play.

Guy to Watch: Jacob Vargas plays Javier nicely; you really believe in Javier and Shade's budding romance.

Scene Worth the Rewind: Shade and her boyfriend dancing up a storm in his living room—with his mother. Oh, and did we mention that his mom is deaf?

Fun Factoid: Trudi (Ione Skye) and Darius (Donovan Leitch) are real-life brother and sister. Director Allison Anders has an amazing family background herself. She survived a rough-and-tumble childhood, periods spent in foster care, and early motherhood. She often incorporates aspects of her life story in her films.

Watch This One With: All your small-town friends. At last, a movie that doesn't presume everyone lives in either New York or L.A.

Movies with the Same Vibe: GETTING TO KNOW YOU, GIRLS TOWN.

HOW THIS MOVIE HELPS

Movies are the great escape, but they can also make you feel like everyone else is dancing the night away in some penthouse. In the real world, jobs are tough and boring, families are often fractured, and the richness and wonder that life can bring comes in sweet little moments, not giant, endless years of perfection. Allison Anders seems to understand this better than most. GAS FOOD LODGING is a story about a girl that seems real and a life that feels like one that someone might actually live. It won't make things better between you and your difficult sib but it just might make you feel better seeing a really complicated, really honest portrayal of sisters up on the screen. If your only problem with your sister was her stealing your clothes or prom date, you'd be a TV character, wouldn't you? You're not, and she's not the kind of girl who's going to get it together by the next commercial break. So give yourself a break from those expectations and pull up to GAS FOOD LODGING.

Get Over It

MOOD CONTROL

1 2 3
4 5 6
7 8 9
10 11 12

▶ **Press PLAY**
if you're feeling:

1 ADVENTUROUS
2 Ambitious
3 Artsy
4 Cynical
5 Depressed
6 HEARTBROKEN
7 Hopeful
8 Insecure
9 Misunderstood
10 OVERWHELMED
11 Playful
12 Weird

2001 ULTIMATE GIRL RATING: ♣ ♣

DIRECTOR: Tommy O'Haver
BIRTHPLACE:
Mainstream Hollywood
FILE UNDER:
Breaking Up, Cracking Up
RATED: PG-13

STARRING: Kirsten Dunst, Ben Foster, Melissa Sagemiller, Sisqó, Shane West, Colin Hanks, Zoe Saldana, Mila Kunis, Swoosie Kurtz, Ed Begley Jr., Martin Short

THE PROBLEM

The love of your life has flown the coop and everyone has long since lost patience with you. Well, you can't help it. Life sucks. It feels like it's over; still, you go through the motions. You put a lot of energy into convincing people that you're fine now, just so that you don't lose all your friends too. You're not fine, though, and you remember that every night, when you stare in a daze at the ceiling. Time supposedly heals all wounds, but it must be on some kind of semester abroad, because every fiber of your being is still bleeding. Get over it, they say. You say, "I am." You think, "I can't."

The Reel Deal: Berke (Ben Foster) met Alison (Melissa Sagemiller) when he was seven, re-met her when he was in high school, and spent sixteen blissful months being her devoted boyfriend. Then, one day, out of the blue, she sits him down for "the talk." After the break-up, he is a crumpled shell of a man, shuffling down the halls, lethargically agreeing to go clubbing and out on weird dates just to show people, namely his friend Felix (Colin Hanks) that he's trying to put Alison behind him. Things go from bad to worse when Alison takes up with Striker (Shane West), a new student at their school with a boy-band CD under his belt and a dubious-sounding British accent. Obsessed with getting Alison back, Berke decides to try out for the school musical, a ridiculous rock-opera version of Shakespeare's *A Midsummer Night's Dream*. Presiding over the production is Dr. Desmond Forrest Oates (Martin Short), a hilarious, egocentric tyrant with putdowns that make Simon Cowell seem like Paula Abdul in comparison. The romantic triangle of the play is mirrored in the movie, as Berke and Striker compete for Alison's attention. Assisting Berke in his quest to become a major thespian is Felix's younger sister, Kelly (Kirsten Dunst), who clearly has a crush on Berke. As the opening night of the show looms, production and romantic disasters pile up like broken stagelights in this fast-paced, slightly off-center teen comedy.

Girl to Watch: Kirsten Dunst underplays her glamour nicely as Kelly Woods, a sweet, talented girl who more than deserves the hapless hero's affections.

Guy to Watch: Ben Foster is always worth watching, whether in this film, the amazing *Liberty Heights* (1999), or as his compellingly confused character on the HBO series *Six Feet Under*. One minute he's John Cusack, all cuteness and star power, the next minute he's a boy too genuinely ordinary to be in film, just a guy you might know from your French class. In a world where every teen actor looks like he met Calvin Klein at

a loft party, this is a pretty cool thing. Martin Short is, as always, riotously funny as the pathetic drama kingpin.

Scene Worth the Rewind: Although this is a romantic comedy, the pace is too breakneck, the tone too funky for the romance to take center stage. Our favorite bits involved musical exuberance—Berke's comical audition for the musical and Dennis' wonderful version of "September" sung over the closing credits, with the full cast in major dance mode.

HOW THIS MOVIE HELPS

Watching Berke try to "get over it" will not convince you to rip up your last photo of the one that got away and get on with things. GET OVER IT does offer a pretty entertaining diversion, a chance to laugh at yourself, and a reminder that you never know when time will finally catch up with you and let you off the hook. We're not saying that you have to be in your school's upcoming rock-opera, but it's good to join something, or try something different. One day you'll have that feeling of relief you get when you suddenly realize that an all-consuming headache went away without you even noticing. Trust us, that headache will go away someday, and a new, cuter, more devoted headache—er, we mean boyfriend—will take its place.

Getting to Know You

MOOD CONTROL

```
 1    2    3
 4    5    6
 7    8    9
10   11   12
```

▶ Press PLAY
if you're feeling:

1 Adventurous
2 Ambitious
3 ARTSY
4 CYNICAL
5 Depressed
6 Heartbroken
7 Hopeful
8 Insecure
9 Misunderstood
10 OVERWHELMED
11 Playful
12 Weird

1999 **ULTIMATE GIRL RATING:**

DIRECTOR: Lissane Skyler
BIRTHPLACE: Indie U.S.A.
FILE UNDER:
Every Person Tells a Story
RATED: R

STARRING: Mark Blum, Zach Braff, Leo Burmester, Bo Hopkins, Heather Matarazzo, Mary McCormack, Bebe Neuwirth, Chris Noth, Jacob Reynolds, Tristine Skyler, Michael Weston

THE PROBLEM People think they have it rough at home if mom has limited their clothing allowance or dad tells boring stories about his college years. They just don't get it, do they? Some kids have it a lot rougher than that. How do they cope? In GETTING TO KNOW YOU, they tell stories, and in doing so rewrite their own dark histories.

The Reel Deal: Every town has one: a dumpy bus station filled with sad people and their sad stories. Judith (Heather Matarazzo) is a shy, intelligent girl who arrives at one of those bus stations with more mental than physical baggage. She and her brother, Wesley (Zach Braff), are leaving behind the dregs of a lousy childhood. Their alcoholic, self-absorbed parents just had their final fight, leaving Mom zombied out in some state-run hospital and Dad wanting nothing more to do with his kids. Wesley is heading off to Syracuse University to study pre-med, Judith is off to a foster home. Kicking around the station is Jimmy (Michael Weston), a boy who claims to remember Judith from one of the many schools she's attended. He's filled with stories about the people in the station, and Judith kills time by listening to his stories—stirring tales about a girl and a gambler, a woman coping with her husband's nasty temper, and a policeman with really bad luck. Interspersed with Jimmy's stories are flashback scenes that show how Judith and her brother got to this tough place in their lives. Wesley scoffs at Jimmy's posturing, but Judith finds his openness endearing, wondering if maybe there's still someone in that dismal town worth holding on to. How depressing you find this movie probably depends on how much you identify with the characters. It can be difficult to watch kids who have been through so much; sometimes you're relieved that you can relate—or you may be relieved that you can't.

Girl to Watch: Heather Matarazzo was the feisty, activist best friend in THE PRINCESS DIARIES. Here, she plays a girl a lot like someone you might know, the kind of girl who hides a world of pain behind a shy smile and a put-on positive attitude.

Guy to Watch: Michael Weston is captivating as the cute and talkative Jimmy. Zach Braff's quiet, serious Wesley is worlds away from his mischief-loving lead character on TV's "Scrubs," except for the interest in medicine, of course.

Scene Worth the Rewind: It's interesting to watch the dance between Jimmy and Judith as they slowly begin to connect. Movies usually hurry this part along to get to the big action. In GETTING TO KNOW YOU, this *is* the big action, and it feels like it's happening in real time.

Watch This One With: Your more serious friends.

Movies with the Same Vibe: WHITE OLEANDER, GIRLS TOWN, RUNNING ON EMPTY.

HOW THIS MOVIE HELPS

This is hardly an escapist film, especially if you've dealt with a tough home life yourself. You see what amazing resources Judith and Wesley have developed, but it's still hard to believe how little their unbelievably self-absorbed parents have given them. You can decide which is more poignant to watch: Wesley's determination to climb out of that mess and never look back, or Judith's need to believe that there's hope yet for parental approval. This little film is beautifully made, filled with funny and interesting moments, and more honest about the challenges of raising yourself into adulthood than all the "What to Wear to the Prom?" movies can offer. So even if your home life is a breeze compared to these kids, you might like to go deep with tales that take twists and turns, tug at your heart, and throw a bit of hope your way when you most need it. Check it out; this might be your stop.

Ghost World

MOOD CONTROL

1 2 3
4 5 6
7 8 9
10 11 12

▶ Press PLAY
if you're feeling:

1 Adventurous
2 Ambitious
3 ARTSY
4 CYNICAL
5 Depressed
6 Heartbroken
7 Hopeful
8 Insecure
9 Misunderstood
10 Overwhelmed
11 Playful
12 WEIRD

2001 **ULTIMATE GIRL RATING:** ♣ ♣ ♣

DIRECTOR: Terry Zwigoff
BIRTHPLACE: Indie U.S.A.
FILE UNDER: Ebony and Irony
RATED: R

STARRING: Thora Birch, Scarlett Johansson, Steve Buscemi, Brad Renfro, Illeana Douglas

THE PROBLEM If there's a more cynical girl than you at your school, you haven't met her. You look at all the kids around you who are anxiously awaiting the next big stage of life and wonder, "What are they thinking?" Life itself is a stage in your book, and we're just actors in someone's idea of a sick comedy until they decide to turn the lights out. At least, that's what you think on your good days. The problem? There actually isn't a big problem. You like being this way. Your big goal in life? Avoiding one.

The Reel Deal: Enid (Thora Birch) and Rebecca (Scarlett Johansson) are ending their senior year poised on the brink of—well, not much. They view graduation, the prom, and the summer ahead with all the excitement of houseflies in a jar. Bonded by their mutual dislike of almost everyone they meet, they pass their days mocking strangers and even dissing their only other friend, Josh (Brad Renfro). Rebecca is pushing Enid to rent an apartment together and get moving toward some kind of future, but Enid has little energy for that. The one event that does energize Enid is playing with the affections of an eccentric loner they stumble upon, Seymour (Steve Buscemi), who has a dull desk job by day but lives (if you can call it living) for his collection of 78 rpm records and old advertisements. At first, Enid is just amused by Seymour's tragic life, but she gradually finds herself admiring him for caring so much about something. As Enid drifts away from Rebecca and finds she can't shake herself of Seymour, she realizes that life happens, whether you mock it or make plans. GHOST WORLD is one of those movies that shows summer the way it really is for lots of people without the means or inclination to spend every minute at the beach, working on the perfect tan. Summer means long hours of hanging out, wasting time, and almost missing the structure and purpose that the school day brings. (We said almost.)

Line That Says It All: "I don't want to meet someone who shares my interests. I hate my interests."

Girl to Watch: Enid is every hipper-than-thou girl at every school whose smug sense of isolation puts a barrier between herself, her friends, and her feelings.

Guy to Watch: He's hardly a boy, but Steve Buscemi is perfect as the tragic Seymour, the guy who looks up at you with hope at every sad little coffee shop.

Scene to Rewind: Most scenes in this movie are too perfectly poignant to sit through again. For laugh-out-loud funny, check out the unprintable note the girls leave their friend Josh when he's not home.

Fun Factoid: GHOST WORLD is based on a famous adult comic book by Daniel Clowes.

Watch This One With: Cynics and art-house lovers.

Movies with the Same Vibe: DONNIE DARKO, HEATHERS. Also check out *Walking and Talking* (1996), a more mainstream indie film featuring two friends who can talk about anything, until one of them gets engaged. Then everything gets weird.

HOW THIS MOVIE HELPS

Enid can hardly help herself get a handle on life, much less help you. But sometimes it's nice to see a heroine that's not fending off cute boys while checking her perfect look in the mirror. One of the joys of indie films (once you get used to the subtlety and strangeness) is the sense that the script was not written by a team of Hollywood studio execs to be smooth and perfect. Like life, this film seems to amble along not quite sure of its destination. Isn't that how we often feel, half aware of our own story? You don't have to be the most eccentric girl at school to relate to Enid's distancing act from her own life. If your answer to the question "I've got spirit, how 'bout you?" is a bemused shake of the head, GHOST WORLD might be right up your alley.

Girlfight

2000 **ULTIMATE GIRL RATING:** ♣ ♣ ♣

DIRECTOR: Karyn Kusama
BIRTHPLACE: Yo, Brooklyn
FILE UNDER: Girl Rocky
RATED: R

STARRING: Michelle
Rodriguez, Ray Santiago,
Paul Calderon, Jaime Tirelli,
Santiago Douglas

THE PROBLEM

They think you have a violent streak. Maybe you hit people, maybe you just yell a lot. Maybe they're right—maybe the world is just too stupid to deal with, and you can't take it sometimes. Wouldn't it be great if they admired your strength and toughness instead of fearing it? What if the thing you're good at—letting people have it—was considered a talent? Well, welcome to boxing.

The Reel Deal: Diana Guzman (Michelle Rodriguez) lives in a Brooklyn housing project with her sensitive brother, Tiny (Ray Santiago), her boorish father (Paul Calderon), and a chip on her shoulder the size of Alaska. Not that she doesn't have reason to be angry. Her father's emotionally abusive manner was no doubt a factor in her mother's suicide, and Diana can't hide the contempt she feels for him. Her anger shows up daily at school, where she falls into fighting the way the rest of us fall into breathing. Things start to change for her the day she goes to pick her brother up from his boxing lesson. Tiny would rather go to art school than learn to box, but his father is trying to toughen up his somewhat effeminate son. Diana becomes entranced with the agility and fierceness of the boxers and asks Tiny's trainer, Hector (Jaime Tirelli), to give her lessons. Hector refuses at first, but then decides that her money is as good as anyone else's. Soon, Diana becomes obsessed with boxing, intrigued by a handsome fellow boxer (Santiago Douglas), and finds that her whole attitude about school and life is lifted by spending time in the ring. Now if she can only keep her father from finding out what she's up to.

Line That Says It All: "This equality thing has gone too far."

Girl to Watch: Michelle Rodriguez as the indomitable Diana. She was picked from hundreds of girls in a huge casting call, and this is her first film. Can you tell? We can't either.

Guy to Watch: Santiago Douglas' Adrian is so cute. Too bad he finds the idea of a hot girl who can knock guys out so confusing.

Scene Worth the Rewind: The fight scenes are really interesting and show you how boxing matches actually work. None of that "final knockout with the fallen guy slowly crawling to his feet at the last second, to the swelling of heroic music" stuff.

Fun Factoid: The director, Karyn Kusama, is a boxer herself. (Can you say labor of love?) And take a look at the science teacher. He's played by John Sayles, a famous indie movie director and the executive producer of this film. (That means he helped get it made.) He also writes deeply personal films: check out *Return of the Secaucus 7* (1980) and *Brother From Another Planet* (1984).

Watch This One With: Your brothers, your boyfriend, or any sexist in need of a wake-up call.

Movies with the Same Vibe: BEND IT LIKE BECKHAM, OUR SONG, LOVE AND BASKETBALL.

HOW THIS MOVIE HELPS

What if anger and rage weren't considered bad things? Maybe if you're a volatile kinda girl, you should check out one of the let-'em-have-it sports. If boxing isn't your thing, what about the martial arts, or just running down the road, your lungs burning, your tendons stretching, pretending you're chasing a bad guy who you're gonna throw into your squadcar? Your mother always said, "Channel your energy," and who knew? Turns out she was right. So get pumped, or pumping, or whatever it is you want to do to make that fierceness work for you. You're sick of being read the riot act. Let's have your fans rioting in the streets instead.

Until fairly recently, it was rare for women to direct movies. Women are still under-employed in the director's chair, but it's no longer unusual for your favorite films to be female-fueled. Some are included in this book, and here are a few more that you may have missed on your way to *The Matrix*.

Desperately Seeking Susan (1985)

Director Susan Seidelman must have had a good time making this funny movie about longing for a more exciting life, mistaken identity, true love, and a certain very cool leather jacket. Did we mention Madonna costars?

But I'm a Cheerleader (1999)

Director Jamie Babbitt paints a candy-colored, cartoonlike vision of a normally serious subject: the attempt by some groups to "cure" homosexuals. It all begins when a perky, blonde cheerleader finds herself shipped off to True Directions, a rehab camp for gay teens.

This Is My Life (1992)

From Nora Ephron, the director of *Sleepless in Seattle* (1993) and *You've Got Mail* (1998), this film is a humorous, honest look at a mom who starts to rise in her career and how her success affects her two daughters. A great movie for any teen who ever got the phone call: "Sorry, honey, I'll be home late. Can you make dinner?"

Mississippi Masala (1992)

Director Mira Nair paints an evocative picture of Indian life in the New South in this interracial romance between an Indian girl and an African-American guy (played by Denzel Washington).

The Anniversary Party (2001)

This clever, scathing serio-comedy is codirected by and costarring Jennifer Jason Leigh and Alan Cumming. We see a Hollywood party deteriorate into a night of revelation, long-buried emotions, and tortured-artist angst. Very indie, very "Sophisticated Themes" (as the ratings people like to say).

Children of a Lesser God (1986)

Director Randa Haines gave us this beautiful and popular movie based on an award-winning play. The subject is a new teacher at a school for the deaf who befriends an obviously bright young deaf woman who graduated from the school and is now a janitor there. Marlee Matlin won an Oscar for this, her first film performance.

Girl, Interrupted

MOOD CONTROL

1	2	3
4	5	6
7	8	9
10	11	12

▶ Press PLAY if you're feeling:

1 Adventurous
2 Ambitious
3 ARTSY
4 Cynical
5 DEPRESSED
6 Heartbroken
7 Hopeful
8 Insecure
9 Misunderstood
10 Overwhelmed
11 Playful
12 WEIRD

1999 **ULTIMATE GIRL RATING:** ♣ ♣ ♣ ♣

DIRECTOR: James Mangold
BIRTHPLACE: Mainstream Hollywood
FILE UNDER: Life in Lock-Up
RATED: R

STARRING: Winona Ryder, Angelina Jolie, Clea DuVall, Brittany Murphy, Elisabeth Moss, Jared Leto

THE PROBLEM

Sometimes it's all you can do to get out of bed in the morning. So the very thought of planning a magnificent future for yourself just makes you want to crawl under the covers and hide. Crazy people have it made, you think; no one expects anything of them. You sometimes wish you could just go live in one of those places where your days consist of strolling the grounds, sipping tea, and talking to a soothing therapist. You're not crazy. You just want a vacation from having to keep it all together.

The Reel Deal: GIRL, INTERRUPTED is based on Susanna Kaysen's memoir of her eighteen-month stay in a mental hospital after her ingestion of alcohol and pills convinced everyone that she was a danger to herself. Susanna (Winona Ryder) turns out to be significantly more stable than her new companions: Georgina (Clea DuVall), despondent Daisy (Brittany Murphy), and

Lisa (Angelina Jolie), whose mix of charisma and cruelty draws all the girls into her web. In a series of utterly compelling episodes, GIRL, INTERRUPTED shows life inside a mental hospital in the '60s, when women were sometimes locked up simply for living at a more dramatic pitch than their peers. Susanna becomes fond of most of the women who make up her new world, and draws

Scene Worth the Rewind: There's a hilarious scene at an ice-cream parlor that will remind you of every time you and your friends cut up in public.

Watch This One With: Anyone who struggles to feel good about herself and her place in the world. You don't have to be in lock-up to wonder if anyone else feels a little crazy just living in this world.

Movies with the Same Vibe: CRAZY/BEAUTIFUL, GIRLS TOWN.

comfort from the structure and routine built into her endless days. "Don't put down roots here," a savvy nurse warns her, and we learn along with Susanna the dangers of trying to avoid reality. Not just a cautionary tale, the movie is a story of female bonding, bucking the system, and the heartbreak of being unable to fix the ones we love.

Line That Says It All: "Have you ever confused a dream with life?"

Girl to Watch: Winona Ryder offers us a peek into this unusual world. Angelina Jolie burns up the screen with her wild-eyed Lisa; she'll stay with you long after the credits roll.

Guy to Watch: Jared Leto gives a nice, understated performance as Susanna's boyfriend, Toby, who can't imagine why she'd choose this cuckoo's nest over an escape into the real world with him.

HOW THIS MOVIE HELPS

Strong characters and good acting helped make this movie massively popular with teenage girls. But it offers more than that. Girls can relate to the feeling that life is too hard to handle, that it would be great to be airlifted out of your world for a while so you could get a handle on things. Unfortunately, psychiatric hospitals aren't the spas we wish they could be, and those in the throes of serious mental illness aren't enjoying their stay. Those of us who are reasonably mentally healthy have to look for our pockets of sanity elsewhere: a friend who understands us, a plan for the future that changes what we don't like about the present, and movies that remind us that even though we may not have it all together, that's different from falling apart.

Girls Town

MOOD CONTROL

I	2	3
4	5	6
7	8	9
I0	II	I2

▶ Press PLAY
if you're feeling:

I Adventurous
2 Ambitious
3 ARTSY
4 CYNICAL
5 Depressed
6 Heartbroken
7 Hopeful
8 INSECURE
9 Misunderstood
I0 Overwhelmed
II Playful
I2 Weird

1996 ULTIMATE GIRL RATING: ♣ ♣ ♣

DIRECTOR: Jim McKay
BIRTHPLACE: Jersey
FILE UNDER: Band of Sisters
RATED: R

STARRING: Lili Taylor, Bruklin (Idina) Harris, Anna Grace, Aunjanue Ellis, Ramya Pratt, Asia Minor

THE PROBLEM

You have your best buds, and you don't know what you'd do without them. Sometimes it really feels like it's you and your friends against the world. Still, there are some things that even they don't know about you, about what you've gone through. You don't know why you haven't told them. Embarrassment? Shame? You don't want them looking at you differently? You don't know. So you stuff that little piece of info into a diary, or into the back of your brain, and get on with it. But sometimes you wonder, "How close can we really be if I can't share the scary stuff too?"

The Reel Deal: Four close high school friends in a blue-collar part of New Jersey break a lot of stereotypes. Two are African-American, two are white, three are getting ready to go to college, one is a single mother who has been held back in school so many times someone says, "What is she? Forty?" They have a friendship truly based on who they are, not who they're trying to impress.

In the beginning of the film we see one of the girls, Nikki (Aunjanue Ellis), walking down the street and hear what her head is filled with: brutality, the sound of sirens, the harsh noise of life. What's the matter with her? We suppose it's not much when we find out that she's on her way to Princeton. Yet her friend Emma (Anna Grace) can't believe that she hasn't signed up for housing yet. "You're going to wind up in the cafeteria," Emma teases her. The next day, Nikki's reason for stalling out on her future becomes horribly clear. She has committed suicide. Her friends rush over to her house and are met with kind yet firm silence from Nikki's mom. So they steal her journal and find out that she was raped while working as an intern at a local magazine. This tragic incident gets the girls really talking. They discover that they've all suffered some sort of violation by men. Emma was raped by a classmate, and as Patti (Lili Taylor) puts it, "You don't want to do it, a guy wants to do it, he's gonna get it. You call that rape, I've been raped by every guy I've gone out with." The three friends realize how much they've held back from one another, and how much it hurts a friendship and your own sense of self not to share these stories. Soon, they decide to do more than share: they decide to get some revenge. That's when things get really interesting.

Line That Says It All: "If this was a movie, we would have shot fifty people by now."

Girl to Watch: All the young women are great.

How You Know It's a Movie: They look a little older than high school girls, don't they? But the dialogue is so natural that you can forget that.

Scene Worth the Rewind: Don't try this at home, but we couldn't help enjoying the scene where the girls vandalize a jerk's car to get revenge.

Fun Factoid: This movie was shot over several months, and the women improvised a lot of the scenes. So if it sounds like real people saying what pops into their minds sometimes, that's because they are. Pretty cool, huh?

Watch This One With: Your girls in the hood.

Movies with the Same Vibe: OUR SONG, GAS FOOD LODGING, RIVER'S EDGE.

HOW THIS MOVIE HELPS

It's really easy to say you've got best friends and that you tell them everything. Yet when you really need them, when there's a risk involved, do you still let them in? It's fun to whine about relationships and bad-hair days, but just how willing are you to let your friends know the serious stuff? Are you afraid that they'll go away if you share your biggest problems? We're afraid that you'll go away if you don't—not necessarily kill yourself, but deny your dreams and plans and get stuck in a dark place with creepy memories. Tell somebody what really happened and it's like a flashlight lighting up your spirit. Make your best friends earn their title, won't you?

Good Will Hunting

MOOD CONTROL

1	2	3
4	5	6
7	8	9
10	11	12

▶ Press PLAY if you're feeling:

1 Adventurous
2 Ambitious
3 Artsy
4 CYNICAL
5 Depressed
6 Heartbroken
7 HOPEFUL
8 INSECURE
9 Misunderstood
10 Overwhelmed
11 Playful
12 Weird

1997 **ULTIMATE GIRL RATING:** ♣ ♣ ♣ ♣

DIRECTOR: Gus Van Sant
BIRTHPLACE: Mainstream Hollywood
FILE UNDER: Genius in the Rough
RATED: R

STARRING: Robin Williams, Matt Damon, Ben Affleck, Stellan Skarsgård, Minnie Driver, Casey Affleck, Cole Hauser

THE PROBLEM

You know you have a talent for something, but it's more embarrassing than gratifying. You don't know why, but ambition strikes you as a stupid thing. You just don't see the point of working hard to make something of yourself. All those big successes out there, are they really any happier than anybody else? You don't know, and you don't want to find out. Why are you this this way? Are you lazy? Afraid to test yourself, to find out that you're wrong about your gift, or even worse, that you're right? Fine. We'll shut up already. Just rent GOOD WILL HUNTING....

The Reel Deal: South Boston is a tough place, and few come tougher than Will Hunting (Matt Damon). He toils as a janitor at prestigious MIT by day and goes out drinking with his buddies at night, trying to put a childhood filled with abuse behind him. Yet despite his determinedly blue-collar life, he can't ignore his desire to use his phenomenal brain. When nobody's looking, he memorizes huge history texts, and impulsively solves a notoriously difficult math problem left on a hallway chalkboard. The complicated equation is a breeze for the brilliant Will; he has no way of knowing that a professor left it out there for his students to puzzle over for weeks. Astonished to find it solved the next morning, the professor eventually discovers that Will, the janitor, was the mystery mathematician. He's dying to work with the gifted prodigy, but Will responds to the attention by going out and getting himself arrested. Professor Lambeau (Stellan Skarsgård) shows up in court to make a deal: he'll get psychiatric help for Will so that he can work with him. Lambeau looks up an old friend, Sean Maguire (Robin Williams), a gifted therapist from Will's neighborhood who made a mess of his career but works well with people. Maguire is joined by Will's best friend Chuckie (Ben Affleck) and a delightful Harvard student named Skylar (Minnie Driver), who is trying to get Will to recognize that turning his back on a decent future is crazier than thinking a Southie can leave the hood without betraying the only people who ever cared about him.

Line That Says It All: "You don't know about real loss, 'cause it only occurs when you love something more than you love yourself."

Girl to Watch: Minnie Driver plays Skylar without a trace of affectation. See her in *Ella Enchanted* (2004) or old episodes of *Will and Grace* and you will see that she can play anyone.

Guy to Watch: Matt Damon is powerfully affecting as the tough-as-nails Will Hunting.

Scene Worth the Rewind: The bar scene is a fun piece of one-upmanship. Too bad that in real life being smart and knowing stuff isn't the cool sport of kings that it is in this scene.

Soundtrack Note: The late singer-songwriter Elliot Smith stumbled into fame when his song "Miss Misery" was picked up for the film and later nominated for an Oscar. It was quite a night for GOOD WILL HUNTING; Ben and Matt earned a Best Original Screenplay award, and Smith, in a thrift shop tux and a bewildered expression, played his sweet, sad song in between all the other razzle-dazzle numbers.

Watch This One With: Anyone who hasn't seen it yet.

Movies with the Same Vibe: ORDINARY PEOPLE, FINDING FORRESTER.

HOW THIS MOVIE HELPS

GOOD WILL HUNTING shows that inside every belligerent, impossible guy is a hurt child waiting to be loved. (Or at least, it would be nice to think so.) Whether or not WILL makes you forgive that guy who wouldn't let you get too close, at least you'll understand a certain type of the male species better. What makes this film different from so many movies about damaged men is Skylar, a female character who'll wait patiently for her man to get his act together—but she won't wait forever. Welcome to the new world, fellas.

Gregory's Girl

MOOD CONTROL

1	2	3
4	5	6
7	8	9
10	11	12

▶ Press PLAY if you're feeling:

1 Adventurous
2 Ambitious
3 ARTSY
4 Cynical
5 Depressed
6 Heartbroken
7 HOPEFUL
8 Insecure
9 Misunderstood
10 Overwhelmed
11 PLAYFUL
12 Weird

1981 ULTIMATE GIRL RATING: ♣ ♣ ♣

DIRECTOR: Bill Forsyth
BIRTHPLACE: Scotland
FILE UNDER:
Scottish Rite of Passage
RATED: PG

STARRING: John Gordon Sinclair, Dee Hepburn, Jake D'Arcy, Clare Grogan, Robert Buchanan, Billy Greenlees

THE PROBLEM

When first love hits, it does so without warning. One minute you're fine, the next minute you're a lunatic with idiotic thoughts and a new, permanently stupid, expression. What can you do? You're smitten. It would be nice if the object of your affection had some idea that you were alive, but first love doesn't really bother with that. Whether or not your love is returned, it inhabits your body like some weird disease that only you know you have. Unless you're Gregory, of course. Then the whole world knows.

The Reel Deal: This movie is so darn cute you'll want to pinch its little Scottish cheeks. Gregory (John Gordon Sinclair) is the kind of teenage boy who is too awkward for his height and too enthusiastic for his own good. He loves soccer (called football in the U.K.) but he's terrible at it because of that whole awkward stork thing. One day, a new player comes out to salvage the team, and it turns out to be a lovely, confident girl named Dorothy (Dee Hepburn). Gregory is only momentarily humiliated by the fact that she's ten times better than he is; Cupid strikes before that can be much of an issue. Running down the field, muscles flexing, golden hair flying, Dorothy has an athletic grace that leaves Gregory slack-jawed and numb, like a cartoon character just before he falls over from a punch. Dorothy is faintly bemused by Gregory's persistent attempts to catch her attention, but he barely makes her radar screen. His friend Steve (Billy Greenlees), who's happy to inform Gregory that he hasn't got a chance, is not much help. Yet finally, a miracle strikes: it appears that Dorothy has consented, at last, to a date. How that date develops, in surprising and hilarious ways, is indicative of the film's entire tone. GREGORY'S GIRL is a true homage to the great adventure that awaits when you dare to give love a whirl.

Girl to Watch: Dee Hepburn's Dorothy, who was bending it like Beckham while Beckham was still a schoolboy. These days, a story about a girl who outkicks her male soccer teammates would be a half-hour special on the Disney Channel. But in 1981? Ahead of the game.

Guy to Watch: John Gordon Sinclair is terrific. You can practically see the Clearasil on his face. What American filmmaker dares to show a teen with less than perfect skin?

Scene Worth the Rewind: Gregory and Dorothy's date is such a funny scene. You'll love just keeping track of all his expressions: nervous, confused, delighted, relaxed. Also, keep an eye out for the boy in the penguin costume. Every movie should have one.

Fun Factoid: This movie was made for a tiny amount of money, even by 1981 standards, and was a minor splash here and in Europe. Leave it to those Scots to make a sensitive, coming-of-age story that manages to be hysterically funny even as it's tugging at your heart.

Watch This One With: Tea and shortbread. Forget the people.

Movies with the Same Vibe: LUCAS, FLIRTING, SIXTEEN CANDLES.

HOW THIS MOVIE HELPS

GREGORY'S GIRL is one of those movies that people stumble upon in the video store, snatch up, and take home to show their roommates what they've been missing. The fashion and hairstyles are humorously dated, but the writing and emotions ring true year after year. In a world where it's scary to admit you're not jaded, Gregory's openness is a breath of fresh air. Need a sea change from the cynicism? Spend a night being GREGORY'S GIRL.

Hairspray

MOOD CONTROL

1	2	3
4	5	6
7	8	9
10	11	12

▶ **Press PLAY**
if you're feeling:

1 Adventurous
2 Ambitious
3 Artsy
4 Cynical
5 DEPRESSED
6 Heartbroken
7 Hopeful
8 INSECURE
9 Misunderstood
10 Overwhelmed
11 Playful
12 WEIRD

1988 **ULTIMATE GIRL RATING:** ♣ ♣ ♣

DIRECTOR: John Waters
BIRTHPLACE:
Indie America
FILE UNDER:
Beehive and Behave
RATED: PG

STARRING: Sonny Bono, Ruth Brown, Divine, Colleen Fitzpatrick, Michael St. Gerard, Debbie Harry, Ricki Lake, Leslie Ann Powers, Jerry Stiller, Shawn Thompson, Pia Zadora, Ric Ocasek

THE PROBLEM

You're in the need for some good old-fashioned girl empowerment. Yet so many movies along that line are as earnest as an after-school special. Bore me later, please. What you want is a film that lifts you up while having all the reality of a candy-colored dream sequence. Remember those talking fish that everyone used to buy as gag gifts? They were ridiculous, to be sure, but also sort of charming—kind of like HAIRSPRAY.

The Reel Deal: Tracy Turnblad (Ricki Lake) wants nothing more in life than to be on the *Corny Collins Show*, a local dance program that's a lot like a MTV beach party, except that it's 1962, so the dancers have clothes on. One obnoxious *Collins Show* princess named Amber is horrified that plus-size Tracy wants to be on the show, even though Tracy is the better dancer of the two.

She is equally horrified that Tracy is a devout integrationist who wants to see diversity in skin color and size on the Corny Collins set. Amber and her equally creepy parents (Debbie Harry and Sonny Bono) do everything they can to stop the radical Tracy Turnblad from integrating the show, but Tracy and her friends—including a hunky new beau—fight the good fight, with plenty

Line That Says It All: "Free Tracy
Turnblad!"

Girl to Watch: Yes, it's Talk Show Ricki,
younger, plumper, and shakin' it like a
Polaroid picture. And her mom? The late,
great drag queen Divine. When this single
mom says she's both a mother *and* a father
to her girl, she means it.

Guy to Watch: This is the most normal
movie John Waters ever made. So who is this
talented weirdo, anyway? Look for him as
the deranged psychiatrist near the end of the
film.

Watch This One With: Your weirdest
friends. This one is off the wall, but in a
good way.

Movies with the Same Vibe:
HAROLD AND MAUDE, CAMP.

of cool dance moves to boot. Since this
movie was made in the wink-wink, nudge-
nudge '80s by famously eccentric filmmaker
John Waters, it's played more for cheesy
laughs than serious drama. But wait—is that
a lump in your throat? It's so hard to believe
that the world was that segregated, and so
cool to think that plenty of kids tried to do
something about it in their own way. Despite
the strange outfits and hilarious hairstyles,
HAIRSPRAY winds up touching you with its
flavorful homage to the Baltimore of Waters'
youth—the good, the bad, and the big hair.

HOW THIS MOVIE HELPS

In the crazy, mixed-up world of John
Waters, it seems Tracy is one good-
sized girl who never heard that she
was supposed to be a self-deprecating
wallflower. Watching her go for the
spotlight with the boy of her dreams
is just a blast. HAIRSPRAY is a satire
with heart, and it even made it to New
York as a celebrated musical. Tracy
Turnblad fights to get on local TV
and winds up a Broadway star—how
cool is that?

Harold and Maude

MOOD CONTROL

1	2	3
4	5	6
7	8	9
10	11	12

▶ Press **PLAY** if you're feeling:

1 Adventurous
2 Ambitious
3 Artsy
4 Cynical
5 DEPRESSED
6 HEARTBROKEN
7 Hopeful
8 Insecure
9 Misunderstood
10 Overwhelmed
11 Playful
12 WEIRD

1971   **ULTIMATE GIRL RATING:** 🍿🍿🍿🍿

DIRECTOR: Hal Ashby
BIRTHPLACE: Mainstream Hollywood, Indie Heart
FILE UNDER: Oddball Romance Classic
RATED: PG

STARRING: Ruth Gordon, Bud Cort, Vivian Pickles, Cyril Cusack, Charles Tyner, Ellen Geer, Eric Christmas, G. Wood

THE PROBLEM

You look around and wonder where everyone gets their energy for life. We're born, we die—what's the point? A fear and obsession with death—*that* you can understand. Yet your world is filled with people always telling you how great it is to be young, how you have your whole life ahead of you. Ahead for what? To grow old and sick and grumpy, snapping at the Assisted Living staff for trying to make you go to a pottery class? Who needs it? Ah, but to grow old like Maude—everybody needs that. . . .

The Reel Deal: Harold Chasen (Bud Cort) is a poor little rich boy who lives with his freakishly uptight mother in a large mansion. He's like a well-dressed zombie, putting in his time without really feeling much of anything. His hobbies include pretending to commit suicide and going to strangers' funerals. At one such event, he meets Maude (Ruth Gordon), a seventy-nine-year-old woman who loves life as much as Harold hates it. Pretty soon, they're hanging out, stealing cars for joyrides, and comparing world views. Harold finds his heart melting over Maude's utter self-confidence and enthusiasm for her various odd pursuits. In no time at all, deep feelings develop between them, much to the chagrin of everyone in Harold's life.

Line That Says It All: "L-I-V-E, Live! Otherwise, you got nothing to talk about in the locker room."

Girl to Watch: Maude. Okay, so she's almost eighty. We still promise you'll find that Maude to be more with it than anyone at your school.

Guy to Watch: Bud Cort's Harold is compelling in every scene.

Scene Worth the Rewind: Our "since 1980" rule is broken for this movie due to its funky, modern sensibility. HAROLD AND MAUDE is so weirdly hilarious that every scene is pure gold. Harold's first visit to Maude's house is particularly magical. But what about the opening scene? And that final, surprising image? Oh never mind. Just rewind the whole thing and watch it again.

Soundtrack Note: Who sings those sweet little folk songs sprinkled throughout the film? It's the singer Yusaf Islam, formerly known as Cat Stevens, who was a huge folk-pop god before he became a serious Muslim and disavowed his musical past.

Fun Factoid: This movie was pretty much ignored when it first came out. Then, through word of mouth, it built a following, and has been a cult classic for decades, à la *Rocky Horror Picture Show* (1975). Maude was just another character in Ruth Gordon's illustrious stage and screen career. Yet Bud Cort never really escaped his Harold persona, poor guy. Oh well. If you're only famous for one film, this isn't a bad one.

Watch This One With: Your friends who can appreciate a movie that's fairly offbeat. Most viewers love HAROLD AND MAUDE, but some people find it too weird to enjoy.

Movies with the Same Vibe: RUSHMORE, REALITY BITES, GHOST WORLD. Also check out *Benny & Joon* (1993), an off-kilter romance featuring Johnny Depp and Mary Stuart Masterson.

HOW THIS MOVIE HELPS

Maude is so inspirational, you don't have to be a suicidal preppie to fall in love with her magical personality. We don't learn a lot about Maude's past, but enough to know that her attitude comes from an active decision to be happy, not from a long, lucky streak. The message she gives to Harold is simple: "Live!" She doesn't just mean stay alive, she means fill your days with meaning and passion for what you do. Her total acceptance of him is amazing. Who accepts you to that degree? No one? Well, find someone out there who will. Who knows? Maybe it's you.

Heathers

MOOD CONTROL

1   2   3
4   5   6
7   8   9
10   11   12

▶ Press PLAY if you're feeling:

1 Adventurous
2 Ambitious
3 Artsy
4 CYNICAL
5 Depressed
6 Heartbroken
7 Hopeful
8 INSECURE
9 Misunderstood
10 OVERWHELMED
11 Playful
12 Weird

1989   **ULTIMATE GIRL RATING:** ♣ ♣ ♣

DIRECTOR: Michael Lehmann
BIRTHPLACE: Mainstream Hollywood
FILE UNDER: My Boyfriend's Back and There's Gonna Be Trouble
RATED: R

STARRING: Winona Ryder, Christian Slater, Shannen Doherty, Lisanne Falk, Kim Walker, Penelope Milford, Glenn Shadix, Lance Fenton

THE PROBLEM   The popular crowd at your high school is out of control and must be stopped. Their snobbery, their casual cruelty to those born with less fortunate skin or body types, their complete rejection of non-members and slavish demands of conformity to would-be members leaves you the choice of suffering their tyranny or betraying your true self to gain inclusion to their clique. It's practically murder-inducing, isn't it? Well, the juvenile justice system is no cakewalk and college is just a short escape hatch away. Rid your brain of dangerous thoughts and enjoy this fantasy instead.

The Reel Deal: Veronica Sawyer (Winona Ryder) is a pretty, brainy girl who puts some effort into joining the most popular crowd at school, the Heathers (so called because three of the formidable quartet go by that name). Soon, Veronica realizes that she's permanently locked into friendship with these horribly shallow and spiteful people who revel in humiliating those they view as their genetic inferiors. In the tradition of "be careful what you wish for," Veronica, seeking release from this oppressive tribe, hooks up with a charismatic loner, J.D. (Christian Slater), who takes her desire to murder her supposed "best friend" at face value. In a panic, Veronica conspires to pass the homicide off as a suicide, a ploy that is effective beyond her wildest dreams. Soon she and J.D. are in the center of a tragedy trend that sweeps the school, and this bizarre and twisted turn of events brings out the hypocrisy in everyone: teachers, parents, and students. Veronica loves J.D., but soon has to wonder if she is hooked up with a romantic rebel or a complete psycho.

Line That Says It All: "She's my best friend. God, I hate her."

Girl to Watch: Winona Ryder is great. You know you're watching something completely different when the sympathetic heroine is a murderess.

Guy to Watch: Christian Slater. They say he mimics Jack Nicholson a little too much in this movie. Who cares? The young Jack had it all, and so does Christian in this devilish satire.

Scene Worth the Rewind: There's a rally at school to help the kids deal with all the crazy, tragic events. Its corny ineffectiveness will ring true for many.

Fashion to Catch: The Heather kilts are hilarious. Popular princesses can make anything cool, even knee socks.

Watch This One With: Your favorite unpopular people. Not a movie to watch with your friend who still enjoys *The Little Mermaid* and whose turn-offs are sushi and mean people.

Movies with the Same Vibe: ELECTION, PUMP UP THE VOLUME.

HOW THIS MOVIE HELPS

HEATHERS is definitely not a movie for anyone who has recently dealt with a suicide at school, because, in your pain, you might feel that the movie makes fun of that. The biting satire is not for everyone; we talked to teens who love it and teens who roll their eyes at its macabre humor. We see it as a movie that makes clever fun of the way teens use each other and are used in return by the adults in their lives. HEATHERS takes jabs at a society that tends to candy-coat the real anguish that teens can suffer at the hands of the popular kids at school. In this touchy, post-Columbine society, are teens still allowed to have murderous fantasies? Maybe, if they rent them....

Honey

2003   **ULTIMATE GIRL RATING:** ♣ ♣

DIRECTOR: Bille Woodruff
BIRTHPLACE: Mainstream Hollywood
FILE UNDER: Hip-Hop Cinderella
RATED: PG-13

STARRING: Jessica Alba, Lil' Romeo, Mekhi Phifer, David Moscow, Zachary Williams, Joy Bryant, Missy Elliot, Anthony Sherwood, Lonette McKee, Wes Williams

THE PROBLEM   You love hip-hop culture and music, but feel burnt out on the stereotypical portrayal of guns and valuing money over everything. That isn't you. That isn't the people that you know. Well, that isn't HONEY, either. So come meet her. You girls might get along.

The Reel Deal: Honey Daniels (Jessica Alba) is a Bronx bartender and dance teacher who would love to start shaking it in some dance videos. She gets her big break when white music video director Michael Ellis (David Moscow) sees her in a club. The next thing she knows, she's in there with Jadakiss and Sheek, and choreographing for Ginuwine. With even Missy Elliott admiring her moves, Honey appears to be on a straight shot to stardom. We see her achieving her dream, all the while keeping it real by hanging out with her best girl, Gina (Joy Bryant), and finding love in the hood with barbershop owner Chaz (Mekhi Phifer). Yet when she turns down Ellis' advances at a party, Honey sees just how fast stars can go down in flames. Just as she's arranging to put some underprivileged kids in a video, Ellis does everything in his power to see to it that her dreams are destroyed and that she'll never shake her booty in this town again.

Line That Says It All: "I don't know why you just can't teach ballet at a nice uptown school."

Girl to Watch: Jessica Alba does a nice job with Honey, a role that was originally intended for Alliyah before her tragic death. Some critics find her dancing isn't up to snuff, but most were too riveted by her amazing abs to notice.

Guy to Watch: We love Romeo, and promise not to call him Lil' to his face.

How You Know It's a Movie: Every scene screams urban fairy tale, so lovers of edgy hip-hop films might roll their eyes. There's nothing gritty about this story; in fact, there's plenty that would fit right into a Hallmark Hall of Fame film. So the critics, of course, kicked it to the curb. Still, lots of teenage girls thought HONEY was sweet.

Soundtrack Note: Well, you know you're going to hear Missy Elliot ("Hurt Somethin' ") and Jadakiss ("J-A-D-A"). Blaque, Sean Paul, Yolanda Adams, Ginuwine, and many other folks are in the mix as well.

Watch This One With: Your girls. Dance along, no one's looking.

Movies with the Same Vibe: SAVE THE LAST DANCE, CENTER STAGE. Also check out *8 Mile* (2002) with Eminem. He's just a sensitive poet, right? Check out *Breakin'* (1984), but don't look for plot, look for moves. Then there's *Krush Groove* (1985), another old-school fave that's worth watching just to see Run-DMC.

HOW THIS MOVIE HELPS

Sure, the story line is a bit implausible. And, yeah, maybe a dancer who spends her days miming sex moves for videos shouldn't be too shocked when a sleazy director wants some payback for the big time. Still, we found the idea of somebody loving hip-hop dance and culture yet standing up to the sexism and materialism of the music industry kinda cool. Jessica Alba plays a girl whose values are too strong to change with her fortunes, who can't wait to give back when she gets the opportunity. For that reason, it might be nice for young teens to get a taste of HONEY.

How to Deal

MOOD CONTROL

① ② ③
④ ⑤ ⑥
⑦ ⑧ ⑨
⑩ ⑪ ⑫

▶ Press **PLAY**
if you're feeling:

1 Adventurous
2 Ambitious
3 Artsy
4 CYNICAL
5 Depressed
6 HEARTBROKEN
7 Hopeful
8 INSECURE
9 Misunderstood
10 Overwhelmed
11 Playful
12 Weird

2003 **ULTIMATE GIRL RATING:** ♣ ♣ ♣

DIRECTOR: Clare Kilner
BIRTHPLACE:
Mainstream U.S.A.
FILE UNDER: Love Hurts
RATED: PG-13

STARRING: Mandy Moore, Allison Janney, Peter Gallagher, Trent Ford, Alexandra Holden, Dylan Baker, Nina Foch, Mary Catherine Garrison

THE PROBLEM You want to believe in love. But how can you? Every couple you know winds up brokenhearted, possibly starting with your own broken-up home. One minute your best friend is babbling about some incredible person, the next she's sobbing on your shoulder and vowing to hate all men until the day she dies. If nobody stays together, how are you supposed to stay convinced that true love exists?

The Reel Deal: Poor Halley (Mandy Moore). Her local radio DJ dad (Peter Gallagher) is a baby boomer embarrassment who is divorcing her mom and blithely moving on to a younger blonde. On the day that her parents finalize their divorce, she learns that her sister, Ashley (Mary Catherine Garrison), is engaged and her best friend, Scarlett (Alexandra Holden), is madly in love. She tries to be happy for the lovebirds, but identifies more with the bitterness of her mom (Allison Janney). Halley sees love as an inevitable car wreck, and can't understand why everyone she knows keeps getting in their cars and starting the engines. She's finally tempted to get into the game herself when she gets to know charming and persistent Macon Forrester (Trent Ford), but a host of plot twists (this movie could be called *Twister*) keeps her true feelings from surfacing.

Line That Says It All: "Oh Macon, I think I like you too much already to go out on a date with you."

Girl to Watch: Mandy Moore, naturally. We weren't watching her in THE PRINCESS DIARIES and thinking, "Wow, she can sing and act." Yet after seeing her nuanced work here as well as her hilariously charged up character in *Saved!* (2004), we think Mandy might have more than a nice singing voice and a great publicist. Some girls get all the luck....

Guy to Watch: Macon Forrester, played by Trent Ford. You just want to brush that hair out of his eyes, and...

Scene Worth the Rewind: The wedding scene is so goofy that it's worth watching twice. Turning your "special day" into Reality Radio—how romantic! Not.

Eye-Rolling Time: There's a funeral that ends in an amazing aerial shot you film buffs will love. But you're watching it thinking, "Why was that character even in the movie? Just to die, so we could have this touching scene?" Welcome to the Person as Plot Device trick. Kinda bogus, huh?

Watch This One With: Friends whose parents are divorced.

Movies with the Same Vibe: 10 THINGS I HATE ABOUT YOU, SHE'S ALL THAT.

HOW THIS MOVIE HELPS

Okay, so maybe in real life a girl would only resist Macon Forrester for about ten minutes. But that feeling of panic when you really like someone yet can already imagine losing them forever is nicely shown in Moore's pretty, frightened face. If you've ever been lied to before, ever thought love would last forever only to watch it dissolve into a mocking memory, then you know why Halley is tempted to choose solitude over such risky business. Weighing the pros and cons of romance, Halley hardly sees a role model of perfection in any of the relationships going on around her, and realizes that she'll have to come up with her own game plan. Despite its title, HOW TO DEAL isn't exactly a manual about how to improvise a life. Still, it offers an absorbing example for the rest of us.

I Capture the Castle

MOOD CONTROL

1 2 3
4 5 6
7 8 9
10 11 12

▶ Press PLAY
if you're feeling:

1 Adventurous
2 Ambitious
3 ARTSY
4 Cynical
5 Depressed
6 HEARTBROKEN
7 Hopeful
8 Insecure
9 Misunderstood
10 Overwhelmed
11 Playful
12 WEIRD

2003 ULTIMATE GIRL RATING: ♣ ♣ ♣ ♣

DIRECTOR: Tim Fywell
BIRTHPLACE: England
FILE UNDER: Life Beyond the Castle Walls
RATED: R (for brief glimpses of naked female forms)

STARRING: Marc Blucas, Rose Byrne, Sinéad Cusack, Tara Fitzgerald, Romola Garai, Bill Nighy, Henry Thomas, David Bamber, Henry Cavill, James Faulkner, Sarah Woodward

THE PROBLEM You have almost nothing, but you won't settle for some kind of "making do" life, even though people might think you should be grateful for the scraps they throw under the table. Good food and hot water are nice, but what is life without hope for the perfect ending? They probably call you picky, and it's true. You want a meaningful life and a soul mate to share things with—a life that *you* pick, that lives up to the plans you have for yourself. **Nothing?** You don't have nothing. Living with integrity—that's a lot.

The Reel Deal: It's 1930, in the British countryside, and the only thing stranger than the rundown stone castle we see in this film is the family that lives in it. The Mortmains are true bohemians. James Mortmain (Bill Nighy) locks himself away in a turret room all day, supposedly to finish writing his second great novel. Reduced to poverty and barely scraping by on the royalties of his first book, written some twelve years earlier, the family is counting on a breakthrough. Completely disdainful of their situation is James' daughter, the beautiful Rose (Rose Byrne), a fiery, melodramatic redhead who only dreams of marrying rich and escaping her dank, dark castle home. Her literary sister, Cassandra (Romola Garai), the narrator of this captivating tale, is more supportive of her dad. She, too, is a writer, and her obsessive diary entries chronicle the adventures that ensue when wealthy American brothers show up to look at the castle, which they own now that their father has passed away. Two teenage sisters, two brothers—it sounds like the perfect set-up for a double romance, doesn't it? I CAPTURE THE CASTLE is, indeed, a romance, but it has far more twists and turns than that classic genre usually includes. As Rose closes in on her rich American, both she and Cassandra discover that the simple ideas they formed about love while locked up in their castle bear little resemblance to what really happens to the heart when the drawbridge is let down.

Line That Says It All: "I love. I have loved. I will love."

Girl to Watch: Romola Garai is perfection as Cassandra. It's a tough job: she must look beautiful one minute, plain the next, and come across as both wise beyond her years and hopelessly naive.

Guy to Watch: The Americans, played by Henry Thomas and Marc Blucas, are both compelling. One's an uncomplicated hunk; the other is a cryptic poet. Take your pick.

Scene Worth the Rewind: Cassandra's stepmother, Topaz (a magnetic Tara Fitzgerald), is horrified that her husband has invited the rich Americans over for supper. With no warning—and no money—she manages to put together a lovely meal with décor that looks inspired by a *Town and Country* party

spread. It's the kick-off to a bewitching evening filled with romantic intrigue.

More About That Rating: It's sad that the ratings board had to slap an R on this film, all for two scenes: Topaz Mortmain "moonbathes" in the nude, and later, Cassandra does the same, part of a family ritual that is far more whimsical than erotic.

Watch This One With: Friends who appreciate stories about ideal love, art over money, or eccentric families.

Movies With the Same Vibe: HAROLD AND MAUDE, THE SLUMS OF BEVERLY HILLS, ROOM WITH A VIEW.

HOW THIS MOVIE HELPS

Life is seldom simple, but so many movies boil problems down to a formula: if you do *x*, then *y* will always follow. Sometimes all we want is an escape, so a formula is just fine. I CAPTURE THE CASTLE is different; it sneaks up on you and offers more. It shows us a girl for whom life will never be easy, because she refuses to live in the world of practical solutions. Does that make Cassandra a hopeless victim of her own romanticism, or a brilliant architect of a rewarding future? Your answer to that question says a lot about your expectations of life. If you suspect they could be higher, you might want to check out I CAPTURE THE CASTLE.

I'm the One That I Want

MOOD CONTROL

1 2 3
4 5 6
7 8 9
10 11 12

▶ Press PLAY
if you're feeling:

1 Adventurous
2 Ambitious
3 ARTSY
4 CYNICAL
5 DEPRESSED
6 Heartbroken
7 Hopeful
8 Insecure
9 Misunderstood
10 Overwhelmed
11 Playful
12 Weird

2000 ULTIMATE GIRL RATING: 🐾 🐾 🐾

DIRECTOR: Lionel Coleman
BIRTHPLACE: Indie U.S.A.
FILE UNDER: Stand Up and Cheer for Ms. Nasty

RATED: R (for hilarious, profane talk)
STARRING: Margaret Cho

THE PROBLEM

You are so sick of other people's rules and expectations. You have made a practice of tuning out the noise, but sometimes that isn't enough. What you wouldn't give to have a microphone, a supportive crowd, and ninety minutes to say exactly what you feel about your culture, your gender, your career, your body, your mother, your relationships, your life! Uncensored, unedited, unabashed. What would you give to be Margaret Cho for one night?

The Reel Deal: Margaret Cho is a stand-up comedienne from San Francisco with a sardonic voice and hilarious in-your-face opinions about everything in her life. She played the comedy clubs throughout the '80s, until a comic's dream job landed in her lap: a TV sitcom centered around her Korean-American viewpoint, starring Cho herself. Cho was apprehensive that her quirky, edgy take on life would be watered down for mass consumption. Other cast members on the show were also concerned: A lot was riding on this first Asian-American sitcom. Cho and her team were assured that they would be delighted with the results of *All-American Girl*. That turned out not to be the case. Cho was immediately ordered to lose weight, and her cynical, wickedly funny persona was transformed into a sort of faux-punk Valley Girl that only offended those hoping to see a truly innovative comedy. The show was soon cancelled, and a crestfallen Cho turned to drugs and alcohol in her disappointment. It took time, but eventually she cleaned up her act (not her comedy act, she's still Ms. Nasty there) and turned a horrific time in her life into a fantastic comedy routine. I'M THE ONE THAT I WANT shows us the Margaret Cho she was meant to be. Hollywood wanted her skinny and giggling; Cho preferred a little more weight and a lot more mouth. The result is a performance that slowly grows on you, builds with humor and little pathos, and leaves you gasping at her daring wit. Cho's sharp brand of humor hits us where we live, and gets us laughing at our own misguided priorities. We leave the theater resolving to live the way she does, as an independent spirit refusing to let Hollywood standards rule her life. What's more all-American than that?

Line That Says It All: "I have a lot of gay friends. When I was a little girl, I used to pray to God to surround me with beautiful men. I guess I should have been more specific."

Girl to Watch: Go Cho!

Scene Worth the Rewind: Cho's imitation of her Korean-born mother's phone calls are classic comedy. You'll keel over laughing, particularly if your mom speaks English as a second language (or it just feels like she does).

Watch This One With: The fairly graphic sex talk and language might make it a little awkward to watch with your mom or dad sitting next to you on the couch. Your friends, though, will be entertained.

Movie with the Same Vibe: PUMP UP THE VOLUME. Also check out *Notorious C.H.O.* (2002).

HOW THIS MOVIE HELPS

It seems like pop culture runs our lives. We've been conned into thinking that being on TV should be our ultimate goal. Well, in Margaret Cho's case, she's been there, she's done that, and she's back to tell us that it's better to be real than really famous. You'll be inspired by how Cho is able to take her most humiliating public experiences and mine them for comedy. But I'M THE ONE THAT I WANT is more than just a string of jokes. It's a call to arms for anyone who refuses to feel bad for being original. Cho's TV show bombed, but Cho herself triumphed, and now more people will see her comedy DVDs than those who saw that lousy show. We would say that Cho gets the last laugh, but if you rented I'M THE ONE THAT I WANT, then you're still laughing.

The Incredibly True Adventure of Two Girls in Love

MOOD CONTROL

1	2	3
4	5	6
7	8	9
10	11	12

▶ Press PLAY if you're feeling:

1. ADVENTUROUS
2. Ambitious
3. Artsy
4. Cynical
5. Depressed
6. HEARTBROKEN
7. Hopeful
8. INSECURE
9. Misunderstood
10. Overwhelmed
11. Playful
12. Weird

1995 ULTIMATE GIRL RATING:

DIRECTOR: Maria Maggenti
BIRTHPLACE: Indie U.S.A.
FILE UNDER: The Elle Word
RATED: R

STARRING: Laurel Holloman, Nicole Ari Parker, Dale Dickey, Stephanie Berry, Maggie Moore, Kate Stafford, Sabrina Artel, Toby Poser

THE PROBLEM

You think romantic movies are great—you just can't relate to dreaming about the hot leading guy. Or maybe a good friend of yours is gay or bi or questioning or...whatever—you just want be able to understand what they're going through. Occasionally movies show girls who like other girls, but everyone makes such a big deal about it. It's turned into a huge political thing. Isn't it just supposed to be about love?

The Reel Deal: Evie (Nicole Ari Parker) has just about everything going for her. She's from a prosperous African-American family, she's pretty and popular, and she seems destined to glide through life trouble-free. Randy's (Laurel Holloman) life, on the other hand, is a little more complicated. Her loving family is composed of her lesbian aunt and her partner, and she struggles through school, preferring her gas station attendant job, where she fools around with the gruff mechanic's wife. Evie is applauded wherever

Sad Fact: When this movie came out, it was mainly shown in art houses to audiences filled with gay and straight adults. People really liked it, but the teenage girls who might have benefited from seeing people like themselves up on screen couldn't find this film anywhere.

Watch This One With: Straight friends, gay friends, anyone who likes a funny, sweet love story.

HOW THIS MOVIE HELPS

It's true that before this movie came out, there were almost no "normal" representations of gay women in pop culture. It's still not exactly the prime-time norm, but things are better now, and what a relief. Young lesbians need to see themselves portrayed as regular people on the screen, straight teens need to get beyond the myths and the hype and see how gay relationships unfold exactly like hetero hookups. Yet the best reason to see THE INCREDIBLY TRUE ADVENTURES OF TWO GIRLS IN LOVE is that it's a fun film about one of those terrific couples that look like they'd never even notice each other on the bus. Does renting this movie necessarily scream, "I am gay!"? We don't think so. You rented *Lord of the Rings*. Do people assume you're a hobbit?

she goes; Randy is taunted as a dyke and greets the world with a tougher stance. When Evie stops at Randy's station, they warily begin to talk, and something happens between them. The INCREDIBLY TRUE ADVENTURE OF TWO GIRLS IN LOVE lives up to its whimsical title. It's not a hand-wringing after-school special about forbidden love. It's a funny, charming tale about two girls who happen to adore each other.

Line That Says It All:
"God, Evie, you are so sheltered."
"Then unshelter me."

Girl to Watch: Laurel Holloman and Nicole Ari Parker are both terrific. You really believe they're a couple.

Scene Worth the Rewind: The motel hunt scene is pretty funny. You know how sometimes in life, things can get just a little out of hand? We thought you did.

A League of Their Own

MOOD CONTROL

1 2 3
4 5 6
7 8 9
10 11 12

Press PLAY if you're feeling:

1 ADVENTUROUS
2 AMBITIOUS
3 Artsy
4 Cynical
5 Depressed
6 Heartbroken
7 Hopeful
8 Insecure
9 Misunderstood
10 Overwhelmed
11 PLAYFUL
12 Weird

1992 | **ULTIMATE GIRL RATING:** ♣ ♣ ♣

DIRECTOR: Penny Marshall
BIRTHPLACE: Mainstream Hollywood
FILE UNDER: Baseball Heroines
RATED: PG

STARRING: Geena Davis, Lori Petty, Madonna, Rosie O'Donnell, Tom Hanks, Garry Marshall

THE PROBLEM Everyone is so impressed that you're good at something that's not traditionally a "feminine" activity. But, what's the big deal? Girls are doing everything these days. Besides, you're not trying to make history. You're just trying to do your thing.

The Reel Deal: As World War II loomed, it looked as though baseball teams would break up and all the players would be sent to war. Some enterprising businessmen began the All-American Girls' Professional Baseball League to keep fans coming to the ballpark. For seven years, all-girl teams traveled the country, amazing crowds with the fact that you didn't have to wear trousers to throw and hit well. These early professional female ballplayers weren't raging feminists, just girls with good arms who loved playing the game. A LEAGUE OF THEIR OWN is a fictionalized account of some of these women. It tracks a few seasons as the women ballplayers, one of the best of whom is pretty Dottie (Geena Davis), who hand-in-hand with her sister, Kit (Lori Petty), work with their cynical coach (Tom Hanks), gradually impressing their boss and each other with how well they work together as a team. This movie does a nice job of chronicling their challenges and triumphs in a way that feels realistic to the time they lived in, rather than rewriting history. Still, even though this team ran the bases half a century ago, we see a modern theme in their struggles to be taken seriously by the guys.

Line That Says It All:
"There's no crying in baseball!"

Girl to Watch: Geena Davis is great as Dottie. She's the best on the team and finds this talent both gratifying and confusing.

Guy to Watch: Tom Hanks as the girls' coach. He thinks he picked the loser straw in life when he first gets this job. Hanks himself said in a recent interview that he wanted to play a guy who was a bit of a mess, one who had been beaten up and had given up on life. It's fun to watch his character learn to appreciate how special these women are, and how they renew his spirit.

Scene Worth the Rewind: The tryouts, which take place in little towns all over the country, are some of the most entertaining moments of the movie.

Fun Factoid: The movie begins and ends with a scene at the Baseball Hall of Fame, where the women's league was finally honored many years later. A LEAGUE OF THEIR OWN was based on a true story, and some of the real women ballplayers were used as extras in the movie's finale.

Watch This One With: Your team, of course.

Movies with the Same Vibe: LOVE AND BASKETBALL, BEND IT LIKE BECKHAM.

HOW THIS MOVIE HELPS

It's nice to see that women from our great-grandmothers' generation could kick it up on the field. Of course, as soon as the men came back from war, the women returned to the home and gave them back their bats and balls. Now that women are going to war as well, do we get half the playing fields? Not yet. The good news is that every time a girl plays hard and sticks with her sport, another barrier stands a chance of being broken. Did *you* go to practice today?

Legally Blonde

MOOD CONTROL

1	2	3
4	5	6
7	8	9
10	11	12

▶ Press PLAY if you're feeling:

1 ADVENTUROUS
2 Ambitious
3 Artsy
4 Cynical
5 Depressed
6 Heartbroken
7 HOPEFUL
8 Insecure
9 Misunderstood
10 Overwhelmed
11 PLAYFUL
12 Weird

2001 · ULTIMATE GIRL RATING: 🍿🍿🍿🍿🍿

DIRECTOR: Robert Luketic
BIRTHPLACE: Mainstream Hollywood
FILE UNDER: Barbie Has a Brain
RATED: PG-13

STARRING: Reese Witherspoon, Luke Wilson, Selma Blair, Matthew Davis, Victor Garber, Jennifer Coolidge, Holland Taylor, Ali Larter, Jessica Cauffiel, Oz Perkins, Alanna Ubach, Linda Cardellini, Meredith Scott Lynn

THE PROBLEM

No one takes you seriously because your appearance and/or interests might not be of the serious sort. Yet underneath it all, you have a brain and guts and confidence; you just know that you can do anything you put your mind to. So there! Hmm, *you're* not the one with the problem.

The Reel Deal: Elle Woods (Reese Witherspoon) is finishing up her college career in triumph. She has a straight-A average in fashion merchandising, a handsome, ambitious boyfriend (Matthew Davis), a group of great sorority sisters, and a superlative sense of style that cannot be suppressed. But her perfect world is shattered when, instead of pulling out an engagement ring, her boyfriend, Warner, pulls out a breakup speech. He's on his way to Harvard Law School and thinks that if he's ever going to be a senator, he needs a serious girlfriend, not a blonde cupcake with a little dog and a manicure addiction. Heartbroken, Elle quickly decides to apply to Harvard herself, just to get Warner back. She studies like crazy for the LSAT, the big law school entrance exam, and puts together an application video that is so hilariously strange that the admissions committee can't figure out why they shouldn't let her in. The rest of the movie takes us to Harvard, where Elle finds that even her new-found Ivy League credentials might not be enough to get Warner back. It turns out that he's spent the summer getting engaged to a vicious preppie (Selma Blair), and even the gentle attentions of a cute older law student, Emmett (Luke Wilson) can't soften the blow. Many questions remain: Can Elle get Warner back? Can she survive Harvard Law School? Can Harvard survive Elle Woods? Just seeing this frosted cupcake try to get a grip on the Ivy League scene would probably be entertaining enough, yet in a surprising twist, LEGALLY BLONDE depicts Harvard bending to Elle more than the other way around. *Harvard*. If we could only harness the incredible force of Reese Witherspoon for the good of the planet...

Line That Says It All:
"You got into Harvard Law?"
"What? Like, it's hard?"

Girl to Watch: Reese Witherspoon—pretty as a picture, tough as nails.

Guy to Watch: Bruiser Woods, Elle's stylish Chihuahua.

Scene Worth the Rewind: Elle's law school application video is a comic treat.

Watch This One With: Anyone. About ten times.

Movies with the Same Vibe:
CLUELESS, BRING IT ON. Also check out *Legally Blonde 2* (2003).

HOW THIS MOVIE HELPS

The sequel, *Legally Blonde 2: Red, White and Blonde*, was also fun, but never reaches the giddy heights of this first frothy effort. Underneath the bubbly surface of LEGALLY BLONDE lies a serious (well, not *so* serious) social commentary about class issues. Elle Woods has money, but her glamour-girl surface is deemed too cheap for the upper-crust crowd. In an earlier film, she would have learned to tone down her look to win the respect of the brainy bunch. What makes LEGALLY BLONDE so much fun is Elle's refusal to lower her standards—or her hemline. Despite the touch of romance in the air, this is really a movie about a young woman realizing that being smart is even more fun than being cute—and being both can get you a multipicture deal. We watch LEGALLY BLONDE for the fun of it, but the movie holds a worthwhile reminder for us all: if someone thinks you're not good enough for them, don't prove them wrong. Prove yourself right.

❶ PRESS PAUSE: Movie Heartbreak How-Tos

What happens when the one you love won't love you back? You mope around. You don't eat; you don't sleep (or you sleep all the time). You stare gloomily out the window with red-rimmed eyes and a stuffed-up nose, hair that hasn't been combed and three-day-old outfits. In the movies, when the heartbroken heroine is told by her consoling friends, "Gosh, you look terrible," it's a big fat lie. She looks, in fact, fantastic, the practiced brooding expression on her face only underscoring her otherwise conventional beauty. That's fine with us. We look to the movies to learn how to weep attractively and brood with style. Because no one expresses their sorrow or gets even as well as someone for whom devastating loss is a fictional situation. The rest of us? It's not pretty. Come back when we're sane.

Test your Cinema Heartache Reaction (CHAR) and match the lovelorn behavior to the movie:

1 *Mystic Pizza* ___

a Agreed to play chauffeur for beloved and his date

2 *Some Kind of Wonderful* ___

b Wrote many folk songs about lying, cheating ex

3 *Bring It On* ___

c Wrote poem about him, read it in English class

4 *Say Anything* ___

d Went to prom without him, a show of strength

5 *Center Stage* ___

e Dumped tons of fresh fish into his convertible

6 *10 Things I Hate About You* ___

f Wrote about her feelings in newspaper article

7 *Pretty in Pink* ___

g Dumped the romance, kept the professional opportunity

8 *Never Been Kissed* ___

h Surprised his cheating face in the dorm room, kicked him to the curb

Answers: 1-e, 2-a, 3-h, 4-b, 5-g, 6-c, 7-d, 8-f

Little Darlings

MOOD CONTROL

1	2	3
4	5	6
7	8	9
10	11	12

▶ Press PLAY
if you're feeling:

1 ADVENTUROUS
2 Ambitious
3 Artsy
4 Cynical
5 Depressed
6 HEARTBROKEN
7 Hopeful
8 INSECURE
9 Misunderstood
10 Overwhelmed
11 Playful
12 Weird

1980 | **ULTIMATE GIRL RATING:** 🌸 🌸 🌸 🌸

DIRECTOR: Ronald F. Maxwell
BIRTHPLACE: Mainstream U.S.A.
FILE UNDER: Virgin Marys
RATED: R

STARRING: Tatum O'Neal, Kristy McNichol, Armand Assante, Matt Dillon, Margaret Blye, Nicolas Coster, Krista Errickson, Alexa Kenin, Abby Bluestone, Cynthia Nixon, Simone Schachter

THE PROBLEM You're a virgin, and you feel like a freak. Or you feel fine about it and wonder why it's such a big issue for everyone else you know. Is virginity a magical line that, once you cross it, changes your world forever? Is sex a gift you give someone you love, a gift you give yourself, or just an item on your shopping list? People think your generation is sex-obsessed? More like sex-confused, you say....

The Reel Deal: Ferris (Tatum O'Neal) and Angel (Kristy McNichol) are two girls who are unlikely to inhabit the same planet, much less the same summer camp. Ferris is a rich girl who gets everything she wants, Angel is a tough street kid used to nothing but trouble. The two take an instant dislike to one another, and a rivalry ensues. In different ways, these two fifteen-year-olds aim to seem wise beyond their years and reluctantly confess their virginity to one another. They then hatch a plot to see who will be the first to lose her virginity while at camp. Ferris goes after handsome camp counselor (Armand Assante), while Angel sets her sights on a boy her own age, Randy

(Matt Dillon). The two seductions go very differently, and have an unexpected impact on both girls. On the surface, LITTLE DARLINGS sounds like a raunchy summer sex comedy, and the ad campaign definitely emphasizes that angle. Actually, it's a story that will ring all too true for lots of girls, centering on the notion that sometimes what we think we want and what we wind up wanting are two very different things.

Line That Says It All: "Don't laugh… but do you care about me a little?"

Girl to Watch: McNichol's feisty Angel is the one to watch here.

Guy to Watch: Randy, played by Matt Dillon, who was a pretty major hunk back in the day.

Scene Worth the Rewind: Seeing Angel look so vulnerable near the end of the movie as she realizes that "the first time" is not a throwaway item.

Fun Factoid: *Sex and the City*'s Sarah Jessica Parker was all over the teen movie scene, but check out a very young Cynthia Nixon (*Sex and the City*'s Miranda) here as a crunchy granola type.

Watch This One With: The same friends that you discuss all the personal stuff with. The hairstyles and language of LITTLE DARLINGS may be dated, but what Ferris and Angel do and feel will ring a bell for some of you.

Movies with the Same Vibe: FAST TIMES AT RIDGEMONT HIGH, THE SLUMS OF BEVERLY HILLS.

HOW THIS MOVIE HELPS

Back when LITTLE DARLINGS was made, movies hardly ever showed girls talking to each other about sex. Many considered this movie to be a light, slightly sleazy comedy, and most critics failed to note just how revolutionary the film's dialogue was. What's fresh about this movie is the girls' view of sex as something to be checked off a list. A "virginity contest," or some other version of sex-as-competitive-sport, could easily be happening in just about any school today. How do you feel about that? It probably depends on your values, life experience, and worldview—our feelings about intimacy are as varied as our body types. LITTLE DARLINGS does a nice job of showing that sex is a connection that lingers in both the mind and the body long after the fact. Showing the significance of that, without pretending to have all the answers, is what makes LITTLE DARLINGS worth the watch.

Little Women

1994   ULTIMATE GIRL RATING: ♣ ♣ ♣

DIRECTOR: Gillian Armstrong
BIRTHPLACE: Mainstream Hollywood
FILE UNDER: We Are Family/ I Got All My Sisters With Me
RATED: PG

STARRING: Winona Ryder, Gabriel Byrne, Trini Alvarado, Samantha Mathis, Kirsten Dunst, Claire Danes, Christian Bale, Eric Stoltz, John Neville, Mary Wickes, Susan Sarandon

THE PROBLEM How do you find your true path in life? People always talk about following your dream and being true to yourself, but what they don't mention is that sometimes, in order to go for the thing you really want, you have to turn down something—or someone—equally wonderful.

The Reel Deal: The March sisters stick close to one another and their beloved "Marmee" (Susan Sarandon) while their father is off in the Civil War. Their fairly quiet days are enlivened by the sudden appearance of Laurie (Christian Bale), the handsome and charming nephew of their wealthy neighbor, Mr. Lawrence. Laurie admires the quiet beauty of the oldest sister, Meg (Trini Alvarado), but falls hard for the far more lively, free-spirited Jo. (That's right—Laurie is a guy, Jo is a girl. Just go with it). Jo (Winona Ryder) develops a wonderful friendship with Laurie, but is horrified to find that his attentions are romantic in nature. Jo is hardly ready to settle down to that life; she longs to move to New York City and become a real writer. Meanwhile, drama abounds for all the sisters: Meg enjoys the attention of Laurie's kind-yet-poor tutor (Eric Stolz), little Amy (Kirsten Dunst) wins the heart of their frosty

Guy to Watch: Christian Bale is pretty yummy as Laurie, but you can see why Jo had trouble thinking of him as a romantic figure. Um, right?

Scene Worth the Rewind: The scene where Laurie confronts Jo with his feelings is a classic.

Watch This One With: Anyone you let see you cry.

Movies with the Same Vibe: CIRCLE OF FRIENDS.

Aunt March (Mary Wickes), and young Beth (Claire Danes), a gentle soul almost too good for this world, has been feeling poorly lately....The only thing old-fashioned about LITTLE WOMEN is its quaint title; author Louisa May Alcott was way ahead of her time with her tale of a plain-Jane heroine who charms suitors and editors alike with her beguiling mix of vulnerability and fierce independence. LITTLE WOMEN is Jo's story, but you'll fall in love with the whole March family and wish for a large house full of sisters all your own.

Line That Says It All: "Don't be such a beetle! I could never love anyone as I love my sisters!"

Girl to Watch: Winona Ryder does a nice job with Jo, no small feat when you're following in the footsteps of Katharine Hepburn, who played her in the original 1933 version.

HOW THIS MOVIE HELPS

In the best of families, we can observe the dreams and schemes of our siblings with compassion, knowing that understanding each other's differences helps us to define ourselves. In the worst of families, everyone sacrifices their individuality to the strong stamp of group approval. Parents can have a big effect on sibling harmony (or lack of it), but in the end, the decision to bond or battle with our brothers and sisters belongs to us. When a rivalry starts in the crib, it's kind of hard to remember who started it. Does it matter? Don't wait until you move out to get to know your siblings. A best friend might be right down the hall, "borrowing" your favorite shirt.

The Lizzie McGuire Movie

MOOD
CONTROL

1 2 3
4 5 6
7 8 9
10 11 12

▶ Press PLAY
if you're feeling:

1 ADVENTUROUS
2 Ambitious
3 Artsy
4 Cynical
5 Depressed
6 Heartbroken
7 Hopeful
8 INSECURE
9 Misunderstood
10 Overwhelmed
11 PLAYFUL
12 Weird

2003   **ULTIMATE GIRL RATING:**

DIRECTOR: Jim Fall
BIRTHPLACE: Mainstream Hollywood
FILE UNDER: Pop Princess in Pastaland
RATED: PG

STARRING: Hilary Duff, Adam Lamberg, Alex Borstein, Yani Gellman, Ashlie Brillault, Clayton Snyder

THE PROBLEM

Nothing really magical or even interesting will ever happen in your life. You're just sort of there, unless, of course, you're making a fool of yourself, then everybody notices. Some people seem destined to win all the trophies in the award shows of life. Who's operating the spotlight these days, and when are they ever going to shine it on you?

The Reel Deal: On TV, Lizzie McGuire (Hilary Duff) spends her junior high days falling all over herself, just short of out of it. In the movie version, life gets a lot better after a calamity-filled intro that exists mainly to establish the running Lizzie jokes. After a humiliating graduation, Lizzie and her pal Gordo (Adam Lamberg) head off for a trip to Italy with her nemesis Kate (Ashlie Brillault), laid-back Ethan (Clayton Snyder), and their fierce chaperone, high school principal Miss Ungermeyer (Alex Borstein). You could say the fantasy begins when the kids check into what appears to be a five-star Roman palace on a school-trip budget. Yet it really heats up when Italian pop star Paolo (Yani Gellman) spies Lizzie in a crowd and realizes that she's the spitting image of his

Guy to Watch: Okay, maybe Lizzie is pining for Paolo and Gordo is pining for Lizzie, but we kinda love her goofy friend Ethan, who gets all the best lines.

Eye-Rolling Time: We keep waiting for evidence on either the big or small screen that Kate deserves to be more popular than Lizzie. Nope, no help here. Maybe that's the point of popularity. Maybe it goes to whoever needs to have that power. Maybe it's caused by random forces in the universe. (Uh-oh. Are we sounding like Lizzie now?)

Watch This One With: Your little sister and her friends.

former singing partner, Isabella (Hilary Duff, as well). A mild little romance springs up between them, and Lizzie's friends cover for her while she zips around town with Paolo on his scooter. An amazing opportunity allows Lizzie to finally shed her klutz image, yet she has a ways to go in the "understanding guys" department.

Line That Says It All: "Goodbye Lizzie McGuire, hello fabulous."

Girl to Watch: Hilary Duff glows like the sun, even when she's falling down a flight of stairs. Lucky girl. Alex Borstein's sharp-tongued chaperone is a riot.

HOW THIS MOVIE HELPS

THE LIZZIE MCGUIRE MOVIE won't win any awards, but it's a pleasant fantasy about the privileges and perils of being plucked from the crowd. Sure, it's all silly fun, but there's a real message in here about remembering to trust and value the people who've known you forever. Hilary Duff knows that lesson well—she's made a movie that her loyal TV fans are bound to enjoy.

Love and Basketball

MOOD CONTROL

1	2	3
4	5	6
7	8	9
10	11	12

▶ Press **PLAY** if you're feeling:

1 ADVENTUROUS
2 AMBITIOUS
3 Artsy
4 Cynical
5 Depressed
6 HEARTBROKEN
7 Hopeful
8 Insecure
9 Misunderstood
10 Overwhelmed
11 Playful
12 Weird

2000   ULTIMATE GIRL RATING: 🍿🍿🍿🍿

DIRECTOR: Gina Prince-Bythewood
BIRTHPLACE: Mainstream Hollywood
FILE UNDER: Full-court Romance
RATED: PG-13

STARRING: Glenndon Chatman, Jess Willard, Chris Warren Jr., Kyla Pratt, Alfre Woodard, Naykia Harris, Harry J. Lennix, Debbi Morgan, Dennis Haysbert, Sanaa Lathan, Omar Epps

THE PROBLEM Maybe you're into the same sport/art/field of study that your guy is, and maybe he thinks it's all good. But when push comes to shove, does he want you to achieve to the same degree that he does? What if you're just as good? What if you're better? What if you play to win at any cost? Is that still "all good" or does he look for another partner off the court?

The Reel Deal: Just as Monica Wright (Sanaa Lathan) enters adolescence, her family moves to an affluent neighborhood in Los Angeles, next door to a bona fide NBA star and his son, Quincy (Omar Epps). Quincy takes a shine to her immediately; the same "tomboy" quality that concerns her family makes her a great companion in his book. They play a lot of basketball, and she holds her own, impressing him to no end. They stay friends throughout high school, each the star of their basketball team. Quincy's home life isn't as smooth as his life on the court, and Monica's house is a safe haven when the fighting kicks up. They make eyes at each other at a dance, but can't bring themselves to turn that into something more. Eventually, they're both recruited by the University of Southern California and keep playing basketball throughout college. At this point,

Monica sees the unfair discrepancy between men's and women's basketball—he gets the perks and the lure of an NBA contract, while she combats penalties and plays to tiny crowds, awaiting little in the way of a professional future. Romance between them blooms, but it becomes hard to treat each other well when basketball treats them so differently.

Line That Says It All: "You wanna be my girl?…We can play ball and ride to school together, and when you get mad I gotta buy you flowers."

Girl to Watch: Like most girls, Sanaa Lathan is such a great mix of toughness and femininity, but it's rare for the movies to show that common blend. Alfre Woodard is her mother, and she inhabits the role with perfection.

Guy to Watch: Omar Epps is great. It can't be easy to jump into your dad's game and make it your own.

Watch This One With: Your squad.

Scene Worth the Rewind: The comparison of their two games: Monica sweating it out in front of tiny crowds vs. the huge, Hollywood hype that Q's games get. Makes you wonder.

Fun Factoid: Writer and Director Gina Prince-Bythewood was a college athlete herself, and really wanted to tell a sports story from a girl's point of view. Her unique perspective shows: the emphasis of LOVE AND BASKETBALL is much more on training, strategy, and the meaning of ambition than a countdown to victory. The movie is purposefully set in the late '80s, before the WNBA formed and women players in this country had a professional option.

Movies with the Same Vibe: GIRL FIGHT, BEND IT LIKE BECKHAM. Also check out *Personal Best* (1982), an '80s film about two runners who are competitors and girlfriends, and really struggling to combine the two.

HOW THIS MOVIE HELPS

Aggression is part of life. You need it to battle your way through red tape and challenging assignments. You need it in dark alleys and lighted arenas. Play is fueled by aggression, and if you don't play, you can't win. Yet sometimes it seems as though girls drop out of sports because it's just too hard to be rough-and-tumble in a world that usually prefers us to be sweet and petite. LOVE AND BASKETBALL shows us a girl who can play tough and care deeply, who doesn't think her love of the game is any weaker than that of Mr. NBA Jr. Monica Wright is "all about ball," even without the big crowds and flashy contracts. If that's what aggression brings out in a girl, bring it on.

Lucas

MOOD CONTROL

1	2	3
4	5	6
7	8	9
10	11	12

▶ **Press PLAY** if you're feeling:

1 Adventurous
2 Ambitious
3 Artsy
4 CYNICAL
5 DEPRESSED
6 HEARTBROKEN
7 Hopeful
8 Insecure
9 Misunderstood
10 Overwhelmed
11 Playful
12 Weird

1986 ULTIMATE GIRL RATING:

DIRECTOR: David Seltzer
BIRTHPLACE: Mainstream Hollywood
FILE UNDER: Getting Pummeled by Love
RATED: PG-13

STARRING: Corey Haim, Kerri Green, Charlie Sheen, Courtney Thorne-Smith, Winona Ryder, Tom Hodges, Ciro Poppiti, Guy Boyd, Jeremy Piven

THE PROBLEM You're in love with a dream. Well, not an actual dream, but a person who may as well be a figment of your sleeping subconscious for all the hope you have of getting that person to love you back. Part of you is constantly coming up with schemes to get the object of your affection to feel the same way. Part of you doubts it will ever happen. It's hard being split in two like this—the crazy you, the sad you. What will make you whole?

The Reel Deal: Lucas (Corey Haim) is the classic smart, sweet, short incoming high school freshman, the kind of boy you laughingly compare to the bearded giants walking the hall beside him. In the summer before school starts, he meets a pretty new girl, Maggie (Kerri Green), and they strike up one of those nice friendships you can have with a neighbor when it's hot and slow and quiet outside. They spend a lot of time together doing the kind of fun summer activities that don't have anything to do with your age or social status at school. Lucas falls in love with his more mature neighbor; Maggie grows fond of Lucas, but hardly thinks she's met the new love of her life. She's still kind to him when school starts, but loses her heart to Cappie (Charlie Sheen), a good-looking football player who sees Maggie as a refreshing change from his tired romance with his long-time girlfriend Elise (Courtney Thorne-Smith). Lucas is devastated by Maggie's budding relationship, and gets it into his otherwise brilliant head that he can win Maggie over by joining the football team himself. Great idea, huh?

Line That Says It All:
"The equipment doesn't fit."
"No, it's you that doesn't fit."

Girl to Watch: Kerri Green plays Maggie as confident with Lucas, unsettled with Cappie—just the way we all can switch in different social settings.

Guy to Watch: Corey Haim is wonderful as Lucas. Charlie Sheen's character Cappie is surprising too. A football player who always gets the girl, he's still not the jerk most movies would turn him into.

Scene Worth the Rewind: The flirtation between Cappie and Maggie in the school laundry room is pretty swoon-worthy, with the kind of cute, dopey talk that takes control of your mouth when your brain is on sensory overload.

Fun Factoid: Most of the kids in this movie went on to have amazing film and/or TV careers—don't they look familiar? Corey Haim's career flourished in the '80s, but didn't do so well after that. Poor Lucas.

Watch This One With: Your favorite underdogs.

Movies with the Same Vibe: GREGORY'S GIRL, WIN A DATE WITH TAD HAMILTON. Also check out *Angus* (1995) and *My Bodyguard* (1980), two other good films about loveable misfits.

HOW THIS MOVIE HELPS

This sweet, surprising film nicely portrays the anguish of loving someone who may not be able to love you back. It's refreshing to see a teen movie in which people win and lose in the game of love, but it doesn't necessarily make them enemies of one another. Movies usually prefer to portray unrequited love as the reason for a revenge-filled story line, or they make it seem that just wanting someone badly enough will bring them to you, like Sabrina the Teenage Witch whipping up a spell. Despite its Big Applause ending, LUCAS is still more like real life when it comes to finding love. If you're a character in real life, your chances are still pretty good for a happy ending—it just might take a little change of cast, and a lot more time than the length of a movie.

The Man in the Moon

MOOD CONTROL

1	2	3
4	5	6
7	8	9
10	11	12

Press PLAY if you're feeling:

1 Adventurous
2 Ambitious
3 ARTSY
4 Cynical
5 Depressed
6 HEARTBROKEN
7 Hopeful
8 Insecure
9 MISUNDERSTOOD
10 Overwhelmed
11 Playful
12 Weird

1991 **ULTIMATE GIRL RATING:**

DIRECTOR: Robert Mulligan
BIRTHPLACE: Mainstream Hollywood
FILE UNDER: Rural Rivalry
RATED: PG-13

STARRING: Sam Waterston, Tess Harper, Gail Strickland, Reese Witherspoon, Jason London, Emily Warfield, Bentley Mitchum, Ernie Lively

THE PROBLEM

Everyone occasionally has crushes on people that don't return the feeling. It's called unrequited love, right? It sucks. Unfortunately, there are a few variations on the theme. There's someone who used to like you but doesn't anymore, someone who would like you if you were closer to their ideal...and a million other permutations too lame to go into. What about that person who likes you and thinks you're a terrific person, but somehow you just don't make them get weak in the knees? You tell yourself that love will grow, you tell yourself that they feel more than they're admitting to themselves, you tell yourself a lot of things. Then they meet someone else, and you see in their eyes the look you've been giving them for months. You know, right then and there, that it's "game over." Like we said, it sucks. At least it happens to Reese Witherspoon too.

The Reel Deal: The time is 1957, the setting is a small town in Louisiana. For fourteen-year-old Dani Trant (Reese Witherspoon), life is all about running through the woods, dreaming about Elvis, and learning the ropes of being a teenage girl from her glamorous seventeen-year-old sister, Maureen (Emily Warfield). Dani is ready for deeper emotion than pining for The King, and she gets it when an old family friend moves back to town with her handsome, seventeen-year-old son, Court (Jason London). Dani and Court become friends, and he returns her affection to some extent. They go swimming together and share some special moments, and eventually a little romance does develop. But it means so much more to Dani than Court, who is aware of Dani's youth and inexperience. Inevitably, he meets her sister, Maureen, and they fall for one another as effortlessly as Dani fell for Court. Court's guilt over not caring for Dani enough, and Dani's angry heartbreak will ring true for anyone who has ever felt the unfair fickleness of love. A tragedy near the end of the movie turns this three-hankie picture into a "just bring me the whole box of Kleenex" affair, but in a good way.

Line That Says It All: "When two people really care about each other, they try to understand each other, don't you think?"

Girl to Watch: Reese Witherspoon, starring in her first movie. She's adorably baby-faced, yet already showing the steel-jawed spunk we see in later incarnations.

Guy to Watch: Jason London. Nobody wants to fight with her sister over a guy. But catch Court shirtless, riding around on some farm equipment, and see how well your family harmony holds up.

Eye-Rolling Time: There's a lot of soft-focus scenes of people running in fields. Oh, and the ending is *so* melodramatic. You have to just put on your jammies, grab your favorite stuffed animal, and buy into the poignancy.

HOW THIS MOVIE HELPS

If we want to be catty, we can start by simply enjoying watching prom queen–perfect Reese Witherspoon pine over some almost attainable guy. This movie is much too touching to stop there, though. It's seriously cathartic for anyone who has lost someone not because he was a jerk, or because he fell for some strumpet, or for any other reason that makes it easier to move on. Sometimes the pain of love stays with you because a truly great guy just couldn't see fit to love you as much as you loved him, and you can only truly see that when he goes on to love someone else. (Of course, with any luck the other woman won't be your sister.) We all need a good wallow from time to time. See this sentimental little memory poem if you need to wallow just a little bit longer.

Mean Girls

MOOD CONTROL

```
1    2    3
4    5    6
7    8    9
10   11   12
```

▶ Press PLAY
if you're feeling:

1 Adventurous
2 Ambitious
3 Artsy
4 CYNICAL
5 Depressed
6 Heartbroken
7 Hopeful
8 Insecure
9 MISUNDERSTOOD
10 OVERWHELMED
11 Playful
12 Weird

2004 ULTIMATE GIRL RATING:

DIRECTOR: Mark S. Waters
BIRTHPLACE:
Mainstream Hollywood
FILE UNDER:
Rules of the Jungle
RATED: PG-13

STARRING: Lindsay Lohan, Rachel McAdams, Lacey Chabert, Amanda Seyfried, Tina Fey, Lizzy Caplan, Tim Meadows, Amy Poehler, Ana Gasteyer, Neil Flynn, Daniel Franzese, Jonathan Bennett, Rajiv Surenda

THE PROBLEM

The girl-on-girl crime at your school has gotten way out of hand. Even when you're not the victim, you feel the effects of living in the war zone. Every time someone says, "There aren't really cliques at our school," you look up to see some popular witch lying her miniskirt off to impress the adults. Just once you'd like someone to make a teen movie that shows the complexity of navigating these treacherous waters, where a girl in a bikini is really a shark in disguise. *Mean Girls* just might be your lifeboat.

The Reel Deal: Clueless Cady Heron (Lindsay Lohan) knows as much about modern high school life as your Great-Grandma Edna. That's because she's been off playing The Wild Thornberries with her professor parents in the wilds of Africa, where she was homeschooled through her entire educational career. Yet when Mom gets tenure at Northwestern University, Cady finds herself facing a much fiercer jungle—in the form of a North American high school. On her lonely first day, she is mocked by everyone but soon is befriended by goth-punk hybrid Janis Ian (Lizzy Caplan) and her funny, très gay friend Damian. Yet Cady's good looks also draw the attention of the Plastics, a trio of pretty, calculating girls ruled by the infamous Regina George (Rachel McAdams). Initially horrified by their interest in Cady, Janis soon sees a grand opportunity: Cady can "infiltrate" the Plastics, enabling Janis and Damian to gain the upper hand with this insidious clique.

Cady finds that becoming a Plastic is as easy as falling off a log—provided that the log is made up of your morals and you're willing to watch them sink out of sight. In the space of one short, hilarious movie, Cady goes from saint to sinner and back again, trying to find her place in a jungle that makes the one she grew up in look like a children's petting zoo.

Line That Says It All: "Half the people in this room don't like me, and the other half only like me because they think I pushed someone under a bus."

Girl to Watch: Lindsay Lohan. It's a multi-layered, complex role—comedy with an edge and then some. Lohan pulls it off.

Guy to Watch: Make a note of super-sized, super-talented Daniel Franzese in the now-requisite role of Gay Boy Sidekick. His Damian makes every throwaway line worth recyling. A real keeper.

Scene Worth the Rewind: MEAN GIRLS is rich with great little moments that lose none of their strength on repeated viewings.

Movie to Watch With: Your clique. Can you find yourselves in the cafeteria? Of course not. We never see ourselves in stereotypes, do we? And this movie celebrates stereotypes, in a way.

Movie with the Same Vibe: HEATHERS, PUMP UP THE VOLUME, THE BREAKFAST CLUB. Also check out *American Beauty* (1999), if you favor films that have fun slamming the suburban dream.

HOW THIS MOVIE HELPS

Do you need a name for the girls who run the school with venomous smiles? MEAN GIRLS gives you one: The Plastics. Silly and slight, the film nonetheless offers more than a good time for anyone who wants a movie that shows all the horrors of high school. It nails the way a pretty new girl instantly has more clout than a regular-looking old one, how some people use fear of abandonment to keep their buds in line, and how your popularity or lack of it can be based on a random rumor. Will MEAN GIRLS give you an escape plan? We're afraid not. Yet you'll recognize everything you see in the halls, everyday, only instead of inwardly cringing, walking fast, head bowed, so the hungry lions don't see or smell your fear, this time you'll look the insanity straight in the eye and laugh, really hard. How fetch is that?

Mermaids

MOOD CONTROL

① ② ③
④ ⑤ ⑥
⑦ ⑧ ⑨
⑩ ⑪ ⑫

▶ Press PLAY
if you're feeling:

1 Adventurous
2 Ambitious
3 Artsy
4 CYNICAL
5 Depressed
6 Heartbroken
7 Hopeful
8 Insecure
9 MISUNDERSTOOD
10 Overwhelmed
11 Playful
12 WEIRD

1990   ULTIMATE GIRL RATING: 🍿🍿🍿

DIRECTOR: Richard Benjamin
BIRTHPLACE: Mainstream Hollywood, Indie Feel
FILE UNDER: The Virgin Daughter
RATED: PG-13

STARRING: Cher, Bob Hoskins, Winona Ryder, Michael Schoeffling, Christina Ricci, Caroline McWilliams, Jan Miner, Betsy Townsend, Richard McElvain, Paula Plum

THE PROBLEM   Your mom thinks she's such a hottie. She's pretty cute, but c'mon! She's your mom. It's *your* turn to be cute and her turn to be, you know, there for you, supportive, nurturing, obsessed with raising money for band uniforms, attractive yet asexual, like a normal mom. Okay, maybe not asexual, but at least focused on what you need to survive high school. If she would only step up to the plate, you could deal with the big hair and the slinky outfits.

The Reel Deal: Rachel Flax (Cher) is what used to be called a "loose woman." She's also the mother of Charlotte (Winona Ryder) and Kate (Christina Ricci), who are forced to move from town to town to escape their mother's failed relationships. Defiantly sexy and nonmaternal, Mrs. Flax is a constant source of embarrassment to the older Charlotte, who turns to prudish dress and behavior in reaction to her mother's risqué reputation. Charlotte fantasizes about being a nun, and is thrilled when their move to Massachusetts puts them a stone's throw away from an actual convent. Yet proving to be even more thrilling is the handsome handyman Joe (Michael Schoeffling) that

works for the nuns. Charlotte is terrified that
her attraction to him means she'll turn out
just like her mother. Meanwhile, her mom
is having some problems of her own. The
town's genial shoe salesman, Lou Landsky
(Bob Hoskins), seems good for a few laughs.
Unfortunately, he digs his heels in and wants
a real relationship with Rachel, and doesn't
go away no matter how badly she behaves.
Is it time for another move?

Line That Says It All: "Charlotte, I
know you're planning a celibate life, but
with half my chromosomes it might be
tough."

Girl to Watch: Winona Ryder does a
great job with the offbeat roles. Charlotte's
discovery of love and lust is painfully true—
and painfully funny.

Guy to Watch: Michael Schoeffling or life
in a convent? Hmmm, what to do, what to do.

HOW THIS MOVIE HELPS

If you have a larger-than-life, self-
absorbed parent (or two), you can
either bow out of life like Charlotte
wants to do, or embrace it like
Charlotte may decide to do. You can
blame a challenging parent for a lot
of things, but it's not their fault if
you decide to hide in their shadow.
Mrs. Flax is no walk in the park, yet
MERMAIDS refuses to judge her, and
actually shows her slowing down long
enough to give Charlotte some pretty
useful advice. As you watch Charlotte
go from future nun to passionate
woman, you get the sense that, in
daring to think about what she wants
instead of what she doesn't, she may
finally make a move of her own.

Mona Lisa Smile

2003 ULTIMATE GIRL RATING: ♣ ♣ ♣

DIRECTOR: Mike Newell
BIRTHPLACE: Mainstream U.S.A.
FILE UNDER: The Art of Independence
RATED: PG-13

STARRING: Julia Roberts, Kirsten Dunst, Julia Stiles, Maggie Gyllenhaal, Ginnifer Goodwin, Dominic West, Juliet Stevenson, John Slattery, Marcia Gay Harden, Topher Grace, Laura Allen

THE PROBLEM

You get really mad at your friends when they say that your boyfriend rules your life. You don't want to hear it, but deep in your heart you know it's a little bit true. Or maybe you aren't in a relationship right now, but still believe that a boyfriend is more than just a nice addition to life, that he will fix everything that's wrong with you. It might be time to travel back to 1953 and sit in on Katherine Watson's class. No need for a time machine—sounds like you're already there.

The Reel Deal: With women flooding law and medical schools in record numbers these days, it's hard to believe that many girls of a certain social standing once attended college for reasons that had nothing to do with a career. It was seen as a way to mingle with girls of your same background and to gain knowledge of art, history, and culture so that you'd make a charming and gracious companion for your husband and a learned helpmate for your children. In other words, it was a way to earn your "Mrs. degree." For some, the area of study mattered little; getting into a good school gave you access to the Ivy League–educated movers and shakers who were considered to be the choicest husbands. MONA SMILE SMILE portrays Wellesley College in 1953 as being just such a place. The story centers around the students' reactions to Katherine Watson (Julia Roberts), a free-spirited young professor from the West Coast who shakes up her class with her radical ideas. An art history teacher, she is appalled rather than impressed to learn the first day of class that her students memorize, rather than thoughtfully consider, their lessons. She teaches them to read the wild map of a Jackson Pollack painting, but more importantly, she gets them to realize that learning is about questioning as much as it is about simply absorbing what you are shown.

Line That Says It All: "See past the paint, let us open our minds to a different idea."

Girl to Watch: Maggie Gyllenhaal as Giselle Levy. She steals nearly every scene she's in.

Guy to Watch: Dominic West as Bill Dunbar. He's a more three-dimensional love interest than the younger guys in this film.

Scene Worth the Rewind: There's a confrontation between Giselle Levy and Betty Warren (Kirsten Dunst) that's very touching. You'll wish all the fights you had could end with such mutual empathy.

Watch This One With: Friends who don't mind kind of a slow movie with lots of "message speeches." You either find that sort of thing really inspiring (like the teens who love this film) or you fall asleep and drool into your lap.

Movies with the Same Vibe: STAND AND DELIVER, MYSTIC PIZZA, CIRCLE OF FRIENDS. Also check out *Dead Poets Society* (1989).

HOW THIS MOVIE HELPS

Our world may be noisy, but it's still pretty easy to sleepwalk through it, not really questioning the path of least resistance. The best teachers may be annoying at times, but they can wake us up from our slumber with their constant challenges to the status quo. Sometimes we love their ideas, sometimes we think they're nuts. Often, we appreciate them more a few years down the road, when we realize that we've grown and look back to realize that the change all began years ago, when we were trapped in a room with a force of nature who cared enough to shake us up. The nice thing about being an agent of change is that you don't have to get a teaching degree to do the job. MONA LISA SMILE may inspire you to startle your friends into some action of their own. What do you get out of it? Their amazement at being provoked into living more consciously will be your paycheck.

Moulin Rouge!

MOOD CONTROL

1 2 3
4 5 6
7 8 9
10 11 12

▶ **Press PLAY if you're feeling:**

1 ADVENTUROUS
2 Ambitious
3 ARTSY
4 Cynical
5 Depressed
6 Heartbroken
7 Hopeful
8 Insecure
9 Misunderstood
10 Overwhelmed
11 Playful
12 WEIRD

2001 ULTIMATE GIRL RATING: ♧♧

DIRECTOR: Baz Luhrmann
BIRTHPLACE: Aussie-American Intergalactic Hybrid
FILE UNDER: Fantastical Musical Kaleidoscope
RATED: PG-13

STARRING: Nicole Kidman, Ewan McGregor, John Leguizamo, Jim Broadbent, Richard Roxburgh, Garry McDonald, Jacek Koman, Matthew Whittet

THE PROBLEM Realism bores you. You feel as though you should go through life draped in velvet, like an opera diva. They call you a "teenage drama queen," but you don't care. If other people want to slump along in blue jeans and work hard to blend in with the pack, that's their right. You prefer to seek out the extraordinary and create art out of everyday experience. Don't tell Dad, but Baz Luhrmann must be your true biological father.

The Reel Deal: This enchanting modern musical is set in Paris around 1900. Satine (Nicole Kidman) is a cabaret singer at the Moulin Rouge. She's also a high-class woman-of-the-evening type who longs to be taken seriously as an actress. Although she acts like someone who has the world by the tail, we know that Satine is dreading her impending liaison with a rich duke (Richard Roxburgh), an incredibly jealous tyrant.

On the night of her scheduled rendezvous with the duke, she meets Christian (Ewan McGregor), a handsome but penniless playwright who passes himself off as the duke to gain entrance to her boudoir. Faster than you can say "sing a love song," he enters her heart as well, and promises that his next play will transform the Moulin Rouge into a legitimate theater. The love between Christian and Satine is fierce, but it is threatened by many outside forces, like their economic circumstances and the fury of the jilted duke, to name just two. Then there's that nasty cough of Satine's....

Line That Says It All: "My gift is my song, and this one's for you."

Girl to Watch: Nicole Kidman has never been more gorgeous, and who knew she could sing?

Guy to Watch: Ewan McGregor. He lights up the screen.

Soundtrack Note: The music is all over the map in this story. Bravely, Luhrmann decided that audiences would accept the use of modern rock in a historical tale if the songs conveyed the right feeling. As a result, we see Christian on the rooftop with Satine suddenly break into an Elton John ballad. Later, Satine performs a Madonna number; even Nirvana makes an appearance at the Moulin Rouge. This will strike some people as strange, but MOULIN ROUGE! is such a dazzling, peculiar peacock of a film that it's best just to go with the flow.

Watch This One With: Your fellow drama queens. You don't even need to be in drama, you just have to love visual flair and sensual overload.

Movies with the Same Vibe: EVER AFTER, THE PRINCESS BRIDE, ROMEO + JULIET. Also check out *Cabaret* (1972).

HOW THIS MOVIE HELPS

Satine has a difficult life, to say the least, but she sure knows how to wow an audience. So does MOULIN ROUGE! Baz Luhrmann's strangely arresting movie shows us a life far from the one we truly lead; the film floats us into a universe filled with passion and color. There's nothing wrong with wanting to inject a little dazzle into your everyday life. Sometimes an eccentric confection like MOULIN ROUGE! can inspire your own artistic vision. Isn't that what art is for, to show us a way to reinvent the world? Some choose to put a spotlight on what's most real in life. Good for them. You may prefer to create a world too extraordinary for ordinary living. Good for you. Can we come visit?

⏸ PRESS PAUSE: Some Great Movies Are Drawn That Way

Some of the most amazing action sequences, the most beautiful romances, the most captivating stories about overcoming challenges and discovering your hidden gifts can be found in the kind of movies that are drawn rather than captured on celluloid. What attracts us to animation? The visuals are incredible and the story lines know no bounds. Animation allows the writer to tell a tale in ways that wouldn't be possible if he or she were limited to the laws of physics.

The movies listed here made us laugh or cry, or took our breath away. Not just for kids, some of these animated features even made us think in a new way about our own lives. (Kind of a far cry from Saturday morning cartoons, don't you think?) So throw one of these on the stack the next time you hit the video store for a break from real life. It'll be a journey you won't soon forget.

Spirited Away (2001)
The height of Japanese anime. A ten-year-old girl's journey takes her far from home and family. Simply gorgeous.

Waking Life (2001)
Put your thinking cap on because this one's very intellectual and esoteric: a roving conversation about everything under the sun. True-life dialogue put into the mouths of animated characters of all shapes and sizes.

Finding Nemo (2003)
Did you miss this splendid fish tale? Swim back and check it out.

The Little Mermaid (1989)
Okay, so she loses her voice to get her guy. We don't like that part, but you gotta love Ariel and her wacky desire to join the dysfunctional human race.

Kiki's Delivery Service (1989)
An earlier effort from the creators of SPIRITED AWAY. Kiki is another girl with spunk and energy to burn. She's a young witch who leaves home to make her way in the world.

If you missed these classics of animation or claymation, don't put off seeing them: *A Bug's Life* (1998), *Beauty and the Beast* (1991), *Chicken Run* (2000), *The Lion King* (1994), *Monsters, Inc.* (2001), *Shrek* (2001), *Toy Story* (1995), and *Wallace & Gromit* (various shorts).

Muriel's Wedding

MOOD CONTROL

1	2	3
4	5	6
7	8	9
10	11	12

▶ Press PLAY
if you're feeling:

1 ADVENTUROUS
2 Ambitious
3 Artsy
4 Cynical
5 Depressed
6 Heartbroken
7 HOPEFUL
8 INSECURE
9 Misunderstood
10 Overwhelmed
11 Playful
12 Weird

1994   ULTIMATE GIRL RATING: 🍀🍀🍀🍀

DIRECTOR: P.J. Hogan
BIRTHPLACE: Australia
FILE UNDER:
Muriel vs. the Mean Girls
RATED: R

STARRING: Toni Collette,
Bill Hunter, Rachel Griffiths,
Sophie Lee, Rosalind
Hammond, Belinda Jarrett,
Pippa Grandison, Jeanie
Drynan

THE PROBLEM

Okay, so you're a bit of a mess. That's no excuse for people to be so unkind. You don't deserve the awful treatment you often receive. At least, that's what you think most of the time. Yet it's hard to keep building yourself up when everybody seems to be standing around you with demolition equipment, eagerly awaiting the next tear down. What ammunition do you have against such ruthlessness? If you could handle the abuse, you wouldn't be such a mess, would you? Oh well. At least there's music, and fantasy, and sleep to get away from it all. Will there ever be more than that?

The Reel Deal: Muriel Heslop (Toni Collette) is most likely the most put-upon girl in Porpoise Spit, Australia. Her siblings are obnoxious, her father tosses out cruel comments like they were candy bars, and her sweet mother is so burdened that she's unable to give Muriel much in the way of helpful advice. Even her friends are a disappointment—the sort of pretty, self-confident girls that will put up with you when they find you entertaining, but toss you as soon as you get embarrassing. Unfortunately, Muriel is eternally embarrassing, always wearing the wrong clothes, without a suave bone in her big-boned body. Her life is presented to us as a walking exercise in humiliation; we only see her happy when she's alone in her room, listening to her beloved Abba tapes and dreaming of her wedding day. Muriel is obsessed with having a perfect wedding in the way that only a girl who has never been in a relationship can be: it's all about the flowers and the dress; the relationship is just an excuse for this wonderful day of love and attention. With her father growing meaner by the day and her high school friends abandoning her, Muriel hits rock bottom at a very young age. Then tragedy has an unexpected dividend, and suddenly Muriel heads off to the tropics, rewarded with a much-needed makeover, a true best friend (Rachel Griffiths), and the promise of a better life.

Line That Says It All: "When I lived in Porpoise Spit, I used to sit in my room for hours and hours and listen to Abba songs. But since I've met you and moved to Sydney, I haven't listened to one Abba song. That's because my life is as good as an Abba song. It's as good as 'Dancing Queen.'"

Girl to Watch: Two women make this movie. Toni Collette is terrific as Muriel, taking her on about ten journeys in one short film. Equally memorable is Rachel Griffiths as Rhonda, the impulsive, rebellious girl who shows Muriel what loyalty is all about.

Scene Worth the Rewind: When Muriel goes onstage at the resort, astonishing her former friends with her awe-inspiring bravado and style.

Soundtrack Note: Years before the Broadway show *Mamma Mia* made Abba hip again, MURIEL'S WEDDING employed the songs of this Swedish pop band to hilarious, charming effect. If you only like gangsta rap or classical music you might cringe at the syrupy sounds, but otherwise, you're guaranteed to smile.

Watch This One with: Your friends who like their highs high, and their lows low.

Movies with the Same Vibe: CIRCLE OF FRIENDS, RUSHMORE.

HOW THIS MOVIE HELPS

We would hardly want to go through what Muriel does to discover what matters most in life. Yet when you think about the sorry state she was in at the opening of the film, you'll put her through anything to help her escape. MURIEL'S WEDDING features a girl who has nothing going for her, but who wishes for eternal love. Her story demonstrates that the specifics of the fantasy don't matter, it's simply the desire for dreams to come true that propel us toward action. What that change eventually brings with it is often a surprise, like when we go to the store to buy one thing and come out with something different. Why do we do that? Because we found something even better.

Mystic Pizza

MOOD CONTROL

1	2	3
4	5	6
7	8	9
10	11	12

▶ Press **PLAY** if you're feeling:

1 Adventurous
2 AMBITIOUS
3 Artsy
4 CYNICAL
5 Depressed
6 HEARTBROKEN
7 Hopeful
8 Insecure
9 Misunderstood
10 Overwhelmed
11 Playful
12 Weird

1988 | **ULTIMATE GIRL RATING:** ♣ ♣ ♣ ♣

DIRECTOR: Donald Petrie
BIRTHPLACE: Mainstream Hollywood
FILE UNDER: Terrific Trio
RATED: R

STARRING: Annabeth Gish, Julia Roberts, Lili Taylor, Vincent D'Onofrio, William R. Moses, Adam Storke

THE PROBLEM

You're living in a small town, or a town that just feels small because you keep bumping into people you don't want to see, family members who judge you, and dreams that don't fare well in the face of reality. It's a time in your life when relationships are the most confusing things in the world—what would you do without your girls?

The Reel Deal: Kat (Annabeth Gish) and Daisy (Julia Roberts) are sisters, JoJo (Lili Taylor) is their best friend, and all three dish up pizza and romantic complications in the Connecticut seaside town of Mystic. Daisy is a beautiful, headstrong girl who views her looks as her ticket out. Her sister, Kat, couldn't be more different; a self-made preppie on her way to Yale in the fall, she views Daisy's obsession with men and sex with derision. Then there's JoJo, their hilarious loudmouth friend who left her man, Bill (Vincent D'Onofrio), at the altar, but loves him just the same. Daisy meets a young, rich guy who seems to adore her, but she worries that she's just the "townie" amusement of the month. Kat gets knocked off her feet by a married architect she's babysitting for, and suddenly understands that judging others is a whole lot easier when desire isn't sending *you* into perilous waters as well.

MYSTIC PIZZA shows us a drama-filled summer in the lives of three young women who are forced to look hard at the reality of their lives. As the choices they make help define their differences, their unflagging support of one another gets sorely tested. Kat and Daisy feel like real sisters, and JoJo seems like a wonderful friend that any two siblings would happily share. Yet triangles are tough, especially during a season of so much change. Fortunately, they all have Mystic Pizza in common, and there's nothing like the simple work of dishing up food and mopping up floors to keep you grounded. Now if only they can clean up the messes they make with guys....

Line That Says It All: "It's tradition—and you don't monkey with tradition!"

Guy to Watch: So many! Julia's Richie Rich dream-boy (Adam Storke) couldn't be cuter, but fisherman Bill shows that Vince D'Onofrio's later success in a variety of roles is no fluke. And look for Matt Damon in a bit part near the beginning.

Girl to Watch: All three women excel in these roles, but this is where Julia captured the world, so keep an eye on her. She's not so toothpick skinny here, which is kind of nice to see.

Fashion to Catch: The clothes are a flash from the past—the '80s, to be precise—but the dress that Julia's character wears for her surprise big date is cute in any decade.

Watch This One With: Your gang of friends from work.

Movies with the Same Vibe: BLUE CRUSH. Also check out *Boys on the Side* (1995).

HOW THIS MOVIE HELPS

There are three great story lines in this film, and I defy anybody not to relate to all three if you live and love long enough: there's the older guy who captures your heart, the cross-class, cross-culture romance that may or may not work in the real world, and the "great guy, bad timing" issue. MYSTIC PIZZA makes you feel like any possible romantic complication can be dealt with if you have your buds by your side, time to heal, and a really great slice of pepperoni on your plate. Dig in!

Never Been Kissed

MOOD CONTROL

1	2	3
4	5	6
7	8	9
10	11	12

▶ Press PLAY if you're feeling:

1. Adventurous
2. Ambitious
3. Artsy
4. Cynical
5. DEPRESSED
6. HEARTBROKEN
7. HOPEFUL
8. Insecure
9. Misunderstood
10. Overwhelmed
11. Playful
12. Weird

1999   ULTIMATE GIRL RATING: ✿ ✿ ✿ ✿

DIRECTOR: Raja Gosnell
BIRTHPLACE: Mainstream Hollywood
FILE UNDER: Wishful-Thinking Whimsy
RATED: PG-13

STARRING: Drew Barrymore, David Arquette, Michael Vartan, Molly Shannon, Leelee Sobieski, John C. Reilly, Garry Marshall, Jeremy Jordan

THE PROBLEM How do you get a handle on the unspoken rules of your high school social life? It seems like you can go from being popular to being nobody pretty quick, but those rules hardly ever work in reverse order. If you could do it all over again, knowing then what you know now, would you make the same choices freshman year? It can take all four years to figure out where you fit in—then there's college, when it starts all over again. Isn't it ironic?

The Reel Deal: Josie Geller (Drew Barrymore) is a bookish, persnickety, twenty-five-year-old copy editor at the *Chicago Sun-Times*. She's forever roaming the halls correcting people's grammar and listening to their dating tales as though they're reciting exotic tribal rituals. For Josie, the dating scene is taking place on foreign soil. She dresses like a nun on holiday and has barely even been kissed before, just a few sloppy experiments in tooth gnashing that she'd rather forget. Josie not-so-secretly dreams of her first real kiss and her first real story for the *Times*. She gets the latter when her over-the-top editor (Garry Marshall) decides that the paper should do an exposé on high school life. He spots the youthful-looking Josie at a story meeting and impulsively commands her to enroll in high school as a senior.

Ecstatic with her first story assignment, Josie conveniently forgets that high school was pure torture for her the first time, when she was called "Josie Grossie" and humiliated on prom night. With a new blonde haircut and flashy clothes, she fairs a little better this time, and she's befriended by a lovely, brilliant girl named Aldys (Leelee Sobieski), whose intelligence and inner determination makes her a more resourceful nerd than Josie ever was. Keeping her post-college identity isn't hard, but everything else is: she can't find a decent angle for her story. No one but Aldys will even talk to her, and her flawless interpretations of Shakespeare send her young English teacher into a troubling tailspin of attraction. Her sweet brother, Rob (David Arquette), comes to both their rescues: he's the kind of childish grown-up who fared far better in high school than adulthood.

The twin pleasures of this film are developing a hot-for-teacher fixation on Mr. Coulson (Michael Vartan) and watching Rob show his sister that popularity is a just a trick: given the right mix of charm and confidence, it can be achieved by lunchtime.

Line That Says It All: "There's a big world out there, bigger than prom, bigger than high school!"

Girl to Watch: Drew Barrymore, as usual.

Guy to Watch: There are Web sites devoted to how cute Michael Vartan is in this movie. There are probably bumper stickers, sweatshirts, and key chains too. Put a few more Sam Coulsons in the classroom and the dropout rate would plunge. How cute is Michael Vartan? Michael Vartan is so cute that—okay, so we have a problem.

HOW THIS MOVIE HELPS

NEVER BEEN KISSED is below sea level on the plausibility meter, but so what? It's a nice fantasy for girl geeks everywhere who wonder if they'd have more luck the second time around. Yet who's to say what getting it right is? Anyone would rather be friends with Leelee Sobieski's character than the three Barbie-clone freaks (recognize Jessica Alba?) who finally accept Josie. It's nice to watch this movie and then look hard at your own social circle. You may not be hangin' with the tip of the pyramid, but your crew is probably filled with some pretty cool people. If not, get out there and make friends with people worth your time and energy. Remember: Josie is the exception. Most of us only get to do this high school thing once. Forget about popularity. You'll survive going to the prom with pals instead of with a date. But those pals you party with? Friendship matters. Get it right the first time.

Not One Less

MOOD CONTROL

1	2	3
4	5	6
7	8	9
10	11	12

▶ Press PLAY
if you're feeling:

1 Adventurous
2 AMBITIOUS
3 ARTSY
4 Cynical
5 Depressed
6 Heartbroken
7 Hopeful
8 Insecure
9 Misunderstood
10 OVERWHELMED
11 Playful
12 Weird

1999 **ULTIMATE GIRL RATING:** ♣ ♣ ♣

DIRECTOR: Yimou Zhang
BIRTHPLACE: China
FILE UNDER:
Mission Nearly Impossible
RATED: G

STARRING: Minzhi Wei,
Huike Zhang, Zhenda Tian,
Enman Gao

THE PROBLEM

You have a problem that just seems to get harder and harder to solve. Everyone is either telling you to give up, or just assuming that at some point you'll realize that your plan is futile. You want to tell them that they're wrong. You want to believe that, with enough perseverance, you can do anything. You want to be Minzhi Wei.

The Reel Deal: You probably know this Chinese film by its pre-translation title: *Yi Ge Dou Bu Neng Shao*. Yes, we're kidding. Seriously, though, this is a terrific movie about a young woman who goes to incredible lengths to find a young boy in a large city. It's one of those films that an interesting teacher might show, where you have a three-part reaction: From "Oh good! We're just watching a film today!" to "Ugh, this seems kind of slow and boring," to

"Whoa. This is so good I may have to beg to stay in at lunch to finish watching it." Wei is a thirteen-year-old country girl who has been brought to a small village to be a substitute teacher. Her qualifications for this job are dubious, but the mayor is desperate; his only teacher has to leave for a month to see an ailing parent, and he needs someone to keep the kids in line. Teacher Gao leaves for his journey with strict instructions that Wei preserve his precious chalk and keep any

All of them. There are *no* professional actors in this film. Wei is played by a real village girl; the mayor is played by the village's mayor; the television station manager is played by the—well, can you guess what he does for a living? It's like the world's coolest home movie.

Line That Says It All: Unless you are fluent in Chinese, you'll have to read the lines as subtitles, and the language is pretty simple and straightforward.

Watch This One With: Your friends who don't mind subtitles and simple, powerful plots. You know, your smart friends.

students from defecting. She's even been offered a bonus if no student deserts during his absence. Wei becomes obsessed with keeping all the kids in attendance so that she can earn the maximum amount of money. She treats one boy's decision to leave the village for work in the city as a major calamity. Determined to track down her charge and bring him home, Wei puts all the children to work to help her raise money for bus fare into the city.

This simple story doesn't throw an MTV-paced avalanche of obstacles in the heroine's way. Instead, she encounters one obvious "Go Home" message after another. Slowly, you realize that Wei is asking impossible things of the universe in her obsessive rescue mission—and that the universe doesn't stand a chance against such awesome persistence.

Girl to Watch: Minzhi Wei as the film's heroine. She's in almost every frame of this dynamic film.

HOW THIS MOVIE HELPS

Watching this simple village girl refuse to give up is an incredible experience; you almost get mad at her for being so much more determined than you might be under the same circumstances. Taking a tip from this pint-sized force of nature might give you the strength you need to pass World History or convince your mom to let you get a piercing, or whatever. Compared to Wei's, our lives are easy enough that it doesn't take much to roll off once the going gets rough, so sometimes it's hard for us to tell: is it worth fighting for or is it worth folding on? Only your inner Minzhi Wei knows for sure.

Ordinary People

MOOD CONTROL

1	2	3
4	5	6
7	8	9
10	11	12

▶ Press PLAY
if you're feeling:

1 Adventurous
2 Ambitious
3 Artsy
4 Cynical
5 DEPRESSED
6 Heartbroken
7 Hopeful
8 Insecure
9 Misunderstood
10 OVERWHELMED
11 Playful
12 WEIRD

1980   ULTIMATE GIRL RATING: ♣ ♣ ♣ ♣

DIRECTOR: Robert Redford
BIRTHPLACE:
Mainstream Hollywood
FILE UNDER:
Perfection Bites the Dust
RATED: R (mainly for language)

STARRING: Timothy Hutton, Judd Hirsch, Donald Sutherland, Mary Tyler Moore, M. Emmet Walsh, Elizabeth McGovern, Dinah Manoff, Fredric Lehne, James Sikking, Basil Hoffman, Scott Doebler

THE PROBLEM

You wear your unhappiness like a second skin. Everyone knows why you're unhappy, everyone understands. Yet, at the same time, they want you to get on with it, get on with life. You're trying. It's not working. How do you recover from the end of the world?

The Reel Deal: Conrad Jarrett (Timothy Hutton) is a bright, handsome kid who lives in a nice house with two parents who love him. He has a great future in front of him and a nightmare behind him. The problem is, the nightmare isn't really behind him, it lives in the pretty house with the nice family right alongside their fine furniture and leafy backyard. Conrad and his older brother, Buck (Scott Doebler, seen in flashbacks), the "golden boy" of the family, were out boating when the weather turned. Conrad made it back to shore, Buck didn't. That simple, horrible fact changed everything about this family. Buck was his mother's (Mary Tyler Moore) clear favorite, and she hasn't looked at Conrad the same way since the accident. Conrad's despair at the family's loss brings on a depression that results in a suicide attempt and a hospital stay.

The interesting thing about ORDINARY PEOPLE is that it begins after all that, as the Jarrett family attempts to get on with life after so much tragedy. For Beth Jarrett, the solution is to stuff her feelings down and keep up appearances. Cal (Donald Sutherland) would like to do that too, but knows that the only way to help Conrad is to talk about how they feel about things. Dr. Berger (Judd Hirsch), a wise and unorthodox psychiatrist, helps both father and son work through terrifically difficult emotions while Beth takes a different tack. Watching this financially blessed but otherwise "ordinary" family cope with extraordinary loss is the subject of this deeply moving, Oscar-winning picture.

Line That Says It All: "Don't admire people too much, they might disappoint you."

Girl to Watch: Mary Tyler Moore is amazing as Conrad's rigid, "perfect" mom. You've met this woman a thousand times. You may even live with her.

Guy to Watch: Timothy Hutton played this sad, sweet preppie just right.

Scene Worth the Rewind: Every scene with Conrad and his doctor. You just want Dr. Berger to follow you around your life, making sense of everything.

Fun Factoid: ORDINARY PEOPLE changed our perceptions of two stars: Robert Redford and Mary Tyler Moore. Long known as a pretty-boy actor, Redford startled us with his talent at directing. Mary Tyler Moore, a beloved comedienne from the '60s and '70s (*The Dick Van Dyke Show*, *The Mary Tyler Moore Show*), was cast against type as the chilly, perfectionist Beth, and finally showed us the amazing range she'd had all along.

Watch This One With: Just about anyone.

Movies with the Same Vibe: RUNNING ON EMPTY, STEPMOM. Also check out *American Beauty* (1999), for a darker look at heartbreak behind the perfect hedges.

HOW THIS MOVIE HELPS

This movie wowed audiences when it won the Oscar for best picture, and continues to impress people who discover it today. It has no current megastars, no special effects (well, there's the storm during the boating accident), no huge plot twists, no stunning visuals. It has something much better: characters that feel real, and dialogue that makes you laugh or cry at every turn. Some might say that the wealthy, upstanding Jarretts have it relatively easy in life, and we won't argue with that. But even though it portrays a family at the top of the food chain, ORDINARY PEOPLE feels like it could be about any family, and any person's journey toward their own true self.

Our Song

MOOD CONTROL

1 2 3
4 5 6
7 8 9
10 11 12

▶ Press PLAY
if you're feeling:

1 Adventurous
2 Ambitious
3 ARTSY
4 CYNICAL
5 Depressed
6 Heartbroken
7 Hopeful
8 Insecure
9 Misunderstood
10 OVERWHELMED
11 Playful
12 Weird

2000 ULTIMATE GIRL RATING:

DIRECTOR: Jim McKay
BIRTHPLACE:
Brooklyn, New York
FILE UNDER:
Keeping It Real Filmmaking
RATED: R (for language)

STARRING: Kerry
Washington, Anna Simpson,
Melissa Martinez, Marlene
Forte, Raymond Anthony
Thomas, Rosalyn Coleman,
Carmen López, Tyrone Brown

THE PROBLEM

Maybe you or some of the kids at your school don't live in a great part of town, but it's just part of life. Still, it gets you down that whenever you go to the movies, they make it look like all inner-city kids think about is how to score drugs or avoid the shootouts on every corner. It's not a picnic, this life, but it's not like *that* 24/7 either. Where's the real urban story on the big screen? Do you have to shoot somebody to get reality into a movie these days?

The Reel Deal: The quietly amazing OUR SONG shows changes in the lives of three fifteen-year-old girls during one hot summer in Crown Heights, Brooklyn. Crown Heights normally gets the media spotlight for riots and other tragedies, but in OUR SONG we see a different world. It's a world filled with family and friends, where the daily indignities of living in poverty are occasionally alleviated by the small pleasures of unexpected treats. Apartment-dwellers swelter in the summer heat without even a fan, and kids learn how to survive school in a tough neighborhood. Movies are a rare luxury, and even nice kids shoplift cheap T-shirts because it's the only way to get something new to wear once in a while. Lanisha (Kerry Washington), Joycelyn (Anna

Simpson), and Maria (Melissa Martinez) form a tight trio at school and in their marching band, the Jackie Robinson Steppers. Lanisha suffers a tough breakup, Maria gets grief for trying to have a life, and Joycelyn lives with a mom who acts more like a preoccupied big sister. The girls are there for each other, though, until a school closing and an unexpected pregnancy force them to contemplate their future.

Line That Says It All: "Life is hard, honey. People leave us. Things fall apart. We have to be strong and walk through this...together."

Girl to Watch: All three leads are wonderful, each in her own way. Kerry Washington brings a special charm to the part of Lanisha (you might remember her from her great performance in SAVE THE LAST DANCE).

Guy to Watch: Raymond Anthony Thomas is so real as Carl, the weekend dad who can't quite live up to his promises.

Scene Worth the Rewind: The girls lay around one night in the dark, in the heat, just talking. They share secret fantasies and fears that lots of girls will find really familiar.

Rating Story: Here's a movie where the rating system is woefully shortsighted. There's no blood and guts, no extreme sex, nothing like the usual stuff that slaps an R rating on a film. But there's lots of cursing, just because that's how these girls talk. (We're pretty sure that you've heard these words before.) Then there's a scene where kids are smoking weed; apparently that's enough to make this film that's all about being fifteen bad for people that age to see.

HOW THIS MOVIE HELPS

We sometimes grow bored watching Hollywood movies—looking at the obvious scenes, waiting for the obvious endings. We're used to that fast-moving, in-your-face style of filmmaking. OUR SONG doesn't have a particularly suspenseful plot, and it doesn't have a typical ending either. But maybe that's okay for a movie that wants to look like real life. We spend one hot, long summer with three interesting girls, watching the good days and the bad, seeing why they are the way they are, how they show different sides of their personalities depending on who they're with. Does that feel real to you? If you live in a tough neighborhood, most movies would say that's your whole story. We don't think so, and neither does OUR SONG. Instead, with great young actresses and conversations straight off the street, this movie reflects the variety of people, ideas, and events you live with every day. What's the ending to your story? Too early to tell. Get on a train, see where it goes. Don't forget to write.

Pieces of April

MOOD CONTROL

1	2	3
4	5	6
7	8	9
10	11	12

▶ Press PLAY
if you're feeling:

1. Adventurous
2. Ambitious
3. ARTSY
4. Cynical
5. Depressed
6. HEARTBROKEN
7. HOPEFUL
8. Insecure
9. Misunderstood
10. Overwhelmed
11. Playful
12. Weird

2003 — **ULTIMATE GIRL RATING:**

DIRECTOR: Peter Hedges
BIRTHPLACE: Indie U.S.A.
FILE UNDER:
Family Alien-Nation
RATED: PG-13

STARRING: Katie Holmes, Derek Luke, Oliver Platt, John Gallagher, Jr., Alison Pill, Patricia Clarkson, Alice Drummond, Sean Hayes, Sisqó

THE PROBLEM

You know those photo Christmas cards people send out where one family member looks out of place? You're that person, the only one who wouldn't put on the matching reindeer sweater, the one left out of everyone's happy scrapbook memories. Try as you might to escape your disapproving family, they keep drawing you back in, time after time. You keep biding time, hoping they'll change, sure they're hoping the same about you. Is there any way out of this waiting game?

The Reel Deal: Heather Burns (Katie Holmes) is a young punk rocker living with her boyfriend, Bobby (Derek Luke), in a gritty section of New York City, happy to be far away from her eternally disapproving family. Though they're not too warm and cuddly, we get the impression that the family once had plenty to disapprove of—April seems like the kind of girl who took a long time to stop self-destructing. Family visits are few and far between, yet when April's mom, Joy (Patricia Clarkson), is diagnosed with cancer, the reluctant April is spurred into some degree of family feeling. When she invites them to the city for Thanksgiving dinner, they feel they have to accept. PIECES OF APRIL cross-cuts between two journeys: her family's bumpy ride into the

Did we mention that this is a comedy? Despite the cancer and dysfunctional family plot-points, hilarity abounds. Just watching April try to mash potatoes (honey, you *cook* them first) is a riot.

Anyone you don't mind crying in front of, because for a comedy there's still lots of weepin' to be had.

WHAT'S EATING GILBERT GRAPE, BEFORE SUNRISE. Also check out *About a Boy* (2002).

bowels of the big city, and April's calamity-filled day of trying to a create a memorable holiday meal with no cooking skills, a broken oven, and the help of neighbors who have problems of their own.

Line That Says It All:
"It was only one memory."
"Sometimes one is a lot."

Girl to Watch: We're not paddling in Dawson's Creek here. Katie Holmes is utterly believable in this edgy role. Patricia Clarkson does a masterful job as her mother, Joy. Don't dwell on whether or not you like Clarkson's character; think of all the different emotions she can communicate with just a few words and expressions. Now that's acting.

Guy to Watch: Derek Luke is great as Bobby, the kind of boyfriend every girl with a tough childhood should be rewarded with in the end.

HOW THIS MOVIE HELPS

We don't have long on this planet with each other. It's true. So do we waste time trying to make unworkable relationships work, or do we move on and find people who can accept us for who we are? The question gets a little trickier when family is involved. PIECES OF APRIL seems to suggest that we shouldn't try for more than is possible with our estranged relatives. Still, maybe we should try for something. Any effort is commendable: an e-mail, a postcard, a meal made with more bravery than talent. Trying to create a family fantasy that never existed is asking for heartache. Yet creating a cranberry sauce from scratch? Anyone can do that. Sometimes the smallest efforts create the sweetest memories.

⏸ PRESS PAUSE: Pick Your Family Movie

In the movie PLEASANTVILLE, a teenage boy is so enamored with a perfect '50s sitcom family that he actually enters the television and becomes their son. We understand his fantasy; movie families can be pretty perfect, can't they? They're often filled with attractive, understanding, encouraging people who look downright loveable. Feel like jumping into the screen yourself? Pick carefully, my friend. Not every movie family is created equal, make a wrong move and you might get the mother from WHITE OLEANDER instead of the father from CLUELESS. In case you ever get this magical opportunity, *The Ultimate Girls' Movie Survival Guide* offers this handy set of clues to help you pick the right kind of video or DVD to submerge yourself in. Do you jump in or step back?

HERE'S WHAT TO LOOK FOR:

Everyone calls the dad "Coach" .... Jump in

Everyone calls the dad "Sir" (even Mom) .... Step back

The mom is pretty in a bland way .... Jump in

The mom is pretty in a trashy way .... Step back

The sibling is older and pretty hot .... Jump in

The sibling is younger and hides a lot .... Step back

There's a big, loveable dog .... Jump in

There's a scrawny, malnourished cat .... Step back

When the parents get angry, they sit the kids down for a talk .... Jump in

When the parents get angry, they give the kind of performance
that says "Oscar" .... Step back

Dinner consists of four courses .... Jump in

Dinner is something people poke at while ignoring one another .... Step back

Developers threaten the neighborhood .... Jump in

The family threatens the neighborhood .... Step back

The police bring the kids home .... Jump in

The police take the parents away .... Step back

Pleasantville

MOOD CONTROL

1	2	3
4	5	6
7	8	9
10	11	12

▶ Press PLAY
if you're feeling:

1 Adventurous
2 Ambitious
3 Artsy
4 CYNICAL
5 Depressed
6 Heartbroken
7 Hopeful
8 Insecure
9 Misunderstood
10 OVERWHELMED
11 Playful
12 WEIRD

1998   **ULTIMATE GIRL RATING:** 🍀 🍀 🍀

DIRECTOR: Gary Ross
BIRTHPLACE: Mainstream Hollywood
FILE UNDER: Skewering the Sit-Com
RATED: PG-13

STARRING: Tobey Maguire, Reese Witherspoon, Jeff Daniels, Joan Allen, William H. Macy, J.T. Walsh, Don Knotts, Marley Shelton, Jane Kaczmarek

THE PROBLEM

You watch "Nick at Nite" and find yourself envying the perfectly manicured lawns and lives of the families depicted in those shows. Mom is always cooking and cleaning, Dad is always home for dinner, and nobody ever raises their voice. You look at your own messy, complicated family unit and think it could use a little PLEASANTVILLE treatment. Well, be careful what you wish for....

The Reel Deal: David (Tobey Maguire) and Jennifer (Reese Witherspoon) are brother and sister who live in a less-than-pleasant universe. Their mom and dad fight over whose turn it is to have the kids for the weekend. David is a TV-obsessed nerd who couldn't get a girl to look at him, and Jennifer is a sex-obsessed surface-skater whose life is about besting her friends with hot clothes and hot guys. It makes sense that the story begins, "Once upon a time," because what happens to them is weirdo fairytale, like something out of *Alice in Wonderland*.

One night, when their mom's out of town, they fight over the remote control; David wants to watch a marathon of his favorite, drippy '50s sitcom, "Pleasantville," which is set in a town of the same name, and Jennifer's set to watch an MTV concert with a date. Yet this remote is no ordinary piece of hardware. It was given to them by a strange television repairman (legendary '50s TV actor Don Knotts), who mysteriously showed up right after their real remote broke. Their tussle causes the new remote to switch on, and the next thing they know they're transported into Pleasantville, the black-and-white nirvana of David's dreams.

In reality, though, they both find it hard to fake their way through a few days of being "Bud" and "Mary Sue," the perfect children of George (William H. Macy) and Betty (Joan Allen). Jennifer immediately gives the town a taste of sex appeal, and even David's mildness is challenged by the town's unwillingness to accept any individuality in its citizens. At one point, Bud, tells his father, "People change." George reacts with total surprise: "They do?" Pleasantville changes—a lot—in this satire of family values, but what makes the movie really interesting is the way that David and Jennifer change as well.

Line That Says It All: "There's some places where the road doesn't go in a circle. There's some places where the road keeps going."

Girl to Watch: Reese Witherspoon. She has such fun with this part, and you see early signs of her LEGALLY BLONDE gumption.

Guy to Watch: Toby McGuire is so endearing as David/Bud, the boy who starts to become a man.

Fashion to Catch: Reese in a poodle skirt, especially when she dons her '50s nerd glasses.

Watch This One With: Your TV-addicted friends.

Movies with the Same Vibe: ELECTION, DONNIE DARKO. Also check out *The Truman Show* (1998).

HOW THIS MOVIE HELPS

We all do it when we're lazy, when we're unsure about what we really want to do—we turn on the TV and let someone dictate our reality. Nothing wrong with zoning out every now and then, but the danger comes when we start to buy in to the values and desires fed to us by the "image machine." Being a fan of a certain show is fun. Feeling as though you would like to retreat into that fabricated world is a sign that it might be time to give the remote a vacation. Real life isn't as silky smooth as what we're spoon-fed by the networks, but PLEASANTVILLE shows us that the tradeoff—a rougher ride that reveals beauty and truth—is totally worth it.

Pretty in Pink

MOOD CONTROL

1	2	3
4	5	6
7	8	9
10	11	12

▶ Press PLAY if you're feeling:

1 Adventurous
2 Ambitious
3 Artsy
4 Cynical
5 DEPRESSED
6 HEARTBROKEN
7 HOPEFUL
8 Insecure
9 Misunderstood
10 Overwhelmed
11 Playful
12 Weird

1986 **ULTIMATE GIRL RATING:** ♣ ♣ ♣ ♣

DIRECTOR: Howard Deutch
BIRTHPLACE: Mainstream Hollywood
FILE UNDER: Rich Little Poor Girl
RATED: PG-13

STARRING: Molly Ringwald, Harry Dean Stanton, Jon Cryer, Annie Potts, James Spader, Andrew McCarthy, Jim Haynie, Alexa Kenin, Kate Vernon

THE PROBLEM

Does where you come from determine who you are? You have the taste and the talent of people who live a life far more glamorous than yours. Do they deserve all they have just because they have it? It doesn't seem fair. And you know it's wrong to be bitter. You know you're better than all that. It's just that sometimes you get tired of being a good sport about a world that you didn't make. Fair enough.

The Reel Deal: Andie Walsh (Molly Ringwald) lives in a tiny house with her unemployed father (Harry Dean Stanton), her closet full of cool, handmade outfits, and her dreams of something better. Andie's mom left when she was little, leaving her nothing but a picture. She loves her depressed dad, but suspects that he's not working too hard on that job search. Every day she deals with being one of the token poor kids in a school full of what she calls "richies." She shields herself from their cruelty by hanging out with her best friend, Duckie (Jon Cryer), a goofy new-waver who not-so-secretly adores her. To Andie's amazement, she also captures the eye of handsome "richie" Blane McDonnagh (Andrew McCartney), a major player in a clique filled with people who disdain anyone not in their tax bracket. As a sweet romance develops between Andie and Blane, both of them are forced to choose between their friends and their feelings.

Line That Says It All: "You said you couldn't be with someone who didn't believe in you. I believed in you. I just didn't believe in me."

Girl to Watch: Molly Ringwald is wonderful in this film. Annie Potts is a blast as Iona, Andie's quirky boss at a downtown record shop.

Guy to Watch: Andrew McCarthy has a slow smile that could melt metal. Jon Cryer is terrific as Duckie.

Scene Worth the Rewind: Duckie's lip-synching performance in the record shop. Inspired.

Eye-Rolling Time: Although James Spader does a nice job as Steff, the smooth-talking villain, he looks way too old to play a high school senior.

Fun Factoid: Writer John Hughes and actress Molly Ringwald were thick as thieves when he wrote PRETTY IN PINK for her to star in. He got the title from a song by the Psychedelic Furs, a band that Molly was really into at the time.

Watch This One With: Anyone who wishes their taste matched their wallet.

Movies with the Same Vibe: THE BREAKFAST CLUB, SIXTEEN CANDLES, MYSTIC PIZZA.

HOW THIS MOVIE HELPS

It takes awhile for Andie to see that everything about her life has made her into the person she has become. "Take all of me or none of me," she seems to say, and that's a self-confidence that money just can't buy. It's good to be reminded of that when we're tempted to hide some aspect of our life that we don't think is good enough for other people. Sure, if you're clever enough, you can "pass" in any environment. But in the end, doesn't that feel like failure? PRETTY IN PINK doles out the rewards pretty neatly, but when we've been pummeled by the unfairness of things, sometimes all we want is to believe that our classy ways will outshine our economic class any day of the week. Should you ever forget that, the Duck Man is at your service, with a little musical reminder....

The Princess Bride

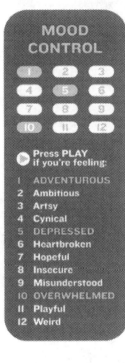

MOOD CONTROL

1	2	3
4	5	6
7	8	9
10	11	12

▶ Press PLAY
if you're feeling:

1 ADVENTUROUS
2 Ambitious
3 Artsy
4 Cynical
5 DEPRESSED
6 Heartbroken
7 Hopeful
8 Insecure
9 Misunderstood
10 OVERWHELMED
11 Playful
12 Weird

1987 ULTIMATE GIRL RATING: ♣ ♣ ♣

DIRECTOR: Rob Reiner
BIRTHPLACE: Mainstream Hollywood
FILE UNDER: Facetious Fairytale
RATED: PG

STARRING: Cary Elwes, Robin Wright Penn, Mandy Patinkin, Chris Sarandon, Christopher Guest, Wallace Shawn, André the Giant, Fred Savage, Peter Falk

THE PROBLEM

Does true love exist? You see it in the fairytales, where the princess swoons and sighs and waits for her true love to rescue her. Fortunately, he always does. Of course, then she's got to spend the rest of her life beholden to the guy. Wouldn't it be better if lovers both fought hard to find their way to one another? True love is a tall order—shouldn't it be a team effort?

The Reel Deal: Like a bedtime story told by your wickedly funny older sibling, THE PRINCESS BRIDE is, on the surface, a tale of adventure and romance. Yet underneath the typical trappings of princesses and evil henchman lies a hilarious parody of all those "long ago in a kingdom far away" adventures. The story begins with a young boy (Fred Savage) who is sick at home, being read to by his grandfather (Peter Falk). The boy is appalled that his grandfather insists on reading him a fairytale—how uncool can you get? Yet gramps promises that this particular tale is unlike any other, so reluctantly the boy settles in for the yarn. He learns of Princess Buttercup (Robin Wright Penn), a self-absorbed beauty who badgers a poor farm boy, Westley (Cary Elwes), who works for her family. Suddenly one day, she realizes that she loves him. Unfortunately, she is soon kidnapped by goons and pursued by the evil Prince Humperdinck (Chris Sarandon), who has his own plans for the princess. The leader of the goons (or at least the most verbal) is a shifty little gnome named Vizzini (Wallace Shawn), who utters the most common phrase in the film when taken aback by events: "Inconceivable!" With him is Fezzik (played by famed wrestler André the Giant), who provides enormous humor value with every expression. They carry the princess off, putting the stalwart Westley through enormous travails to find her. Screaming eels, perilous cliffs, and magical wizards are just a few of the obstacles standing between the young lovers as they fight their way back into one another's arms.

With an exciting plotline and a witty running commentary that mocks the action, THE PRINCESS BRIDE tries to have it both ways, both celebrating and mocking a classic movie genre. Fortunately for those who were involved with the film, it succeeds on both levels, and garnered good reviews and packed movie houses.

Line That Says It All:
"You seem a decent fellow. I hate to kill you."
"You seem a decent fellow. I hate to die."

Girl to Watch: Robin Wright Penn as Buttercup. This princess may be in need of rescuing, but she's also tough as nails, and not about to resign herself to her fate.

Guy to Watch: Cary Elwes is wonderful as Westley. If you were kidnapped by a giant wrestler and a creepy little man with a nasally drone, this is who you'd want on their tail. Mandy Patinkin is also fantastic as Inigo Montoya, a passionate swordsman with a little chip on his shoulder concerning his father's death.

Scene Worth the Rewind: You haven't lived until you've tried to escape a patch of screaming eels. Trust us. It's harder than it sounds.

Watch This One With: Your friends who love fairy tales, and your friends who love witty parodies of movie genres. We recognize that these might be two totally separate groups of friends, but they can get along for one, fun-filled evening.

Movies with the Same Vibe: EVER AFTER. Also check out the *Star Wars* movies.

HOW THIS MOVIE HELPS

THE PRINCESS BRIDE is escapism of the highest order. You'll rent it for the exciting adventures and funny dialogue, but you'll also love the story of Westley and Buttercup, whose love is shown to be a force that exists almost as another character in the film. They're both pretty as a picture and brave, to boot. It's the perfect movie for when you're in that "kinda want to laugh, kinda want to jump out of my seat" mood. THE PRINCESS BRIDE is inspired filmmaking, and it's pretty "inconceivable!" that you won't enjoy the ride.

Maybe you camp out at the theater when the *Harry Potter* and *Lord of the Rings* movies come out, maybe you wait until they're on DVD. Either way, chances are you've seen most of the popular fantasy and sci-fi series: *Star Wars, Star Trek, Back to the Future, The Adventures of Indiana Jones,* and then some. Just what makes imaginary worlds so popular?

To figure it out, all we have to do is look at the day-to-day issues in our world: family, relationships, school, our mental and physical health, and what to do about that little thing called The Future. It's enough to make you want to head off for a galaxy far, far, away or a kingdom long, long ago. True fantasy buffs see it all: the good, the bad, and the just plain weird. The rest of us catch one of these movies now and then, looking for the story lines that have universal themes and characters that ring true no matter what the setting.

This far-from-complete list (no angry letters, please!) offers up a few cool movies that you may remember from childhood, or find more interesting now. Bring this list with you the next time you're looking for a movie experience that's out of this world.

The Dark Crystal (1983)

The Muppet crew creates magic with this engrossing story that combines fairy tales and fantasy.

E.T. The Extra Terrestrial (1982)

Is it humanly possible that you missed this Steven Spielberg classic featuring flying bicycles, the power of love, and the cutest, ugliest alien in history? Don't even talk to us. Just rent it.

Excalibur (1981)

This magnificent British production does the King Arthur legend proud.

Labyrinth (1986)

A teenage girl has to negotiate an incredible labyrinth in order to rescue her baby brother from the King of the Goblins. Don't you hate it when that happens? Rocker David Bowie is an inspired king, and you might recognize a teenaged Jennifer Connelly (*A Beautiful Mind*). Gothic fun.

Ladyhawke (1985)

That guy from FERRIS BUELLER'S DAY OFF (Matthew Broderick) plays a medieval joker in this action-packed fantasy about star-crossed lovers and the thief who may be their only hope.

Willow (1988)

Compelling not-just-for-kids fantasy about a little person's quest to bring an abandoned baby to its rightful home. Great special effects.

The Princess Diaries

MOOD CONTROL

1	2	3
4	5	6
7	8	9
10	11	12

Press PLAY if you're feeling:

1 Adventurous
2 Ambitious
3 Artsy
4 Cynical
5 Depressed
6 Heartbroken
7 Hopeful
8 INSECURE
9 Misunderstood
10 OVERWHELMED
11 PLAYFUL
12 Weird

2001 ULTIMATE GIRL RATING:

DIRECTOR: Garry Marshall
BIRTHPLACE: Mainstream Hollywood
FILE UNDER: Royal Freakout
RATED: PG

STARRING: Julie Andrews, Anne Hathaway, Hector Elizondo, Heather Matarazzo, Mandy Moore, Caroline Goodall, Erick von Detten, Robert Schwartzman

THE PROBLEM Every day of school seems to last a year. You always feel like you're in the wrong place at the wrong time—or maybe you're just the wrong person. If you were suddenly beautiful and popular, every day would be a picnic instead of purgatory, right?

The Reel Deal: Mia Thermopolis (Anne Hathaway) lives with her arty mom, Helen (Caroline Goodall), in an old firehouse in San Francisco. Thanks to her late father, a citizen of the distant, tiny country of Genovia, she can afford to attend a ritzy private school, where she finds few friends among the wealthy preppies that surround her. She can confide in her socially conscious friend Lilly (Heather Matarazzo), whose sweet brother Michael (Robert Schwartzman) barely hides his outsized crush on Mia. One day Mia gets an unexpected visit from her dad's mother, Clarisse Renaldi (Julie Andrews), some old-country grande dame who Mia's never met in her life. The news she hears is shocking: Grandma is not just visiting from Genovia—she *runs* Genovia. She's the queen, which suddenly puts royal blood straight into Mia's gawky veins. Mia learns that she's the princess of Genovia, and Clarisse would like her to move back there

Scene Worth the Rewind: Mia's speech near the end sounds like something a teenage girl might actually come up with, rather than some scriptwriter's polished pearls of wisdom.

Watch This One With: Your friends who enjoyed reading the Meg Cabot series. The movie takes some turns away from the book (movies based on books usually do), but we felt it kept the spirit of Meg's stories intact. And that PG rating makes it the perfect movie to bring the next time you baby-sit.

and take over the family business. Mia is understandably reluctant to agree to running a country when tenth grade is enough of a nightmare. She and her grandmother devise a compromise: Mia will learn how to act like a princess while she decides whether or not to make the move. How her newfound status affects her schoolmates, her friends and family, and her sense of self lies at the heart of this funny, well-made film.

Line That Says It All: "Like I'm not enough of a freak already, let's just slap a tiara on my head!"

Girl to Watch: In acting class, teachers always talk about committing to your character. Anne Hathaway truly commits to this funny, multifaceted character.

Guy to Watch: Robert Schwartzman is adorable as Michael. Not an outsized hunk, just a nice, normal kind of guy used to being overlooked.

HOW THIS MOVIE HELPS

Okay, so you're probably not secretly a princess. But you're secretly something. What is it? A writer? An actress? A topnotch sailor, scientist, mechanic, stand-up comic? Whatever. If you feel talentless and doomed to a life of banality, then you're a secret you're keeping from yourself. People might think they have no special talent or place in this world until a situation forces them to see what other people see: that the world would somehow be a lesser place without them. Would it help if you could get an outside view? Mia got the royal treatment handed to her; you aren't quite that lucky. So listen to those compliments you keep getting about one thing or another. Is there a trend? Maybe people look at you right now and see a dazzling crown.

Pump Up the Volume

MOOD CONTROL

1	2	3
4	5	6
7	8	9
10	11	12

▶ Press **PLAY** if you're feeling:

1 Adventurous
2 Ambitious
3 Artsy
4 CYNICAL
5 Depressed
6 Heartbroken
7 Hopeful
8 Insecure
9 MISUNDERSTOOD
10 Overwhelmed
11 Playful
12 WEIRD

1990   **ULTIMATE GIRL RATING:** ♣ ♣ ♣ ♣

DIRECTOR: Allan Moyle
BIRTHPLACE: Mainstream Hollywood Father, Indie Mother
FILE UNDER: Raise Your Voice, Raise the Roof
RATED: R

STARRING: Christian Slater, Samantha Mathis, Andy Romano, Keith Stuart Thayer, Cheryl Pollack

THE PROBLEM   Nobody sees you, and you're not even sure you want to be seen. Sometimes it's all you can do to get through the day, watching people follow the stupid rules created and enforced by the stupid rule-makers. There's so much you'd like to say about what you see and what you feel. Would it make a difference? Would anybody listen?

The Reel Deal: Every night in a suburb in Arizona, teens tune into the pirate radio station of Happy Harry Hard-on, a foul-mouthed kid with some nasty, though honest, things to say about the parents, teachers, and kids that inhabit his high school world. From pretending to masturbate on air to inciting his peers to go crazy and shake things up in their lives, Harry wreaks disorder in his quiet town. Who is Happy Harry? He uses a voice distorter and a post office box for his address, so no one knows. "I could be the nerd sitting behind you," Harry informs his listening classmates. It turns out that that's pretty much the truth. Harry is in reality Mark Hunter (Christian Slater), an introverted teen from Manhattan who landed against his will in this drab little community. With no friends at school, he tries to keep up with his old New York friends via a ham radio in the basement (remember, this movie was made before the Internet got big). When he stumbles upon an open frequency, he starts his own radio show, and the persona of Happy Harry is born. Hunter's show gives him an outlet for his anger and frustration, and his days are a crazy mix of complete obscurity and wild popularity.

His fame is not without its trials, however. A girl in his English class is closing in on his true identity. Even worse, a suicidal kid has decided that Harry is his lifeline, and Hunter feels ill-equipped to deal with depression of that magnitude. When tragedy strikes, the administration closes in on Hunter, and works hard to put his pirate radio show out of business. Who Mark Hunter becomes, and how his brazen show effects the kids around him is revealed in this inspiring, energetic movie.

Guy to Watch: Christian Slater is the best thing going here. His Harry is nasty, tough, and says too many true things to remember them all.

Girl to Watch: Samantha Mathis as punky poetess Nora. She's the perfect girl for a guy like Harry.

Line That Says It All: "Feeling screwed up at a screwed-up time in a screwed-up place does not make you screwed up."

Watch This One With: Your rebel friends.

Movies with the Same Vibe: HEATHERS, DAZED AND CONFUSED. Also check out Eric Bogosian's *Talk Radio* (1988); it's like this movie's big brother.

How You Know It's a Movie: The insurrection scene near the end is a little farfetched. We'll give them the basic point, though: talk can start a revolution.

Scene Worth the Rewind: All the scenes with Harry on the air. He's one part immature teenage boy, two parts gritty truth-teller.

HOW THIS MOVIE HELPS

Maybe you don't want to rant and rave on the airwaves or the Internet. Yet wouldn't it be cathartic to be able to tell the world just what you think about things without the fear of being grounded or getting suspended from school? Harry does eventually pay the cost for his casual rants, but he also finds incredible freedom in speaking his mind. You don't need a radio show to let it fly. Start a discussion group, a blog, a newspaper of your own. It doesn't matter the size of the audience, it matters that you're making your voice heard. If we gave you a microphone, a dark night, and hundreds of teen listeners, what would you say? Okay, now go find a way to say that.

Reality Bites

MOOD CONTROL

1	2	3
4	5	6
7	8	9
10	11	12

▶ Press **PLAY** if you're feeling:

1 Adventurous
2 Ambitious
3 Artsy
4 CYNICAL
5 Depressed
6 HEARTBROKEN
7 Hopeful
8 Insecure
9 MISUNDERSTOOD
10 Overwhelmed
11 Playful
12 Weird

1994   ULTIMATE GIRL RATING: ♣ ♣ ♣

DIRECTOR: Ben Stiller
BIRTHPLACE: Mainstream Hollywood
FILE UNDER: Driving in the Slow Lane Toward the Real World
RATED: PG-13

STARRING: Winona Ryder, Ethan Hawke, Janeane Garofalo, Steve Zahn, Ben Stiller, Swoosie Kurtz

THE PROBLEM

College sets you up for everything you want to do for the rest of your life, right? That only works for about five percent of any given campus population. The reality is that college can sometimes make you even more confused by giving you a taste of things that are much harder to come by in the real world. It's quite possible to leave seventeen years of schooling less sure of yourself than you were on your first day of junior high. Can't handle that reality? Try this one.

The Reel Deal: Lelaina (Winona Ryder), Troy (Ethan Hawke), Vickie (Janeane Garofalo), and Sammy (Steve Zahn) are recent college graduates. Big deal. Due to personal struggles and a tight job market, they feel like they're back in high school, only this time the rent is due. They are slackers who hang out together constantly.

Lelaina, who works for a morning television show, is already the most ambitious of the quartet. One day she literally runs into a young music executive, Michael (Ben Stiller). Michael convinces her that she can make videos her way without selling out, and they get involved both personally and professionally. This hardly sits well with her

Line That Says It All: "Welcome to the Maxi Pad."

Scene to Remember: The impromptu dance several characters do in a convenience store to "My Sharona" is a classic movie moment. Also, is that Renée Zellweger in a goofy cameo? It is!

HOW THIS MOVIE HELPS

There's nothing too revolutionary going on in REALITY BITES, but it's an entertaining spin on an old truth: no one can tell you who you are meant to be, you have to find that out for yourself. There's a lot of emphasis here on which guy Lelaina picks, which is fun, but the larger message holds well: just make a move. We can wear the hip clothes and have the ironic attitude, but in the end it's just plain fear that keeps us talking about the future without bringing it any closer to reality. Ultimately, it's the choices we actually make (guys, jobs, friends, video edits) that define who we are far more than the endless conversations about what we would do if we could manage to roll off the couch. Enough talk. You can do it. Go make those choices.

roommates, whose post-college reality is more along the lines of cheap dinners and jeans-folding seminars at the Gap. As Lelaina's dreams start to come true (making her own movie, having a relationship with a real "grown-up"), she begins to wonder if she's got the right dreams in mind. Encouraging this confusion is her old friend Troy, who slowly realizes that a hip, ironic stance is fine for a night out with the buds, but it will never win you the girl.

Girl to Watch: It's Lelaina's story, but it's Janeane Garofalo's movie in the end. Her Vickie is alternately exasperating and endearing, the friend you love in spite of yourself.

Guy to Watch: You spend the movie deciding between Stylish Yuppie Michael and Angry Young Rocker Troy. Lelaina makes a choice in the end—thank goodness you don't have to.

Real Women Have Curves

MOOD CONTROL

1	2	3
4	5	6
7	8	9
10	11	12

▶ Press PLAY
if you're feeling:

1 ADVENTUROUS
2 Ambitious
3 Artsy
4 Cynical
5 DEPRESSED
6 Heartbroken
7 Hopeful
8 Insecure
9 MISUNDERSTOOD
10 Overwhelmed
11 Playful
12 Weird

2000 | **ULTIMATE GIRL RATING:** ❀ ❀ ❀ ❀ ❀

DIRECTOR: Patricia Cardoso
BIRTHPLACE: East L.A.
FILE UNDER: Latina Power
RATED: PG-13

STARRING: America Ferrera, Lupe Ontiveros, Ingrid Oliu, George Lopez, Brian Sites, Soledad St. Hilaire

THE PROBLEM

Does where you come from seem to be at odds with where you want to go? Do people think you're ungrateful for wanting more than you have now? Is your ambition embarrassing you? Welcome to Ana's world.

The Reel Deal: Ana Garcia (America Ferrera) is a big girl. Unfortunately, that's all her mother sees, but Ana's so much more than that. She's ambitious, as evidenced by her long trip every morning from East Los Angeles to Beverly Hills High in search of a better education. She's smart, according to a favorite teacher who is trying to get her a scholarship to Columbia University. She's curvaceous and beautiful, according to Jimmy (Brian Sites), the well-off white boy in her class who is mystified by her low self-esteem. Yet none of those things pay the rent, and Ana's family needs her to help out in sister Estela's dress factory. Ana dutifully goes to work with the family, but bristles at the lousy conditions, tedious work, and deplorable pay. She can't believe that these women don't even know they're working in a sweatshop, that they're grateful to a major department store that pays them miniscule wages. As Ana grows increasingly independent, looking seriously into college and enjoying a summer romance with Jimmy, her frantic mother (Lupe Ontiveros) tries every trick in the book to bring her in line. When Ana finally realizes that there's nothing wrong with being a "real woman," no amount of guilt or cruel comments about her weight can erode her sense of self.

Line That Says It All: "It's because I love you that I make your life miserable."
"Don't love me so much."

Girl to Watch: America Ferrera as Ana. She's amazing.

Guy to Watch: Brian Sites. Every girl over size 12 should get a Jimmy.

Scene Worth the Rewind: The scene where the hot and exhausted women strip and compare cellulite and stretch marks is the best. These women embrace their less-than-perfect bodies as part of who they are; they don't hit you over the head with this "positive message," it's just funny and fun to watch.

Fashion to Catch: The evening gowns sewn in the factory are incredible.

Watch This One With: Your amigas who appreciate a film about real girls and real life.

Movies with the Same Vibe: BEND IT LIKE BECKHAM, DOUBLE HAPPINESS, CIRCLE OF FRIENDS.

HOW THIS MOVIE HELPS

How doesn't this movie help? It shows a big, curvy, gorgeous barrio girl standing up to her mother, finding romance, and understanding her family while searching for her true self. It's made by a Latina, about a Latina, but it's for every girl who has ever struggled not to feel invisible. Rent this movie, no matter what your size or background—it will feel like a perfect fit.

River's Edge

MOOD CONTROL

1	2	3
4	5	6
7	8	9
10	11	12

▶ Press PLAY
if you're feeling

1 Adventurous
2 Ambitious
3 ARTSY
4 CYNICAL
5 Depressed
6 Heartbroken
7 Hopeful
8 Insecure
9 Misunderstood
10 Overwhelmed
11 Playful
12 WEIRD

1986   ULTIMATE GIRL RATING: ♣ ♣

DIRECTOR: Tim Hunter
BIRTHPLACE: Indie U.S.A.
FILE UNDER:
Compassion Fatigue
RATED: R

STARRING: Ione Skye,
Crispin Glover, Keanu Reeves,
Dennis Hopper, Roxana Zal,
Daniel Roebuck, Danyi Deats

THE PROBLEM

You're threatening to drown in apathy about life. People seem so ridiculous and annoying that sometimes it becomes hard to stay connected to what really matters. You find yourself thinking about a cute guy at your grandmother's funeral, and you really loved your grandmother. You find all horrors in life equally horrible, which is to say it's hard to feel much of anything anymore. But it's starting to scare you, and that's a good sign.

The Reel Deal: The tragedy of Columbine blew stories like this off the map—but it's still pretty creepy. RIVER'S EDGE was loosely based on an actual incident that made news in the early '80s, in which a teenage boy killed his girlfriend. Teens who knew the couple listened to the murderer brag about his deed for days before informing the authorities that they knew where the missing girl was, and what had become of her. Some kids even sneaked up to where her body was laying for a garish peep show. The media circus didn't focus on the murder, but on the question of how so many kids could have known about it and not gone to the police.

In this fictionalized account of that sordid story, Samson (Daniel Roebuck) kills his girlfriend, Jamie (Danyi Deats), in a fit of…well, not much. He just sort of kills her, then quickly numbs out. Taking over the situation is speed-freak Layne (Crispin Glover), a wild-eyed basket case whose friends are largely afraid of him. Layne decides that while Jamie was their friend too, she's now dead and their job is to protect Samson. The perennially drugged up and drunk crew of friends sort of agrees.

One doubting Thomas is Matt (Keanu Reeves), an amiable stoner who has retained some shred of decency despite his pathetic home life. He gradually emerges as the closest thing the movie has to a hero simply by realizing that some adults should probably be let in on this shocking situation.

Line That Says It All:

"I hear they're having an open-casket funeral for Jamie. I think that's in bad taste." "It is in bad taste. This whole thing is in bad taste. You people are a disgrace to the human race, to all living things, to plants even. You shouldn't be seen in the same room with a cactus."

Girl to Watch: Ione Skye as Clarissa. One
of the most chilling scenes is when Clarissa is musing aloud with a girlfriend about why they don't feel anything, even though Jamie was supposedly one of their best friends.

Guy to Watch: Keanu Reeves. His sweet
slacker persona is perfect for this role.

Scene Worth the Rewind: If you
prefer gritty over sweet, you might really like this intelligently written, honest portrayal of teens living at the edge of society. Any scene

where Ione Skye and Keanu Reeves connect is particularly memorable. The relationship that develops between these two lost kids is like a tiny flicker of hope that tries to warm up this big, dark story.

HOW THIS MOVIE HELPS

In the *Scream* movies, dead bodies are displayed for laughs. There are some comical moments in RIVER'S EDGE, but the repeated shots of a naked dead girl are far from funny, and a grim reminder of what everyone is really refusing to look at. How does this help? It reminds us that death is not a ballad sung at a funeral or teddy bears left by a roadside. It's real and tough and forever, and there's nothing we can do about it. Well, actually, there's a huge thing we can do about it, isn't there? We can choose to live life like it matters, like we appreciate the gifts that we've been given: great friends, sunny days, moments of grace and wonder. We can value each other. We can shake off the easy fog of apathy, toss away the excuses, and really care about people. We can see RIVER'S EDGE and be thankful for the fact that we are not casualties left by the river. And we can understand that the only thing worse than life sucking is losing the opportunity to make it better.

Romeo + Juliet

1996   **ULTIMATE GIRL RATING:** ♣ ♣

DIRECTOR: Baz Luhrmann
BIRTHPLACE:
Mainstream Hollywood
FILE UNDER: Cool Eye
for the Shake Guy
RATED: PG-13

STARRING: Claire Danes,
Leonardo DiCaprio,
Harold Perrineau, Jr., Pete
Postlethwaite, Paul Sorvino,
Brian Dennehy

THE PROBLEM

He was the "Greatest Playwright of All Time," blah, blah, blah. Whatever... you just can't get too interested. Your English teacher keeps saying that Shakespeare's characters were caught up in the same human comedies and tragedies that we play out today, but you just don't see the connection. Couldn't somebody just give Shakespeare a makeover? The dude is *old*.

The Reel Deal: Don't base your term paper on this updated version of Shakespeare's tragic teen romance. In ROMEO + JULIET, the Montagues and Capulets are two feuding families in a Florida city called Verona. Juliet (Claire Danes) and Romeo (Leonardo DiCaprio) meet at a costume party, first seeing each other through a giant aquarium. They quickly fall in love, a love that's impossible given the (literal) war between their two families. Through a series of skirmishes that get out of hand, missed letters and misunderstandings, the young lovers grow to realize that their love is never to be, not in this world anyway. Only after the lovers' tragic end do their families come to realize that some things just aren't worth fighting over.

Line That Says It All: It's Shakespeare. Every line says it all. We like, "If love be rough with you, be rough with love."

Girl to Watch: Claire Danes is wonderful, giving Juliet lots of dimension despite the constant crosscutting of this vibrant, noisy screenplay.

Guy to Watch: Leo's Romeo is a sexy, swaggering guy, yet sensitive when it counts. He's best in his scenes with Danes—it's almost as if she grounds him despite the cacophony that surrounds them.

Scene Worth the Rewind: We love the "balcony" scene, which turns into a romantic dip in the pool. In fact, look for the constant water imagery sprinkled throughout this splashy film.

Soundtrack Note: This movie has a really fun soundtrack. You've got "#1 Crush" from Garbage, songs from Everclear and Butthole Surfers, The Cardigans' "Lovefool," a great version of "Young Hearts Run Free," some cool Radiohead tunes, and more. It's in stores; check it out.

Fun Factoid: An impressive group of young actresses wanted this role: Christina Ricci, Natalie Portman, Jennifer Love Hewitt, Sarah Michelle Geller. They either didn't look old enough or the timing wasn't right, or something, and Clare Danes was picked. (Kind of good to remind ourselves that those girls have to deal with rejection too.)

Watch This One With: Your English class. Bring it to class and beg your teacher—who knows?

Movies with the Same Vibe: MOULIN ROUGE!, 10 THINGS I HATE ABOUT YOU (an updated version of Shakespeare's *The Taming of the Shrew*). Also check out *Hamlet* (2000), featuring Ethan Hawke as Hamlet, and if watching this film got you in the mood for any riff off this classic story, check out Franco Zeffirelli's version (he's the director, and it's pretty interesting), ROMEO AND JULIET (1968). Or perhaps you prefer your doomed lovers dancing? WEST SIDE STORY (1961), is the film version of the smash Broadway musical, taking R + J to gang life in New York during the '50s. Some Broadway musicals don't do as well once they land on celluloid, but this little number won ten Academy Awards.

HOW THIS MOVIE HELPS

ROMEO + JULIET wasn't produced specifically for teens, but it sure tries to make the star-crossed lovers look like kids you might actually know. Sometimes stiff productions of Shakespeare make it hard to see how cool a guy he was; he loved the action sequences and intense emotions as much as the fancy language. Some might argue that ROMEO + JULIET sacrifices substance for style, but we can live with that, if style gets us in the door.

A Room with a View

MOOD CONTROL

1	2	3
4	5	6
7	8	9
10	11	12

▶ Press PLAY if you're feeling:

1 ADVENTUROUS
2 Ambitious
3 Artsy
4 Cynical
5 Depressed
6 Heartbroken
7 HOPEFUL
8 Insecure
9 Misunderstood
10 Overwhelmed
11 PLAYFUL
12 Weird

1985 ULTIMATE GIRL RATING: ♣ ♣ ♣

DIRECTOR: James Ivory
BIRTHPLACE: England
FILE UNDER:
Choose Passion
UNRATED: Brief,
comical backside nudity

STARRING: Maggie Smith,
Helena Bonham Carter,
Denholm Elliot, Julian Sands,
Simon Callow, Patrick
Godfrey, Judi Dench, Daniel
Day-Lewis

THE PROBLEM

You're a good girl, a careful one. You never ruffle feathers, you take the safe route, you know what's of expected of you and try to never disappoint. Great. Day to day, that is the easier path. But should life be, above all else, easy? Feelings in you well up sometimes, feelings that would not receive the stamp of approval. What if you acted on some of those feelings? Wouldn't life be harder? Wouldn't it maybe be better too?

The Reel Deal: Lucy Honeychurch (Helena Bonham Carter) is a proper young British girl who travels to Florence, Italy, with a priggish chaperone, Charlotte Bartlett (Maggie Smith). In Lucy's day (the early 1900s) it was not uncommon for a young woman to have a supervised European adventure before settling down to a stultifying existence as the wife of some carefully selected young man from the family's social circle. In Florence, Lucy and her companion meet the Emersons, also English tourists. Handsome young George (Julian Sands) and his father (Denholm Elliot) are as free-spirited as the women are repressed. They are open with controversial opinions, spouters of poetry, lovers of life. Charlotte finds them kind yet somewhat shocking. Lucy doesn't know what to think of them because she has carefully trained herself to listen to her head rather than her heart. George is immediately smitten with Lucy. One day they are picnicking in a field and he spontaneously kisses her, without any warning. Lucy reels. They part, and she scurries back to England, where marriage soon awaits with a drippy, asexual dolt named Cecil Vyse (Daniel Day-Lewis). That should be that, except that the Emersons soon move into Lucy's village, and she is once again confronted with the life force that is George Emerson, and the feelings that make no sense to her.

Line That Says It All: "He's the sort who can't know anyone intimately, least of all a woman. He doesn't know what a woman is. He wants you as a possession, something to look at, like a painting or an ivory box. Something to own and to display. He doesn't want you to be real, and to think and to live. He doesn't love you."

Girl to Watch: Helena Bonham Carter. She did several period pieces in the '80s. We think casting directors liked her because she always managed to play her characters as vibrant, modern women despite the old-fashioned context.

Guy to Watch: Julian Sands as George. He'll be your cup of tea.

Fun Factoid: A ROOM WITH A VIEW is based on the novel of the same title by E. M. Forster. If your high school English teacher didn't throw him your way, it's a shame. Forster wrote witty and insightful novels that nailed the arrogance of the British class system. Another good book of his is *Passage to India*, also made into a film in 1984.

Movies with the Same Vibe: Also check out *Emma* (1996), the charming Jane Austen story on which CLUELESS is loosely based. This time Gwyneth Paltrow is the busybody.

HOW THIS MOVIE HELPS

A ROOM WITH A VIEW is one of those surprising films that has a rebellious message. It's a period drama, so everyone looks prim and proper and talks like members of the royal family; and it's shocking, simply shocking, when we see any sexual tension. Even if that subculture isn't your thing, however, you can find yourself loving this movie because it's really about love and passion and choosing a conscious life over a mind-numbing existence. You don't need trendy clothes or a cool soundtrack to make that a good message. When Lucy Honeychurch opens her eyes to life's possibilities, she is every girl who ever thought, "Life is short. No more faking my way." It's not only people back in the days of long skirts and afternoon tea who need that nudge. If you need that reminder, right here, right now, check out A ROOM WITH A VIEW.

Okay, maybe your closet isn't as big as Cher's in CLUELESS, and maybe you won't commit crimes for clothes like tragic Tracy in THIRTEEN. Still, fashion is pretty high on your list. Teen movies are a pretty good way to track how styles have changed: can you imagine walking into high school these days with huge shoulder pads and a big scarf knotted on top of your head? (Well, maybe on '80s Day.)

You know which movies have the clothes you'd love to wear; what about the clothes you would have loved to design? If you're one of those people who watches the Oscars mainly to see who won for best costume design, then you're up on this list, which includes, by the way, the sumptuous gowns in A ROOM WITH A VIEW. Whether or not fashion's your main passion, you might want to check out a few of these past winners, which contain both story lines and stylish clothes to die for.

Chicago (2002)
This recent musical had Renée Zellweger and Catherine Zeta-Jones smokin'.

Moulin Rouge (2001)
The whole look of this film was a designer's dream, don't you think?

The Age of Innocence (1993)
A quiet film about stifled passion in the age of dazzling frocks.

Dangerous Liaisons (1998)
Based on an eighteenth-century French novel. Bad behavior never looked so elegant.

Amadeus (1984)
The classical composer Mozart is portrayed as sort of the original punk genius. Visually stunning and lots of fun.

FOR AN INSIDE LOOK AT THE FASHION BIZ, BE SURE TO CHECK OUT

Unzipped (1995)
Long before Isaac Mizrahi charmed hordes of Target shoppers he was making it happen in the elite New York fashion industry. This funny and fairly candid documentary shows Mizrahi at his most charming, and gives us an almost-inside look at the making of a fashion show and its major players: designers, models, journalists, and the legions of hangers-on that go with them. It's almost as much fun as spotting a bargain.

Running on Empty

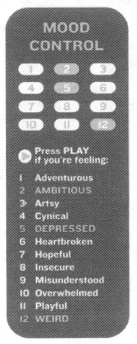

MOOD CONTROL

1	2	3
4	5	6
7	8	9
10	11	12

▶ Press **PLAY** if you're feeling:

1 Adventurous
2 AMBITIOUS
3 Artsy
4 Cynical
5 DEPRESSED
6 Heartbroken
7 Hopeful
8 Insecure
9 Misunderstood
10 Overwhelmed
11 Playful
12 WEIRD

1988   **ULTIMATE GIRL RATING:**

DIRECTOR: Sidney Lumet
BIRTHPLACE: Hollywood Father, Indie Mother
FILE UNDER: My Parents Were Fugitives from the Law and All I Got Was This Lousy T-Shirt
RATED: PG-13

STARRING: River Phoenix, Martha Plimpton, Christine Lahti, Judd Hirsch, Jonas Abry, Ed Crowley

THE PROBLEM You get the feeling that if you leave home to live your own life you're going to disappoint someone terribly: your parents, friends, maybe a boyfriend who plans to stick around town. What are you going to do?

The Reel Deal: The Popes are a nice, seemingly normal family with two parents, two kids, and a dog. The only thing is, the dog is frequently abandoned in the middle of the night as the family suddenly hightails it out of town. In the '70s, Arthur and Annie Pope (Judd Hirsch and Christine Lahti) were part of a radical underground movement that was against the Vietnam War. Trying to hinder the war machine, they blew up a napalm lab, accidentally killing a janitor who was inside the building. They stayed together, flying under the law's radar screen, inventing new names and trying new towns, towing along their growing children, who thought nothing of this lie-filled peripatetic life. Now that Danny Pope (River Phoenix) is in his senior year of high school, things are different. He has his first girlfriend, Lorna (Martha Plimpton), a smart, funny girl who's the daughter of his music teacher—the same music teacher who believes that Danny's talents belong at Juilliard. Going off to college means never seeing his family again, yet staying with them means denying himself the future that his own parents destroyed in a lab decades earlier. Danny's father is adamant that the family should stay together, no matter what. His mother is torn. The conflict in RUNNING ON EMPTY is a powerful one: do Danny's parents love him enough to lose him forever?

Movie with the Same Vibe: MERMAIDS, ORDINARY PEOPLE. Also check out *The Mosquito Coast* (1986), another film where the parental antics take the kids far from normal life.

Line That Says It All: "So now that we've determined that I belong here, let's talk about you."

Girl to Watch: Martha Plimpton. This intelligent, interesting actress should have a much bigger career. Humph. We're mad about that.

Guy to Watch: This is River's movie, and he shines. Tragically, he died just a few years after the movie was released, leaving behind a few films and a lot of promise.

Fun Factoid: RUNNING ON EMPTY received two Oscar nominations. River won one for Best Supporting Actor, and it also received a nod for Best Original Screenplay.

HOW THIS MOVIE HELPS

You don't have to be hiding from the law to feel like your family is isolated from the rest of the world. Maybe your folks are divorced and count on you to help out a lot. Maybe your family is from another country and expects you to play ambassador. Or it could be that you're just a tight-knit group that never does anything without one another. If this is the case, making the decision to strike out on your own could be brutal. Just look at it this way: you're not running the way Danny is—he can't look back. You can do more than look back, you can also keep coming back. They'll always be glad to see you, unless you always arrive flat broke. But that's another movie....

Rushmore

MOOD CONTROL

① ② ③
④ ⑤ ⑥
⑦ ⑧ ⑨
⑩ ⑪ ⑫

Press PLAY
if you're feeling:

1. Adventurous
2. AMBITIOUS
3. Artsy
4. Cynical
5. Depressed
6. Heartbroken
7. HOPEFUL
8. Insecure
9. Misunderstood
10. Overwhelmed
11. Playful
12. WEIRD

1998 ULTIMATE GIRL RATING: ♣ ♣ ♣

DIRECTOR: Wes Anderson
BIRTHPLACE: Hollywood Father, Indie Mother
RATED: R

STARRING: Jasón Schwartzman, Bill Murray, Olivia Williams, Brian Cox, Seymour Cassel, Mason Gamble

THE PROBLEM

You're a leader, at least in your own mind. You have great schemes, wonderful plans, and smart ideas on how to manage your legions of followers. Now all you need are the followers. Everybody thinks your plans are too big and too bold to be believed. "Why are they so afraid?" you wonder. It's like you're surrounded by people who would rather fail at life than be caught trying. Well, that's just not you. Dare to dream big, that's your motto. Any takers?

The Reel Deal: People have all sorts of goals and obsessions in life. Max Fischer's (Jason Schwartzman) obsession is to remain at his prep school, Rushmore, forever. A so-so student, Max excels in many other areas at Rushmore. He runs many clubs and is so politically astute with the teachers that he could operate the United Nations. But Max has a secret. He presents himself as fitting right in with his wealthy classmates, but in reality he is on a scholarship, and his father is a barber. While at school, Max can live out the fantasy of having a much more privileged life than the one he's been handed. He treats the principal like an underling, and finagles anything he needs for his elaborate theatrical productions. Love is the only thing that seems to confound him.

When he meets Miss Cross (Olivia Williams), a beautiful, recently widowed first-grade teacher, he is determined to make her his girlfriend. The fact that she is twice his age doesn't strike him as an obstacle. When Max discovers that Miss Cross is fond of fish, he decides to start a campaign to create a school aquarium in order to win her love. One potential donor is Herman Blume (Bill Murray), an embittered steel tycoon who has sons at Rushmore he can barely tolerate. Amused by Max, Blume becomes his ally in his effort to build the aquarium. Soon, things change dramatically (and hilariously) when Blume too falls in love with Miss Cross.

Line That Says It All: "I guess you've just got to find something you love to do and then do it for the rest of your life....For me, that's going to Rushmore."

Guy to Watch: Jason Schwartzman embodies this goofy, one-of-a-kind character.

Girl to Watch: Olivia Williams is lovely as Miss Cross. Usually, if two guys are going to fight over a hot teacher in a comedy, she looks like Pamela Anderson. This sought-after teacher is pretty, but not flashy, and her intelligence and emotional depth are just as appealing as her flawless skin.

Scene Worth the Rewind: The play Max puts on near the end of the movie is a blast. Forget what you know about school budgets for student productions and just enjoy the extravaganza.

Fun Factoid: The filmmakers were determined to find someone to play Max who seemed like a real person, not a character. They even went to prep schools in New England to find students who might be right for the part. They met Schwartzman at a Hollywood party with someone connected to the film. Just hanging out, listening to him talk, they came to the realization: "This is Max." Although RUSHMORE was his first film, Schwartzman is no stranger to Hollywood. His mother is actress Talia Shire, the sister of Francis Ford Coppola.

Movie with the Same Vibe: HAIRSPRAY. Also check out Director Anderson's other efforts: *Bottle Rocket* (1996) and *The Royal Tenenbaums* (2001).

HOW THIS MOVIE HELPS

The funny thing about natural-born leaders is that they can seem really stupid sometimes. They believe in things no one else thinks will fly, they refuse to notice obvious obstacles in their way. In real life, a kid like Max might be laughed out of existence, but in the imaginary world of RUSHMORE he's a force to be reckoned with. You could say that it's a world that has nothing to do with real life, the way characters keep making odd alliances, the way things keep getting weirder with each new plot development. Or is that just like life? At any rate, we could all use a little of Max's confidence, and we all need our own Rushmore.

Public school, private school, boarding school, military school, a school of fish—just what kind of educational waters do you swim in? We took a look at some movie schools and realized that Hollywood doesn't care how you learn, as long as you bring in the box office.

School most likely to have alien teachers:
THE FACULTY (1998)

Weirdest home-schooling situation:
THE MOSQUITO COAST (1986)

School with the biggest wardrobe budget:
CLUELESS (1995)

Scariest depiction of law school:
THE PAPER CHASE (1973)

Runner-up:
LEGALLY BLONDE (2001)

School with the most obsessive attendance tracking:
FERRIS BUELLER'S DAY OFF (1986)

School with the highest number of hypocrites:
HEATHERS (1989)

Runner Up:
PRETTY IN PINK (1986)

School administration worst at spotting undercover reporters:
NEVER BEEN KISSED (1999)

School with the most over-the-top theater department:
CONFESSIONS OF A TEENAGE DRAMA QUEEN (2004)

Runners-up:
GET OVER IT (2001), FAME (1980)

Save the Last Dance

MOOD
CONTROL

1 2 3
4 5 6
7 8 9
10 11 12

▶ Press PLAY
if you're feeling:

1 Adventurous
2 Ambitious
3 Artsy
4 Cynical
5 DEPRESSED
6 HEARTBROKEN
7 Hopeful
8 INSECURE
9 Misunderstood
10 Overwhelmed
11 Playful
12 Weird

2001 ULTIMATE GIRL RATING: 🍿🍿🍿🍿🍿

DIRECTOR: Thomas Carter
BIRTHPLACE: Mainstream Hollywood
FILE UNDER: Hip-Hop Heartache
RATED: PG-13

STARRING: Julia Stiles, Terry Kinney, Sean Patrick Thomas, Fredo Starr, Kerry Washington

THE PROBLEM

You've lost faith in your gifts and in yourself. Worst of all, the one person who truly believes in you is someone you're not supposed to be with. Says who? His world *and* your world—the whole world. Aren't we supposed to be, like, one world by now? What's up with that?

The Reel Deal: Sara (Julia Stiles) is a talented ballet dancer who was on her way to an audition at New York's famed Juilliard School when a car accident killed her mother. Fate takes her out of her cozy suburban existence and into a rat-hole on the South Side of Chicago with her father (Terry Kinney), a jazz musician she barely knows. School is no picnic either; Sara is the only white student at an all-black school, and nobody is inclined to put down the welcome mat. One classmate,

Derek (Sean Patrick Thomas), a smart kid moving from the street life toward dreams of college, finds her appealing and introduces her to the joys of hip-hop. Her balletic approach to club dancing is humorous, but Sara plows through and learns to appreciate her new neighborhood. Derek's straight-talking sister, Chenille (Kerry Washington), grows to care for her brother's white girlfriend, but doesn't like Sara's assumption that no one should mind the school's academic star hooking up with "the Brady Bunch." Will outside pressure tear Sara and Derek apart? Will she ever return to her dance career? Those answers are obvious. Will black women ever feel good about black men dating white women? Now there's a question the movie brings up wisely and skillfully, with no easy answers at the ready.

Line That Says It All: "We spend more time defending our relationship than actually having one."

Girl to Watch: Stiles is strong, but Kerry Washington's Chenille has all the best lines.

Guy to Watch: Sean Patrick Thomas. Save us a dance.

Scene Worth the Rewind: The Nutcracker princess tries club hip-hop.

Soundtrack Note: Slow, smooth R&B rules the day here, but they kick it up now and then. Overall, the soundtrack has a good mix of music for the club or the couch. "Shining Through" (Fredo Starr and Jill Scoot) and "U Know What's Up" (Donnell Jones) work well here. "Crazy" by K-Ci and JoJo and "All or Nothing" (Athena Cage) are the standouts. Pink adds some fun with her "You Make Me Sick."

Watch This One With: A mixed-race group of friends. Then get into that whole dating issue. Or not. It's your Saturday night.

Movies with the Same Vibe: 10 THINGS I HATE ABOUT YOU, CENTER STAGE, FLIRTING.

HOW THIS MOVIE HELPS

In real life, everyone doesn't just get along in the interest of true love. The reality is that people have lots of preconceived ideas of who we should care about, leaving it up to us to focus on what really matters. SAVE THE LAST DANCE shows an interracial romance in a dramatic movie setting, but every day you know that people are connecting despite differences in culture, religion, and skin tone. When did romance become a sociological state of emergency? How do we move beyond the politics of hooking up? Our leaders are always talking about bringing everyone under a "big tent." Maybe the answer is to get everyone onto a big dance floor.

Say Anything

1989 **ULTIMATE GIRL RATING:** 🍿🍿🍿🍿🍿

DIRECTOR: Cameron Crowe
BIRTHPLACE: Hollywood
Father, Cool Indie Uncle
FILE UNDER:
The Dobler Effect
RATED: PG-13

STARRING: John Cusack,
Joan Cusack, Ione Skye,
Lili Taylor, Amy Brooks,
John Mahoney

THE PROBLEM

Everybody wants something. That's great. But when you look around, it seems like everyone puts on an act to get it. Well, what if you don't have an act? What if your act is just being yourself? Is anybody going to buy that?

The Reel Deal: Diane Court (Ione Skye) and Lloyd Dobler (John Cusack) are in the same graduating class at their high school. But that's where the similarity ends. Diane is brilliant—the class valedictorian—and she's heading off to England for college, as though no university in the United States is smart enough to handle her. In addition, she's drop-dead gorgeous. Lloyd, on the other hand, is just a regular guy. With no plans to join his friends at college or follow his father into the military, Lloyd can think no further than continuing to live with his divorced sister (played by John's real-life sister Joan Cusack) and his little nephew. Sometimes Lloyd thinks he'd like to become a professional kickboxer, but you can tell that not even he believes that's a likely reality.

As graduation looms, the only thing that really grabs his attention is the idea of going out with Diane Court. His best friends (played by Lili Taylor and Amy Brooks)

singer is touching and hilarious. As good as the soundtrack is, her songs about ex-boyfriend Joe are what you'll remember.

Guy to Watch: John Cusack. He even makes shivering look sexy. How is that?

Scene Worth the Rewind: The boom-box scene—it shows what love is all about.

HOW THIS MOVIE HELPS

When you watch a film like SAY ANYTHING, you can believe that just being yourself will let you win the boy, the girl, the job, the college, the whatever. Watching Diane Court, we get to peer inside the mind of "the girl who has everything" to see just how much pressure is involved in keeping that title. It makes sense, doesn't it, that the girl who is known for being extraordinary fantasizes about being totally normal? Yet extraordinary is also a word that applies to John Cusack's character. Lloyd Dobler has stayed a fixture in the minds of many moviegoers because he never compromises, and he never believes that just being a stand-up guy isn't much of anything. We love Lloyd because he knows it's everything.

think she's way out of his league. Undeterred, he calls her house and eventually gets her to agree to go to a grad-night party with him, even though she has no idea who he is. She is charmed by his persistence; as she put it simply to a puzzled friend, "He made me laugh." A funny, touching, one-of-a-kind love story begins that's threatened by family secrets and future plans. Lloyd Dobler stands at the center of it all, with his crooked smile and an ever-present trench coat. Love him or hate him, you'll discover that—well, that you can only love him. What about Diane?

Line That Says It All: "She's a brain trapped in the body of a game show hostess."

Girl to Watch: Ione Skye as Diane. This has to be her best film. The movie is really Cusack's, but the object of his affections is, despite her beauty, so much more than an object, and Skye plays the part with all she's got. Yet we also gotta send props to Lili Taylor. Her obsessive, love-starved folk

Selena

MOOD CONTROL

1	2	3
4	5	6
7	8	9
10	11	12

▶ **Press PLAY**
if you're feeling:

1 Adventurous
2 AMBITIOUS
3 ARTSY
4 Cynical
5 Depressed
6 Heartbroken
7 Hopeful
8 Insecure
9 MISUNDERSTOOD
10 Overwhelmed
11 Playful
12 Weird

1997 | ULTIMATE GIRL RATING: 🐾🐾🐾🐾

DIRECTOR: Gregory Nava
BIRTHPLACE: Indie North America, Mexican Soul
FILE UNDER: Saga of a Shooting Star
RATED: PG

STARRING: Jennifer Lopez, Jackie Guerra, Constance Marie, Alex Meneses, Jon Seda, Edward James Olmos, Jacob Vargas

THE PROBLEM

You want to believe that miracles happen, that dreams come true. You love being a fan, admiring from afar someone who's made it and hasn't forgotten who got them there in the first place. Your own life feels far from the spotlight, and you're not even sure you want the fame. What about the price you would have to pay? Then you think about the drudgery of everyday life and imagine instead thousands of fans worshipping you. It's a million miles away, but maybe someday?

The Reel Deal: SELENA is based on a true story that could have been an after-school special but is so much more compelling than that. Selena Quintanilla (Jennifer Lopez) was a little girl with a powerful voice from Corpus Christi, Texas. Her father, Abraham (Edward James Olmos), saw young Selena's potential when she was part of the family's music act, "Selena y Los Dinos." The family played the county fair circuit, and father and daughter clashed about their sound. He wanted her to start singing in Spanish, she favored disco stars like Donna Summer. Abraham knew that good music came from the center of who you are, and Selena lived in both Mexican and American worlds. Because she loves and admires her father, Selena agrees and learns to speak Spanish as she learns Spanish-speaking songs. Soon she becomes a star of Tejana music—a style of music with Mexican roots and Eastern European musical elements. But Selena never stops loving American music as well. Neither entirely Mexican nor American in nature, Selena's band struggles at times, but her flawless command of both cultures eventually wins over fans on both sides of the border.

When Selena sings—in both Spanish and English—to a packed house at the Houston Astrodome in 1995, she knows she has become a crossover star. Tragically, an argument with a troubled employee over some missing money led to Selena's shooting death just a month after that triumphant night. She remains alive to her legions of fans, and those who continue to discover her cross-cultural talent.

Line That Says It All: "We have to be more Mexican than most Mexicans and more American than most Americans."

Girl to Watch: This early Jennifer Lopez film shows how she just glows on camera. Her resemblance to Selena is an amazing tribute.

Guy to Watch: Jon Seda is wonderful as Chris, the bandmate that becomes Selena's great love. Their romance is friendship caught on fire, a natural evolution that feels just right.

Soundtrack Note: We all know that Ms. Lopez can sing, but Selena's family wanted Selena's voice to be heard, so Jennifer lip-synched for the film. (Could *your* karaoke routine pass as real on the big screen?) If you like the mix of sounds in this movie, there are plenty of Selena CDs for sale.

Watch This One With: Your amigas who like a story that's inspiring and, of course, sad beyond measure. This film focuses much more on Selena's life than on her sudden, tragic death. Yet as you see her climb to fame, and feel how much she deserved it, it's even harder to believe that someone would casually take that all away.

HOW THIS MOVIE HELPS

SELENA is a movie that makes you think, not just about fame and fans and success but about your own mortality. We keep hearing the rumor that no one gets to stick around forever. Do we bemoan that fact, or do we use it as motivation to make our dreams come true? Maybe your dream requires learning two languages and two cultures in order to unify thousands of music-loving fans. Maybe it's not that hard. Either way, you could sit around forever and wonder how your story is going to end. People do that all the time. This movie will inspire you to get out there and make it a story worth hearing.

She's All That

MOOD CONTROL

1	2	3
4	5	6
7	8	9
10	11	12

▶ **Press PLAY if you're feeling:**

1 Adventurous
2 Ambitious
3 Artsy
4 Cynical
5 Depressed
6 HEARTBROKEN
7 HOPEFUL
8 Insecure
9 MISUNDERSTOOD
10 Overwhelmed
11 Playful
12 Weird

1999 **ULTIMATE GIRL RATING:** 🍿🍿🍿

DIRECTOR:
Robert Iscove
BIRTHPLACE:
Mainstream Hollywood
FILE UNDER:
Make Me Over
RATED: PG-13

STARRING: Freddie Prinze, Jr., Rachael Leigh Cook, Matthew Lillard, Paul Walker, Jodi Lyn O'Keefe, Kevin Pollack, Anna Paquin, Kieran Culkin, Elden Henson, Usher Raymond, Kimberly "Lil' Kim" Jones, Tim Matheson, Debbi Morgan, Alexis Arquette, Clea DuVall, Chris Owen

THE PROBLEM

"All the guys love her." Every school seems to have a girl or two who fits this description. What is it about that girl? Maybe there's some strange scent she sends out that attracts all males within a five-mile radius. Maybe she keeps a secret stash of chocolate bars in her purse and hands them out to the boys when we're not looking. Whatever. The point is that most of us aren't like that. Most of us go about our busy lives and are only occasionally lucky enough to find someone worth caring about who cares about us. We'd really like to find that person, but we're not willing to fake a whole new identity to get there. Do you want to throw up when you see girls so desperate to get a guy that they'll hide anything about themselves that he might find uncool—like their personality? Wouldn't it be great if for once you could just be your complicated, difficult, interesting self—and he would have to make all the effort?

The Reel Deal: Laney (Rachael Leigh Cook) is an artistic, self-protective girl who has been overcome with pain and anger since her mother's death many years earlier. Zack (Freddie Prinze, Jr.) is her polar opposite, at least on the surface; he's the most popular guy in school dating the de facto future prom queen. When Zack's Miss Perfect, Taylor (Jodi Lyn O'Keefe), drops him for a guy from the "Real World" television show, Zack's ego takes quite a hit.

Reeling from this disaster, Zack is determined to reclaim his reputation as the most powerful guy on campus. He brazenly bets a friend that he can take any girl in school and turn her into prom queen material. Zack's pals settle on a girl they think will be impossible to glamorize by high school standards. Laney passes by, dropping books and emanating scorn for the universe, and the bet is finalized. Zack bombards Laney with attention (beginning with a pretty funny performance art spoof), determined to win her over and change her into something she never knew she could be. Not to give away the ending, but if you've been on this planet for more than ten minutes, you know who really changes the most, where it counts.

Line That Says It All: "What is this, some kind of dork outreach program?"

Girl to Watch: Rachel Leigh Cook as Laney. One minute loving the attention of the popular kids, the next minute scorning it, she keeps evading stereotypes, just like people off the screen.

Guy to Watch: Freddie Prinze, Jr. as Zack. He drops the total jerk act early enough for you to really root for him.

Fashion to Catch: Laney's weird art getups. What are those layers?

Eye-Rolling Time: Sure, Laney has a temper and dresses weird. But her looks? I'm afraid that SHE'S ALL THAT is one of those movies where the "ugly" girl takes off her glasses and suddenly she's a goddess with clear skin and perfect curves. Oh, yeah, like that ever happens.

Watch This One With: Your artistic friends, or anyone who hates the reality show scene.

Movies with the Same Vibe: 10 THINGS I HATE ABOUT YOU, SIXTEEN CANDLES, GET OVER IT.

HOW THIS MOVIE HELPS

It's pure fantasy, of course, to think that the weird arty girl and the popular jock boy discover that they have matching inner souls. Yet as far as fantasies go, this one is pretty entertaining. There are lots of quirky throwaway lines to listen for, some good music, and other touches that help it rise above standard teen movie fare. Maybe it will even inspire you to get a guy on your own terms, keeping those glasses firmly in place.

⏸ PRESS PAUSE: Leather Jacket or Letter Jacket?: The Game That Helps You Find Your Movie Boyfriend

You'll notice that in teen movies there are only two types of potential boyfriends for the main character to choose from—the hottie jock or the hottie rebel. (Sure, there's always the nerd, but he only gets the girl in movies where he's the star attraction, and this is *your* show). How early in a movie can you tell which guy is Mr. Right (Until College)? Pretty early. Play our game and you'll see.

START HERE

You're a young, beautiful fictional character in a film all about you. (Not a bad start, huh?) At your high school, there's this guy...

If we see him early in the film, walking in slow motion, a gaggle of admirers crowding his long-limbed, confident walk down the corridor, **HE'S THE HOTTIE JOCK!**	If we don't see him for a few scenes, and when we finally do he's slouched over in his seat, chewing on a pen while staring out the window, **HE'S THE HOTTIE REBEL!**
You see him, and gaze longingly. He's nice and all, but he **BARELY KNOWS YOU EXIST.**	He notices *you* right away. **YOU JUST THINK HE'S WEIRD.**
HE'S ALREADY GOT A GIRLFRIEND, of course. She's nearly perfect. But sometimes he looks bored....	**HE DOESN'T KNOW HOW TO FLIRT,** so he just acts mean instead.
Things happen, and HE sees YOU with new eyes. **SOMEHOW, YOU EVEN GET CUTER.**	Things happen, and YOU see HIM with new eyes. **SOMEHOW, HE EVEN GETS CUTER.**
Finally, you get together! **HIS GIRLFRIEND IS ASTONISHED,** but who cares?	Finally, you get together! **YOUR FRIENDS ARE ASTONISHED,** but who cares?

TRUE LOVE REALLY *DOES* CONQUER ALL! THANKS FOR PLAYING.

Sixteen Candles

1984 **ULTIMATE GIRL RATING:**

DIRECTOR: John Hughes
BIRTHPLACE:
Mainstream U.S.A.
FILE UNDER:
Not-So-Sweet Sixteen
RATED: PG-13

STARRING: Molly Ringwald,
Anthony Michael Hall,
Michael Schoeffling,
Gedde Watanabe

THE PROBLEM

You were looking forward to being a teenager, remember? There are some days, however, when you can't imagine why you ever thought this was going to be good thing. It's like you wake up and realize, "Oh, yeah. I've got to do all *that* again." Just the thought of it—dealing with family, high school, friends—makes it a little hard to get out of bed.

The Reel Deal: Samantha Baker (Molly Ringwald) wakes up on the morning of her sixteenth birthday half expecting the world to have changed. Her family will have planned a huge celebration, nature will have kicked in overnight and given her the perfect bod of her dreams, handsome senior Jake (Michael Schoeffling) will have dumped his gorgeous girlfriend in favor of Samantha and her subtler charms. Of course, real life doesn't work this way, and as the morning wears on things spiral in a decidedly downward direction.

In the chaotic rush to prepare for her sister's wedding, Samantha's family has completely forgotten her birthday! She gives them every opportunity to remember the big day, but they're preoccupied with the visiting relatives and wedding plans and hardly notice she's in the house. She even loses her bedroom to her grandparents, who bring along a strange foreign exchange student. Jake is still far from attainable, but the freshman class's ultimate geek is thunderstruck by Samantha and determined to win her over. In this painfully funny comedy, we see Samantha's day as a string of humiliations. Lucky for her she's only a character in a movie.

Line That Says It All: "I can't believe they forgot my birthday."

Girl to Watch: This is the movie that launched the '80s love affair with Molly Ringwald. So often, girls in teen films seem like the most popular girl in school. Molly's characters always seem like someone in your homeroom—or even you.

Guy to Watch: For pure viewing pleasure, Jake is about as cute as boys get. But Anthony Michael Hall plays the geek with such conviction that you want to throw him roses—or comic books.

Scene Worth the Rewind: There are lots of good speeches in this dramatic movie, but the one from the jock is so unexpected.

Eye-Rolling Time: The Asian exchange student is *such* a stereotype. Yuck.

Watch This One With: Your girls, on somebody's sixteenth birthday.

Movies with the Same Vibe: THE BREAKFAST CLUB, PRETTY IN PINK, CAN'T HARDLY WAIT.

HOW THIS MOVIE HELPS

The social catastrophes that abound in this movie bear no resemblance to reality. Or do they? You can look at Samantha's face and think, "I feel that way all the time"—even if no one is selling your underpants. People always tell you it's your imagination when you feel self-conscious, but what if you're just one of those people that always seems to be caught in the act of feeling stupid? If we'd known life was going to be this humiliating, we would have developed an even better sense of humor. SIXTEEN CANDLES is the perfect flick to rent if you're ready to laugh at how hard it is to get through high school with your dignity intact.

Slums of Beverly Hills

MOOD CONTROL

Press PLAY
if you're feeling:

1 Adventurous
2 Ambitious
3 Artsy
4 CYNICAL
5 Depressed
6 Heartbroken
7 Hopeful
8 INSECURE
9 Misunderstood
10 Overwhelmed
11 Playful
12 WEIRD

1998 **ULTIMATE GIRL RATING:** ♣ ♣ ♣

DIRECTOR: Tamara Jenkins
BIRTHPLACE: Indie U.S.A.
FILE UNDER: Sex and the (Bad Part of the) City
RATED: R

STARRING: Natasha Lyonne, Alan Arkin, Bryna Weiss, Marisa Tomei, Charlotte Stewart, Eli Marienthal, David Krumholtz, Kevin Corrigan

THE PROBLEM

You live within spitting distance of the glamorous life, but your life is about as glamorous as a hangnail. Gee, you could make a list of everything you have to deal with that they never seem to show in the movies: a ragtag family life, how weird a sex drive is, how weird guys are about girls, how hard it is to live a normal life when every day brings you indignity. Well, where's that movie? Here's that movie.

The Reel Deal: It's 1976, and the Abromowitz family is hanging on to life in Beverly Hills by the seat of their pants. Most people think Beverly Hills is nothin' but swimming pools and movie stars, but there are some not-so-nice sections too, and this family has sneaked out of every dive apartment complex the town has to offer. Dad (Alan Arkin) can't seem to get a career going, but the kids do well at Beverly Hills High, the terrific public school that keeps

him finding new addresses in 90210, no matter what the consequences.

Daughter Vivian (Natasha Lyonne) sends the family into an uproar just by growing breasts in a short period of time. (Hey, it happens.) She feels ungainly and self-conscious, but her new figure wins the admiration of Eliot (Kevin Corrigan), a guy down the hall in their latest residence. Dealing with her budding sexuality, Beverly Hills High, and the comings and goings of all her crazy relatives is almost more than Vivian can handle. Just in time, young and wild Aunt Rita (Marisa Tomei) appears, fresh out of rehab. Rita is barely able to figure out her plans for breakfast, but in Vivian's opinion, anyone who will tell her the truth about becoming a woman is a role model worth having. Painfully real and really funny, THE SLUMS OF BEVERLY HILLS captures the unique irony in finding your sexuality just outside the Garden of Eden.

Line That Says It All: "You know, I could go to jail for this! There are laws against devirginizing a minor!"

Girl to Watch: The girls steal the show here. Natasha Lyonne is amazing in this funny, poignant real-girl role. Marisa Tomei is terrific too, as the adult we'd all like to have around—some of the time.

Scene Worth the Rewind: This movie is chock-full of crazy moments, but Vivian's bra shopping expedition—with her father, no less—is priceless. Doesn't *that* sound like fun?

Soundtrack Note: This movie could have employed all the greatest hits from the '70s. Instead, they make great use of just one huge track: Parliament's "Give up the Funk (Tear the Roof Off the Sucker)." What a song; what a beat! You will find yourself forced to give up the funk the minute this song comes on. We're not kidding. See the funk fly.

Watch This One With: All your friends in the apartment complex. The rich kids have a million movies to call their own; this one's for you.

HOW THIS MOVIE HELPS

Poor Vivian. She has a ridiculous life, but she's smart and shrewd and capable of figuring out how to make it work. You like the way she admits to some feelings that are hard to admit to, even though girls supposedly are a lot freer now than they were in 1976. Notice how we said "supposedly"? It's still not too cool to admit to being a little sex-obsessed at times. People are so worried about what is going to happen to a girl if she acts on her desires, so some girls just pretend they don't have any. But please, don't try to sell us on that one. We know that can't be true.

Some Kind of Wonderful

MOOD CONTROL

1 2 3
4 5 6
7 8 9
10 11 12

▶ Press **PLAY** if you're feeling:

1 **Adventurous**
2 **Ambitious**
3 **Artsy**
4 CYNICAL
5 **Depressed**
6 HEARTBROKEN
7 **Hopeful**
8 **Insecure**
9 MISUNDERSTOOD
10 **Overwhelmed**
11 **Playful**
12 **Weird**

1987 ULTIMATE GIRL RATING: ♣ ♣ ♣

DIRECTOR: Howard Deutch
BIRTHPLACE: Mainstream Hollywood
FILE UNDER: Three's a Crowd
RATED: PG-13

STARRING: Eric Stoltz, Mary Stuart Masterson, Lea Thompson, John Ashton, Craig Sheffer

THE PROBLEM

Unrequited love, they call it. How about daily injections of self-loathing and pain? That might be a better description. There's an old song that suggests, "If you can't be with the one you love, love the one you're with." Sounds good, but what can you do when your heart doesn't cooperate?

The Reel Deal: Eric Stoltz plays Keith, a sensitive young man who works in an auto shop when he's not going to high school. His best friend since third grade is Watts (Mary Stuart Masterson), a pretty, tomboyish girl who does a great job of alternately teasing and encouraging him. Typical of most of the kids in their rundown neighborhood, they both claim outsider status at their school.

Amanda Jones (Lea Thompson), however, is different. Her beauty and sexy glamour have enabled her to rise up out of the hood and catch the eye of the school's jet set. In most teen movies, this status would make her a complete witch, but Amanda is more interesting than that. Needless to say, most of the guys at school think she's unbelievably hot, and Keith is no exception. He's so focused on getting her to go out with him that he doesn't even notice the great girl who is already in love with him.

"It must be a drag to be a slave to the male sex drive."
"It's not just sex."
"Oh, you want to start a book club with her?"

Mary Stuart Masterson is so great in this. Her look in this movie seems pretty normal now, but it was very "punk" back in the day.

Eric Stoltz is great as a tortured artist. He looks adorably tortured. And is it just us, or is it nice to see a hunk with red hair? The red-haired guys are almost always relegated to the best-friend roles, aren't they?

This isn't as noisy as some of the movies with John Hughes' stamp on them (he wrote the screenplay). One of the small, subtle scenes that really stands out is set in the locker room. You see Watts catching a glimpse of Amanda's amazing body and know she's thinking, "Why do I even bother?"

It seems like most movie soundtracks slap on a bunch of "greatest hits" that you already own. This one offers music that might have been coming from the characters' stereos any day of the week. The character Amanda Jones was no doubt named after the classic Rolling Stones song by the same name ("Miss Amanda Jones"), and a cover of that tune is repeated throughout the film. The Jesus & Mary Chain and Pete Shelley ratchet up the cool factor, and it's a love/hate thing for many when they hear Lick the Tins' "Can't Help Falling in Love." (For us, it's love.)

Movies with the Same Vibe: PRETTY IN PINK, SAY ANYTHING, WIN A DATE WITH TAD HAMILTON.

HOW THIS MOVIE HELPS

SOME KIND OF WONDERFUL does a nice job of reminding us that dreams do come true if you're dreaming the right dream. Yet the question still remains: how do you know if you're not wasting your time? You could ask your friends, but they just might love you too much to give you an honest answer. You could just decide that if it's meant to be it will happen and get on with your life. Easier said than done, right? Too bad unrequited love doesn't come with a playbook that tells you when it's time to either push harder or give up the fight. If it did, maybe we wouldn't need so much chocolate, advice from best friends, and movies like this little gem.

Stand and Deliver

MOOD CONTROL

1	2	3
4	5	6
7	8	9
10	11	12

▶ Press PLAY
if you're feeling:

1 Adventurous
2 AMBITIOUS
3 Artsy
4 CYNICAL
5 Depressed
6 Heartbroken
7 Hopeful
8 Insecure
9 Misunderstood
10 OVERWHELMED
11 Playful
12 Weird

1988 **ULTIMATE GIRL RATING:** 🍿🍿🍿🍿🍿

DIRECTOR: Ramón Menéndez
BIRTHPLACE: Mainstream U.S.A., Indie Soul
FILE UNDER: Math Made Cool
RATED: PG

STARRING: Edward James Olmos, Estelle Harris, Virginia Paris, Mark Eliot, Ingrid Oliu, Carmen Argenziano, Lou Diamond Phillips

THE PROBLEM

You want to do something amazing with your life, but you're not one of those brilliant kids who is going to set the world on fire with your intelligence. How do you know this? Well, you don't get straight As, you think school is hard, and you see the smart kids walking around campus and know that you're not like them. It's tiring to listen to everybody focus on what you should be doing, what you should be learning. If they want you to know this stuff so bad, why don't they make it worth knowing. Then it might be nice to hear somebody say, "That girl? She's smart."

The Reel Deal: STAND AND DELIVER is based on the true story of Jaime A. Escalante, a businessman who returned to the barrios of East L.A. to teach math because he wanted to make a difference. Yeah, yeah, we've heard that before. So had the kids in East L.A. Escalante (Edward James Olmos) realizes that a traditional approach won't reach Tito (Mark Eliot), a big kid who lacks confidence, or Angel (Lou Diamond Phillips), a gang member with a soft side he can't let anyone see. The girls,

Raquel (Virginia Paris) and Lupe (Ingrid Oliu), are just amazed that anyone cares whether or not they understand math.

The next time Escalante shows up for work, he acts just this side of insane. He shouts out strange ideas, and sidles up to students and whispers things. The room grows silent. Small smiles appear. Who is this loco? Eventually, he wins his students' trust by helping both in and out of the classroom. Yet it's not enough for him that kids are showing up for math class and doing their work. He takes them on a field trip, shows them how math is used in engineering. He dreams bigger for them than they'd ever dreamt for themselves. He even gets a bunch of them to give up their summer vacation to study for the advanced placement calculus exam, a test only about 2 percent of high school students pass each year. Can waiting to see if a bunch of kids pass a math test be a nail-biting adventure? We know this sounds insane, but it is.

Line That Says It All:
"You're worried that we'll screw up big tomorrow, aren't you?"
"Tomorrow's another day. I'm worried you're going to screw up the rest of your lives."

Girl to Watch: All the girls feel like real people, ranging from sassy to shy. Escalante says some sexist things to them, just to give them a hard time. But he's totally invested in their education, and they know that.

Guy to Watch: Okay, he's not a boy; he's not even very cute. But Edward James Olmos got nominated for an Oscar for this role, and you don't need to know higher math to figure out why. He's brilliant.

Watch This One With: Your favorite teacher in mind. Raise a bowl of popcorn in a toast to the one who challenged you to think differently.

Movies with the Same Vibe: DRUMLINE, FINDING FORRESTER. Also check out *Lean on Me* (1989) and *Mr. Holland's Opus* (1995).

HOW THIS MOVIE HELPS

Maybe this isn't your year for great teachers. Still, you can remember those who have really inspired you, made you feel like more than a student, like someone who had already achieved in life. There's a lot of talk about mentoring these days, and teachers are just the obvious choice. A mentor can be anybody you pick as a role model, or just a great, older friend. Try to keep one in your back pocket at all times. Who knows? Maybe while you're feeling grateful to somebody for showing you the way, some kid is sending that same gratitude your way. They say, "What goes around, comes around." STAND AND DELIVER isn't about the math, it's about the excitement that comes with success, and knowing that somebody out there cared enough to make sure you achieved it.

St. Elmo's Fire

1985   **ULTIMATE GIRL RATING:** ♣ ♣

DIRECTOR: Joel Schumacher
BIRTHPLACE: Mainstream Hollywood
FILE UNDER: '80s Babies
RATED: R

STARRING: Emilio Estevez, Rob Lowe, Andrew McCarthy, Demi Moore, Judd Nelson, Ally Sheedy, Andie MacDowell, Mare Winningham

THE PROBLEM

You experience a special time with a group of friends, a coming together that feels like you all live in this bubble that can't be broken. Maybe it's summer camp, maybe a great conversation at a great party, maybe college. Everyone gets along, everyone understands each other, and your common language steels you for the foreign world outside your little sphere. But what if the bubble breaks? How do you live without your crew? Without them, who are you?

The Reel Deal: This much-watched drama from the '80s centers around seven friends who have recently graduated from Georgetown University. Kirby (Emilio Estevez) is obsessed with a slightly older woman (Andie MacDowell) and takes up following her wherever she goes. (These days, we'd probably call that stalking, wouldn't we?) Billy (Rob Lowe) can't get his act together to take care of his wife and baby and deal with the odd mess he's made of life. Wendy (Mare Winningham) tries hard to be the perfect little rich girl and makes choices that only please her folks. Too bad she's got a wicked crush on married, messed-up Billy. Still with us? Good. Then there's Alec (Judd Nelson) and Leslie (Ally Sheedy). They look sort of like an up-and-coming power couple, only she's feeling lost and he's feeling a lot of women that aren't Leslie. Kevin (Andrew McCarthy) is one of those depressed writer types who's on a constant search for the meaning of life. Everyone thinks he's gay, but one look at his face and you can see that he's saving himself for Leslie. Lastly, we have Jules (Demi Moore), who seems to be obsessed with money and success. Her banking job could take care of both, but she also has a problem with bad boyfriends and cocaine. See Jules. See Jules unravel fast.

All of these tortured, unhappy grads meet up at a bar called St. Elmo's to hash it out and help each other deal. Yet wounded birds can't be much help to each other—and can even add to the wounds. That's exactly what they do in this entertainingly cheesy, classic '80s hit.

Line That Says It All: "I'm going to try my life without any miracles for a while."

Girl to Watch: This was the movie that launched Demi Moore's career, and she sure looks pretty and falls apart loudly. However, we secretly like the sweet, more subtle, performance of Mare Winningham as Wendy.

Guy to Watch: It depends on your type. They're all pretty watchable, even when what they say is pretty unbelievable.

Fun Factoid: Some journalist somewhere dubbed this gang of popular '80s actors and actresses the Brat Pack. The nickname has followed them throughout their careers. How fair is that?

Soundtrack Note: The Theme from ST. ELMO'S FIRE "Man in Motion" was a monster hit for its creator, David Foster. People flocked to large arenas to hear it sung in concert, then sat there thinking, "Huh? What are these other songs? I just came to hear that one."

How You Know It's a Movie: You always know this one's a movie. It's got nothing to do with how people really talk to each other, and all their breakdowns are unnaturally picturesque. Still, it has some cute Brat Packers, some quirky, surprising moments, and lots of snappy dialogue that works well in this little cinematic bubble.

HOW THIS MOVIE HELPS

If you can deal with the swelling music and the cheese factor, this movie has some good stuff to say about how hard it is to keep the group going when real life pulls us all in different directions. Plus, there are lots of cute guys pining after women in this movie, and we like that. ST. ELMO'S FIRE tries to capture that period in your life when the decisions you make really have consequences for the future. Oh, wait a minute, that's every period in life.

Stepmom

MOOD CONTROL

1	2	3
4	5	6
7	8	9
10	11	12

▶ Press PLAY if you're feeling:

1 Adventurous
2 Ambitious
3 Artsy
4 Cynical
5 DEPRESSED
6 HEARTBROKEN
7 Hopeful
8 Insecure
9 Misunderstood
10 OVERWHELMED
11 Playful
12 Weird

1998 ULTIMATE GIRL RATING: ♣ ♣ ♣

DIRECTOR: Chris Columbus
BIRTHPLACE: Mainstream Hollywood
FILE UNDER: Fractured Family Tales
RATED: PG-13

STARRING: Julia Roberts, Susan Sarandon, Ed Harris, Jena Malone, Liam Aiken, Lynn Whitfield, Darrell Larson

THE PROBLEM

Your folks have split up and one or both have a significant other. But someone who is "significant" to one person can be a royal pain to everyone else. If you're lucky, your parents are able to make polite chitchat with each other, sometimes through gritted teeth. If you're unlucky, they're still waging a world war with you sitting in the middle, the forgotten soldier. If only all these adults could realize that, despite their differences and disillusionment, they're family. What will it take for that day to come?

The Reel Deal: STEPMOM deals with a classic problem for many teens. Mom and Dad get divorced, Dad hooks up with some younger, prettier woman, Mom wants to claw girlfriend's eyes out. In this case, the parents are Jackie Harrison (Susan Sarandon), the perfect soccer mom, and her ex, Luke (Ed Harris). Jackie and Ed are feeling still raw from a tough divorce when Luke gets hot and heavy with Isabel Kelly (Julia Roberts), a successful—and gorgeous—fashion photographer. Isabel's a genuinely nice person who is eager to make friends with Ed's kids, Anna (Jena Malone) and Ben (Liam Aiken). Young Ben is happy to spend time with her, but twelve-year-old

Anna shares her mother's fury at her dad's ability to move on. Nothing Isabel tries is good enough for either Anna or Jackie, who truly hates this woman she considers selfish and irresponsible. From Isabel's perspective, Jackie is some kind of maternal super woman, with perfectly choreographed parenting at all times, someone no one else could ever live up to. After Ben gets lost in Central Park during one of Isabel's photo shoots, Jackie is ready to declare her children entirely off limits to Isabel. Then Ed proposes to Isabel. Jackie is mortified at the thought of a woman she disdains becoming the stepmother to her children. Yet before Jackie can banish Isabel like a furious queen in a fairy tale, she realizes that she needs to give her a chance to learn how to be a mother, and soon. You see, the news at Jackie's last doctor's visit was pretty bad....

Line That Says It All: "Can parents fall out of love with their children?"

Girl to Watch: The focus is on the moms, but Jena Malone plays a confused and furious 'tween with compelling honesty.

Guy to Watch: Ed Harris as Dad. He seems like a real person, not perfect but trying to be.

How You Know It's a Movie: The tragedy is pretty drawn out, for maximum hankie effect. But admit it; you cried.

Fun Factoid: This movie was originally written by real-life stepmom Gigi Levangie—then a ton of other writers got involved. We'd like to think that the best scenes came from her personal experience.

Watch This One With: All your pals from divorced families. The fights, the indignation, the tense custody and scheduling discussions—that part's like a documentary.

HOW THIS MOVIE HELPS

It seems kind of unfair of your folks to be working through their own Shakespearean tragedy at a time when you're being thrust into one yourself, just by being a teenager. STEPMOM offers up a fantasy solution to putting an end to all that petty squabbling. Of course, no one wants cancer making an appearance in order for parents to bond. Ugh. Yet sometimes it takes an outside force to make people look up from their internal obsessions. Short of hiring a referee to show up at one of their tense porch meetings to blow a whistle, what can you do to let your folks know that if they can't learn to get along, you can't get on with your life? Hey, wait. That sounds good. How 'bout you just tell them that?

The Sure Thing

MOOD CONTROL

1	2	3
4	5	6
7	8	9
10	11	12

▶ Press **PLAY** if you're feeling:

1 ADVENTUROUS
2 Ambitious
3 Artsy
4 Cynical
5 Depressed
6 Heartbroken
7 Hopeful
8 Insecure
9 Misunderstood
10 OVERWHELMED
11 PLAYFUL
12 Weird

1985 **ULTIMATE GIRL RATING:** ♣ ♣

DIRECTOR: Rob Reiner
BIRTHPLACE:
Mainstream Hollywood
FILE UNDER:
Rule-breaking Roadtrip
RATED: PG-13

STARRING: John Cusack, Daphne Zuniga, Viveca Lindfors, Nicolette Sheridan

THE PROBLEM

You know this guy. He's almost cool. Then he acts like a complete moron and blows it. You want to believe in your heart that guys want the real thing when it comes to women, but guys like this confuse you. What if they only want the sure thing?

The Reel Deal: If you looked up the phrase "sexually frustrated" in a dictionary, you'd probably see the face of Walter "Gib" Gibson (John Cusack). Girls initially enjoy his off-the-cuff charm, but then he comes on too strong and blows it; or he doesn't come on strong enough, or something. Bottom line: nothing is happening for him with the ladies. After Alison (Daphne Zuniga) disses him at a party one night, he talks to a friend in L.A. who is having a very different college experience. The friend convinces him to come out to California during his next school break with the offer of introducing him to a gorgeous young woman who will have sex with him, no questions asked. She's what's known in the grimy world of guys as "a sure thing." Gib enthusiastically agrees, and finds a ride from the school's ride-share board. Unbeknownst to him, the uptight Alison is catching a ride in the same car, off to see her boyfriend at law school out west.

When the driver gets sick of their squabbling, they're unceremoniously dumped out of the car halfway to nowhere. Somehow, they must work together to find a way to get to Los Angeles without killing each other. (What do you mean, "Will sparks fly instead"? Oh, you've seen a movie before, haven't you?)

Line That Says It All:
"Live a little. Go to bed when you want to and not when you think you should. Eat foods that are bad for you. Talk to people whose clothes aren't color-coordinated. Make love in a hammock. Life is the ultimate experience. You have to experience life in order to write about it." "What was that part after 'hammock'?"

Girl to Watch: Daphne Zuniga as Alison. It's fun to watch this bright, logical girl surprised by her own emotions.

Guy to Watch: John Cusack is always watchable, and he gives this movie its zip.

How You Know It's a Movie: The gorgeous "sure thing" (Nicolette Sheridan) acts like some guy's virtual fantasy girl. Can you say "character created to make a point"?

Scene Worth the Rewind: The scene in the bed-and-breakfast is so romantic and charming. It gives you hope for the Gibs of the world.

Watch This One With: Your classic movie buffs. Then rent *It Happened One Night* (1934), a similar tale from back in the day, and just as funny and fun to watch.

HOW THIS MOVIE HELPS

Just when you decide that all guys are total sex fiends with "only one thing on their mind," as grandmas like to say, a guy surprises you. Maybe he wants someone to really talk to, to have adventures with, to get to know. Maybe he'll be like the guy in this film, someone who is trying to figure out how to be a man instead of a moron. Maybe if we stop focusing on "what guys want" and "what girls want" we can see each other as people. Who wouldn't want that?

10 Things I Hate About You

MOOD CONTROL

1 2 3
4 5 6
7 8 9
10 11 12

▶ Press PLAY
if you're feeling:

1 Adventurous
2 Ambitious
3 Artsy
4 CYNICAL
5 Depressed
6 Heartbroken
7 Hopeful
8 Insecure
9 MISUNDERSTOOD
10 Overwhelmed
11 PLAYFUL
12 Weird

1999 | **ULTIMATE GIRL RATING:** 🍿🍿🍿🍿🍿

DIRECTOR: Gil Junger
BIRTHPLACE: Mainstream Hollywood
FILE UNDER: There's a Thin Line Between Love and Hate
RATED: PG-13

STARRING: Heath Ledger, Julia Stiles, Joseph Gordon-Levitt, Larisa Oleynik, David Krumholtz, Andrew Keegan, Susan May Pratt, Gabrielle Union, Larry Miller, Daryl Mitchell, Allison Janney, David Leisure

THE PROBLEM

In the world of romance, it seems as though there are a few people that everyone is lined up for, and a few people you couldn't give away. You are one of those people. You're not that difficult, you're not that complicated—well, yeah, you are. Still, you imagine that the right person will see through all that and accept you for the difficult, complicated, wonderful person that you are. Where is that person, anyway? Held up in traffic, or what?

The Reel Deal: Seattle's Padua High contains two Stratford sisters, and they're as different as—well, as most sisters are. Bianca (Larisa Oleynik) is gorgeous and sunny, the kind of girl that makes boys line up and take a number. In fact, two guys are dying to take her to the prom, but her father has decided that she can't date until her older sister, Kat (Julia Stiles), is dating as well. (That way, the screenwriters can have their story mimic

Guy to Watch: Heath Ledger gives the "bad boy" role a nice, low-key vibe.

Scene Worth the Rewind: A romantic gesture involving a marching band. Too cute.

Watch This One With: Your sassiest friends. Listen to Kat's comebacks and steal them for future use.

Movies with the Same Vibe: SHE'S ALL THAT, PRETTY IN PINK, THE SURE THING. Also check out *You've Got Mail* (1998): Tom hanks and Meg Ryan flirt over e-mail but fight in person.

Shakespeare's *The Taming of the Shrew*.) The problem is that no guy in his right mind would go near Katarina Stratford. She's cute and clever, but has this tendency to eat people for breakfast. So Bianca's guys hatch a plot to convince Patrick (Heath Ledger), a sort of good-looking social outcast himself, to ask Kat to the prom for $300. If you don't know what romance and complications ensue from here, then you've never been to a movie before. The plot is not the thing here, the players are. Methinks no Shakespearean actor has had as much fun as Stiles and Ledger do in this snappy film.

Line That Says It All:
"People perceive you as somewhat…"
"Tempestuous?"
"'Heinous Bitch' is the term used most often."

Girl to Watch: Julia Stiles does justice to a girl who has to seem both likeable and like a pain in the butt.

HOW THIS MOVIE HELPS

This fantasy might be encouraging on those days when you look around your school and think that if Perky Boy Toy is the only acceptable route, you'd rather just stay off the romance road. But wait. What about that guy in the corner, the one no one ever thinks about, the one who would never approach a girl in a million years? Could he be hiding hilarious impressions of his grandmother, amazing artistic abilities, the best CD collection ever? Would he even know what to do with a girlfriend if he had one? You could, you know, go find out. Just don't play Perky Boy Toy; instead, give him a hard time. The right guy? He'll like that.

Thirteen

MOOD CONTROL

1	2	3
4	5	6
7	8	9
10	11	12

▶ Press PLAY if you're feeling:

1 Adventurous
2 Ambitious
3 Artsy
4 CYNICAL
5 Depressed
6 Heartbroken
7 Hopeful
8 INSECURE
9 Misunderstood
10 OVERWHELMED
11 Playful
12 Weird

2003   **ULTIMATE GIRL RATING:** ♣ ♣ ♣ ♣

DIRECTOR: Catherine Hardwicke
BIRTHPLACE: Indie U.S.A.
FILE UNDER: Lost in Transition
RATED: R (for many reasons)

STARRING: Evan Rachel Wood, Holly Hunter, Nikki Reed, Vanessa Anne Hudgens, Brady Corbet, Ulysses Estrada, Kip Pardue, Jeremy Sisto, Deborah Unger

THE PROBLEM

Let's see: drug use, self-mutilation, casual sex to gain popularity, peer pressure, divorce, financial worries, depression, desire to feel powerfully sexy, desire to be heard, desire to be loved. Got angst?

The Reel Deal: The movie starts with a bang: two young teenage girls, high on inhalants, playing a brutal game of "Hit me as hard as you can; I can't feel anything." In the next scene, we travel back four months to find out why the central character, Tracy (Evan Rachel Wood), a pretty, wholesome teen given to sleeping with stuffed animals and writing poetry, flipped almost overnight into her complete opposite—a poster child for self-destructive teen rebellion.

Tracy first spots her friend Evie (Nikki Reed) at the beginning of seventh grade, when Evie and her girls traipse across campus in revealing black tops and low-rider jeans, leaving a trail of drooling boys in their wake. Tracy disses the gang to her friends, yet all it takes is one insult from Evie to shake Tracy to her core. Soon she does anything she can to prove her worthiness to the Queen of the Hotties, including all manner of drug use, sex with a guy so

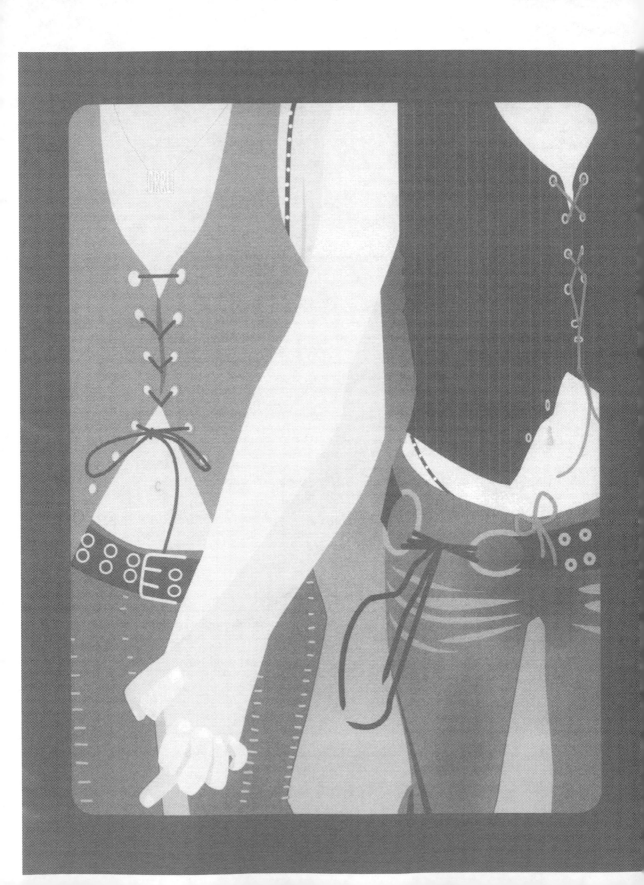

that he'll like her, and arm-slashing with increasingly sharp implements. Ouch.

Some dismiss THIRTEEN as a hysterical cautionary tale. But others see it as an absorbing character study of one girl's painful struggle to find acceptance and love.

Line That Says It All: "You don't understand. It's different this time. She's starting to scare me."

Girl to Watch: Evan Rachel Wood as Tracy and Holly Hunter as her mother both deserve the huge amount of praise they received for these riveting performances.

Scene Worth the Rewind: Which of the twenty harrowing scenes would *you* like to revisit? We'll take Tracy's breakdown in the kitchen; that moment is so real.

Watch This One With: You're going to want to watch it with your friends, but your mom (if she's smart) will want you to watch it with her.

Movies with the Same Vibe: OUR SONG.

About the Rating: There was a lot of talk when this film came out about just what audience it was geared toward. We think it's a fine film for older teenagers, but not at all right for younger teens, even though the main characters are supposed to be thirteen. Some movies are just better seen at a time in your life when you have some distance and perspective on things, and this is one of

them. If you're thirteen and living this life, THIRTEEN will just seem cool to you (kinda missing the point there). If you're that age and much more wholesome, you'll just be grossed out by Tracy's behavior (that could kind of happen at any age).

HOW THIS MOVIE HELPS

Girls who are experiencing or have recently experienced this level of tough stuff might appreciate seeing a fairly honest portrayal of their life. Self-hatred and the inability to handle horrible feelings can lead girls to literally and figuratively cut themselves up, hoping to shed the skin that houses their current, pathetic being. Yet the essence of who we are is too individualistic and extraordinary to die without a fight. As much as we're willing to shuck our old personality to fit in, to matter to others, there's part of ourselves that won't be left behind. That part, the part that doesn't want to grow up, is sometimes the very part that helps us survive the war inside.

13 Going on 30

MOOD CONTROL

1 2 3
4 5 6
7 8 9
10 11 12

▶ Press **PLAY** if you're feeling:

1 ADVENTUROUS
2 Ambitious
3 Artsy
4 Cynical
5 Depressed
6 Heartbroken
7 Hopeful
8 INSECURE
9 Misunderstood
10 Overwhelmed
11 PLAYFUL
12 Weird

2004 ULTIMATE GIRL RATING:

DIRECTOR: Gary Winick
BIRTHPLACE: Mainstream Hollywood
FILE UNDER: Little BIG Girl
RATING: PG-13

STARRING: Jennifer Garner, Mark Ruffalo, Judy Greer, Christa B. Allen, Andy Serkis, Kathy Baker, Phil Reeves, Alex Black, Alexandra Kyle, Sean Marquette, Renee Olstead

THE PROBLEM   You flip through magazines, seeing the woman you want to be someday. She's glamorous, she's a free spirit, and her job is as cool as her clothes. Meanwhile, you're stuck in the present, in a life that's nothing like that perfect world of beauty and achievement. How do you get from Life Sucks to Life Is Sweet? It's not that you want to lose your soul. You just want that gorgeous boyfriend and those amazing shoes. What's wrong with that?

The Reel Deal: Jenna Rink (first Christa B. Allen, then Jennifer Garner) is a 13-year-old saddled with braces and a nerdy taste in clothes, music, and pin-up idols. She's the butt of cruel jokes by the Six Chicks, a half-dozen beautiful monsters who float through the hallways like mean girls on parade. Her best friend is chubby, brilliant Matt (Mark Ruffalo), who she loves with all her heart but is too insecure to recognize and accept his way-beyond-friendship feelings. All she wants is to be the Seventh Chick, date the blond god of that social circle, and grow up to be a glamour queen like the ones she sighs over in *Poise* magazine.

Quicker than you can say "Extreme Makeover," Jenna wakes up and discovers that she now has that life: living in a gorgeous apartment, working at *Poise*, and dating a hunky sports star. The only problem is that she only looks like a 30-year-old Jenna—inside she's a giddy, alarmed 13-year-old who realizes that somehow she's been magically transported into her future. Her former enemies are now her friends, her former insecurities banished by a closet full of designer clothes and the body of her dreams. Yet, still feeling 13, Jenna goes off to search for Matt, the boy she left behind in search of this new life. Matt has transformed nicely himself, but has long ago put his past—including his once all-consuming crush on Jenna—far behind him.

Line That Says It All:
"Jenna, you can't just turn turn back time."
"Why not?"

Girl to Watch: Jennifer Garner. Fans of her hit show *Alias* might be surprised at what a lovable goofball Garner can be.

Guy to Watch: Mark Ruffalo makes a wonderful Matt. We love how he doesn't have a huge reaction to suddenly seeing Jenna again—why should he? His pain over losing her is long gone.

Scene Worth the Rewind: There's a promotional party for *Poise* that's not going very well. Then Jenna has the DJ cue up Michael Jackson's "Thriller."

Movie to Watch With: Your big sister, your younger aunt, your Mom.

Movies with the Same Vibe: FREAKY FRIDAY, PRINCESS DIARIES. Also check out *Big* (1988), which shows Tom Hanks as 13 going on 30 in a very similar fashion.

HOW THIS MOVIE HELPS

What are you willing to leave behind to make your dreams come true? There's nothing wrong with wanting to improve yourself, and achieve a far-off goal. Yet what would happen, 13 GOING ON 30 seems to suggest, if right now we looked around at our life, at ourselves, and decided that things were okay? That we were okay? What would happen? Maybe there's a new freedom we'd feel. Maybe there's even someone we need to look at more closely.

Titanic

1997 **ULTIMATE GIRL RATING:** ♣ ♣ ♣

DIRECTOR: James Cameron
BIRTHPLACE: Mainstream Hollywood
FILE UNDER: Perfect Love, Capsized
RATED: PG-13

STARRING: Leonardo DiCaprio, Kate Winslet, Billy Zane, Kathy Bates, Bill Paxton, Gloria Stuart, Frances Fisher, Bernard Hill

THE PROBLEM

You read about it in books, of course, the one person that you'll meet who will make it all seem worthwhile. Too bad that the relationships you see in real life seem to be about people making deals with each other and growing old together out of habit. Where is the passion? Where is the excitement? Maybe all the great loves happened in the past. Well, if history books were anything like this story, maybe you'd study harder.

The Reel Deal: Rose (Kate Winslet) is an old woman (played by Gloria Stuart) when she sees a television show about treasures brought up from the *Titanic*, the famous "unsinkable" ocean liner that hit an iceberg and sank in 1912, killing more than 1,500 passengers. She notices a charcoal portrait among the other items and contacts explorer Brock Lovett (Bill Paxton) to tell him that she's the woman in the picture, and that it was drawn by her great love, Jack Dawson.

The movie takes us back to that fateful voyage, showing thousands of passengers celebrating their luck to be crossing the seas in the grandest ship that ever left England. Rose is in the upper-class accommodations, accompanied by her mother (Frances Fisher) and horrid fiancé (Billy Zane), a man young

Rose feels forced into marrying. Jack (Leonardo DiCaprio) won a seat on the ship in a poker game, and feels as light about his prospects as Rose feels weighted down by hers. They meet when he keeps her from throwing herself overboard, and Rose warms to him fairly quickly. Rose's irate fiancé doesn't enjoy being thrown over for a lower class artist and promptly frames Jack in a jewelry theft. Tensions are already high when the great ship hits an iceberg, putting all on board in peril. You might think that the romantic triangle would take a backseat when a disaster of this magnitude occurs. Yet romance stays the course, making for a gripping finale to this modern-day classic.

We know you'll stay riveted to the fortunes of Jack and Rose. Yet note also the eerie quality of a ship slowly sinking under the weight of water—and its own grandiosity. Why do we say that? Well, those of you with true Titanic fever have learned that there weren't enough safety precautions taken to ensure the safe rescue of all aboard. That's how convinced the ship builders were that nothing could sink the boat. Since the TITANIC first came out, we've had to learn a lot about preparing for the worst. Yet as Jack and Rose's story clearly suggests, life is also about hoping—and working toward—the best.

Line That Says It All:
"I know what you must be thinking. "Poor little rich girl, what does she know about misery?"

"No, no, that's not what I was thinking. What I was thinking was, what could've happened to this girl to make her feel she had no way out?"

Girl to Watch: Kate Winslet is luminous.

Guy to Watch: Leonardo DiCaprio. Teenage girls flocked to this movie when it was released in theaters, and later bought it on video and watched it over and over. We're pretty sure it wasn't for the ocean view.

Watch This One With: Anyone who loves a good romantic movie. Pass that box of Kleenex.

Movies with the Same Vibe: Find a copy of *The Poseidon Adventure* (1972). It's very '70s, an era when disaster movies ruled the multiplex. It will look awfully dated now, but it's still a good ride.

Fun Factoid: This movie won Oscars for Best Picture and Best Director in 1998, and got nominated for many other awards. We guess people liked it.

HOW THIS MOVIE HELPS

Maybe it's easy to have an idealized relationship when you're trapped on a boat in the middle of the ocean, being attacked by man and nature. The massive popularity of TITANIC shows us that we want life to be more than an accumulation of the day's duties and routines. We want it to be a grand adventure. Maybe by watching this one we feel like a little of that adventure will rub off on us. When it comes to love, nobody wants to capsize—but it would be nice to hear the ocean crashing, wouldn't it?

Uptown Girls

2003 **ULTIMATE GIRL RATING:**

DIRECTOR: Boaz Yakin
BIRTHPLACE:
Mainstream Hollywood
FILE UNDER: Au What a Pair
RATED: PG-13

STARRING: Brittany Murphy,
Dakota Fanning, Marley
Shelton, Donald Faison,
Jesse Spencer, Austin
Pendleton, Heather Locklear

MOOD CONTROL

1 2 3
4 5 6
7 8 9
10 11 12

▶ Press PLAY
if you're feeling:

1 Adventurous
2 Ambitious
3 Artsy
4 Cynical
5 Depressed
6 HEARTBROKEN
7 Hopeful
8 Insecure
9 Misunderstood
10 OVERWHELMED
11 PLAYFUL
12 Weird

THE PROBLEM

You know it's time to grow up, but adulthood just never seemed that appealing. Now that you're almost there, it looks even worse. It's hard to see the benefits of getting up early and being someplace just so you can pay some bills you're used to having mom and dad foot anyway. What's the big reward? Pantyhose? What's going to make taking on all that responsibility worthwhile? Until they present a better argument for adulthood, you're not sure you want to buy.

The Reel Deal: Brittany Murphy plays Molly Gunn. She's cute and rich with a cool, rock-star dad—too bad he died in an accident along with her mother years ago. Molly lives the way you'd expect someone to live who has tons of money and no guidance—her life is a blur of parties, shopping, unmade beds, and unopened mail. Just after her twenty-second-birthday bash,

the lights go out on Molly's privileged existence. When her prim best friend, Ingrid (Marley Shelton), finally gets that mail opened, we learn that all of Molly's money is off somewhere with a thieving accountant.

With no money and no skills, destitute Molly is hardly ripe for employment. Eventually, her friend Huey (Donald Faison), a music talent scout, finds her a job as a nanny for his boss (Heather Locklear), a glamorous record company executive whose husband is in a coma and who has no interest in her eight-year-old daughter, Ray (Dakota Fanning). Molly is a horrible nanny at first. With her kooky, klutzy ways she's far less competent at life than the perennially tense and hyper-organized Ray. Ray is hard to love, yet Molly sees her as a kindred spirit, a poor little rich girl who has had to grow up on other people's timetables. Molly campaigns to get Ray to loosen up, while Molly's friends work to get her to take charge of her life. Oh, and there's this guy…

Line That Says It All:
"Grown-ups never stay friends with kids."
"I don't see any grown-ups here."

Girl to Watch: Brittany is bubbly, but young Dakota Fanning is a true actress.

Guy to Watch: Jesse Spencer's Neal is cute, but the romance between Neal and Molly is the weakest part of the film.

How You Know It's a Movie: This seems like one of those films where lots of people contributed lots of ideas. Maybe a few too many. It's not a very cohesive story, but parts of it are delightful.

Fashion Alert: Molly Gunn has some fun, ethereal, rocker-girl getups. Don't even think about what they must have cost her.

Watch This One With: Your fellow babysitters or nannies.

Movies with the Same Vibe: ADVENTURES IN BABYSITTING, CRAZY/BEAUTIFUL, HOW TO DEAL.

HOW THIS MOVIE HELPS

Watching hapless Molly reassure you that there's someone even more childish than you in the world is fun. Okay, so she's fictional—we'll take our wins where we can get them. It's nice to see her find a way to support herself without denying her playful, quirky persona. If growing up meant leaving your personality back in the toy chest, who would ever do it? UPTOWN GIRLS is a fairytale of sorts, but under all the stardust it delivers a very sweet reminder that sometimes the only way out is up, and that maturity *is* sometimes all that it's cracked up to be.

Valley Girl

MOOD CONTROL

1	2	3
4	5	6
7	8	9
10	11	12

▶ Press PLAY
if you're feeling:

1 ADVENTUROUS
2 Ambitious
3 Artsy
4 CYNICAL
5 Depressed
6 HEARTBROKEN
7 Hopeful
8 Insecure
9 Misunderstood
10 Overwhelmed
11 Playful
12 Weird

1983 **ULTIMATE GIRL RATING:** ♣ ♣ ♣

DIRECTOR: Martha Coolidge
BIRTHPLACE: Mainstream Hollywood
FILE UNDER: Romeo and Juliet Surf the New Wave
RATED: R

STARRING: Nicolas Cage, Deborah Foreman, Elizabeth Daily, Michael Bowen, Cameron Dye, Heidi Holicker

THE PROBLEM You don't like who you're supposed to like. You're not one of those people who wants to stick out, who wants to be seen with the kind of guy that attracts lots of attention and makes you look like a crazy rebel. You tend to go for the kind of guy that everyone likes, the kind that fits in at your parties. So what should you do with your attraction to Mr. Couldn't-Fit-in-if-He-Tried?

The Reel Deal: Julie (Deborah Foreman) is a typical San Fernando Valley girl in '80s California. She's all about big hair, nice nails, and she has a way of talking with her friends that sounds like she's the keynote speaker at an airhead convention. Julie's not an airhead herself, so when she and her handsome-but-annoying boyfriend break up, she finds herself at one of their same old parties, wondering what the point of it all is. The point arrives in the form of Randy (Nicolas Cage) and Fred (Cameron Dye), two punk rockers who look like fish out of water. Randy locks eyes with Julie and decides that she's pretty great, even with the Miss Priss background. He convinces her to ditch the party with him, and before you know it they're falling in love against the background of the punk scene in Los Angeles. It's entertaining to watch Julie and her friend try to make sense of a scene where people dress in ripped and mismatched clothes, and jump around like fish trying to get out of a barrel. Julie thinks Randy is wonderful, but when her friends give her the whole "It's him or it's us" routine, she thinks she may just have to head back to the Valley.

Line That Says It All: "He's, like, totally trippendicular!"

Girl to Watch: Deborah Foreman is charming.

Guy to Watch: It's Nicolas Cage's movie. He smolders as easily as other people breathe. You can picture him jumping into a swimming pool and evaporating all the water with his white-hot intensity. Even in a light romantic comedy, he burns and yearns like nobody's business. Excuse us. We have to go lie down now.

Soundtrack Note: The L.A. new wave scene looks less rough-and-tumble than it was in real life, but the music is authentic. The Plimsouls, a terrific L.A. band from that time, play in one of the club scenes. Their "Million Miles Away" became a big hit after this film. Other big hits featured here are "Melt With You" by Modern English and "Love My Way" by the Psychedelic Furs. Then there's "Johnny Are You Queer" by Josie Cotton, a matter-of-fact song about a girl trying to figure out if the guy she likes is gay. That was considered pretty outrageous subject matter back in 1983.

Watch This One With: Your '80s-obsessed friends.

Movies with the Same Vibe: PRETTY IN PINK, EMPIRE RECORDS, SAY ANYTHING. Also check out *Moonstruck* (1987), which features an older but still smoldering Cage (this time paired with Cher).

HOW THIS MOVIE HELPS

VALLEY GIRL mainly assists you in perfecting your Val Speak before the next big '80s theme party. Yet this surprisingly clever romance, inspired by the Valley girl subculture during its fifteen minutes of fame, reminds us that love sometimes pops up in a form we weren't expecting. If the guy is a jerk, assume your interest in him is just some kind of bored rebel yell. If he's a great guy like Randy, consider the fact that even though your friends may be screaming "makeover," it might be your choice of buds that needs an overhaul instead.

The Wedding Singer

MOOD CONTROL

1 2 3
4 5 6
7 8 9
10 11 12

▶ Press PLAY
if you're feeling:

1 Adventurous
2 Ambitious
3 Artsy
4 Cynical
5 Depressed
6 HEARTBROKEN
7 Hopeful
8 INSECURE
9 Misunderstood
10 Overwhelmed
11 PLAYFUL
12 Weird

1998 ULTIMATE GIRL RATING: 🐾 🐾 🐾

DIRECTOR: Frank Coraci
BIRTHPLACE: Mainstream Hollywood
FILE UNDER: See Adam Sing
RATED: PG-13

STARRING: Adam Sandler, Drew Barrymore, Christine Taylor, Allen Covert, Matthew Glave, Ellen Albertini Dow, Angela Featherstone

THE PROBLEM

Do nice guys really finish last, or do they just say that to get girls? You do see some pretty great people all alone, and some real jerks who have to force their legions of admirers to get in line and take a number. Are girls trained to be charmed by snakes, or do we sometimes have trouble seeing the snake through the grass? Maybe what we need are snake charmers. Or wedding singers.

The Reel Deal: Robbie (Adam Sandler) has long ago relinquished his dreams of being a big rock star and enjoys a busy, fun career as a singer at weddings and bar mitzvahs. He is shocked, therefore, when his fiancée, Linda (Angela Featherstone), leaves him right before their wedding for exactly that reason—his complacency.

Grief-stricken and furious, he bypasses rude and goes straight to insane at his next gig. Julia Sullivan (Drew Barrymore), a pretty, kind waitperson who works at the same banquet hall, befriends Robbie. She tries to distract him by getting him to help plan her wedding to Glenn (Matthew Glave), her wealthy, smarmy fiancé. Robbie realizes that Glenn is a cheating jerk and that he, himself, is in love with Julia. But what can he do-about it? He's just a wedding singer, and recent history has convinced him that that's just not good enough.

You're probably a ways away from worrying about caterers and in-laws (and maybe those obsessions will never make your list). Still, weddings continue to be a box-office draw both for those who crave the big ring and those who could care less. Why? Weddings tell much more than a love story—they're about family, the coming together of different cultures, and how one little decision changes your life in a flash.

Betsey's Wedding (1990)

Alan Alda and Molly Ringwald star in this tale of pre-wedding craziness, which reenforces the viewpoint that what matters most is the guy, not the gown. You want everything just so? Fuhgedaboutit.

My Best Friend's Wedding (1997)

Julia Roberts plays a cantankerous character in this comedy about a woman who suddenly desires her best guy pal just because he's found someone fabulous to marry.

True Love (1989)

This little-known indie film gives an honest portrayal of Italian-American love in the Bronx. As the wedding day grows near, our bride begins to ask herself questions: "Sure, he's gorgeous and devoted, but is he right for me...forever?"

My Big Fat Greek Wedding (2002)

It's the little movie that could—and did. It has more heart than plot, but who cares? MBFGW is the classic American love story: love in the melting pot.

The Wedding Planner (2001)

Unless you alphabetize your old homework papers for fun, J Lo's job will look like a nightmare. The girl herself, however, looks fabulous in this fun romantic comedy.

The Wedding Banquet (1993)

Director Ang Lee first came to prominence with this great movie about a successful, gay Taiwanese-American guy who feels compelled to get married to please his family.

Monsoon Wedding (2002)

This fantastic Indian film by female director Mira Nair features a Punjabi family putting on a wedding far too elaborate for their budget. Meanwhile, the bride is having doubts, and who wouldn't? She only met the guy three weeks ago.

Four Weddings and a Funeral (1994)

Befuddled Hugh Grant and glamorous Andie MacDowell keep meeting up at big events, but the timing is all wrong for them to have a big event of their own.

Fashion to Catch: Everyone is doing the '80s thing, big time. Glenn is very *Miami Vice*: the hair and shoulders get big at night. It's an exaggeration of what went on at the time, but it makes for great visuals.

Soundtrack Note: This soundtrack has a little bit of everything that was popular during that time period in new wave and rock, from the Smiths to The Police to Culture Club. It's not a seamless listen, but the soundtrack might be fun to pick up if you love the movie.

Watch This One With: Your friends who have worked catering jobs with you. At last, a movie about the people *behind* the big event.

Line That Says It All: "Hey, buddy, I'm not paying you to share your thoughts on life, I'm paying you to sing!"

Girl to Watch: Drew Barrymore has great fun with Julia.

Guy to Watch: Sandler is generally low-key and almost boy scout–like in this sweet comedy. Well, except when he goes psychotic.

Scene Worth the Rewind: Robbie's public crack-up after his breakup. It's wrong to laugh when someone's wedding is going down in flames. You just can't help it, though.

HOW THIS MOVIE HELPS

It's refreshing to see a grown man (if we can call Adam Sandler a grown man) really fall apart over the loss of a relationship. It seems like most guys act like nothing even happened when they're dumped. But we know that's not how they really feel—look at all the songs written about dealing with a broken heart. Who writes those songs? Guys, mostly. Maybe we don't want to end up with a total crybaby, but a guy who is willing to show some emotion is pretty cool, even with the scary '80s haircut.

Whale Rider

MOOD CONTROL

I	2	3
4	5	6
7	8	9
10	11	12

▶ **Press PLAY**
if you're feeling:

1. ADVENTUROUS
2. Ambitious
3. Artsy
4. Cynical
5. Depressed
6. Heartbroken
7. HOPEFUL
8. Insecure
9. MISUNDERSTOOD
10. Overwhelmed
11. Playful
12. Weird

2002   ULTIMATE GIRL RATING: 🍿 🍿 🍿 🍿 🍿

DIRECTOR: Niki Caro
BIRTHPLACE: New Zealand
FILE UNDER:
Amazing Slice of Pai
RATED: PG-13

STARRING: Keisha Castle-Hughes, Rawiri Paratene, Vicky Haughton, Cliff Curtis, Grant Roa, Mana Taumaunu, Rachel House

THE PROBLEM

You live in a world where you always feel some kind of stigma about being a girl. Maybe your folks wanted you to be a son, or maybe you're drawn to things boys like to do but live in a community where that just isn't okay. Whatever. The point is that you can't imagine how to convince the people in your life that girls can do anything boys can do. Some people think the battle for women's rights has long been won. We know better, don't we?

The Reel Deal: Pai (Keisha Castle-Hughes) is literally born into a traumatic situation. A baby boy was expected to arrive and emerge as the new leader of the Maori tribe in their small New Zealand village. Instead her mother and twin brother died just as she emerged from the womb. It is the belief among Pai's people that their tribe dates back more than a thousand years to an ancestor named Paikea, who escaped drowning by riding back to shore on the back of a whale. His descendents have always been first-born sons, yet Pai's brother's death seems to have ended the ancient line. Her survival at birth is seen as a disappointment to all but her loving grandmother. Even Pai's grieving father flees New Zealand for the life of an artist in Europe.

Raised by her grandparents, Pai grows into a strong and adventurous girl who's determined to become the next chief despite her gender. Her grandfather grows to love

Rawiri Paratene as Pai's grandfather, Koro. He's so tough on Pai that you want to hate him, but he's just hopelessly old school. You root for him to get a clue in time.

The whale of a finale.

The incredible costumes the kids wear during their school performances. Maybe everyone would look forward to assemblies a lot more if cool warrior costumes were involved.

Your seriously Green party, save-the-whale friends, or anyone who feels their family is hopelessly sexist.

her, but never shakes the belief that his way of life is crumbling, and no girl, even one with chieftain lineage in her blood, can save it. Although Pai realizes that she has the courage and passion to be the next leader of her tribe, there's no way her stubborn grandfather will ever consider training a girl in the ways of a warrior. Pai's persistence is the centerpiece of this amazing film, and you'll gasp at the lengths she'll go to prove she has the stuff.

"She's of no use to me."

Keisha Castle-Hughes as Pai. An incredible performance, subtle yet magnetic. The 2003 Oscars were filled with stunning surprises, and Castle-Hughes' out-of-the-blue Oscar nomination was one of them. She didn't win, but we did see her get to meet Johnny Depp, and it looked like that was more than worth it.

HOW THIS MOVIE HELPS

Despite the film's terrific reviews, it didn't stay in the theaters long enough for most people to catch it. Castle-Hughes' Oscar nomination encouraged video and DVD rentals of the movie, though, and we're glad about that. This haunting, beautiful film is one of the more inspiring movies for girls we've found. Pai's life is tough from the minute she's born, but she stays so focused on her destiny. Here's the bottom line: if Pai can buck centuries of tradition, you can too. She offers a cool lesson on how rebellion can be quiet and still totally effective. Give it a shot.

What a Girl Wants

MOOD CONTROL

1	2	3
4	5	6
7	8	9
10	11	12

▶ Press PLAY if you're feeling:

1 ADVENTUROUS
2 Ambitious
3 Artsy
4 Cynical
5 Depressed
6 Heartbroken
7 HOPEFUL
8 Insecure
9 Misunderstood
10 Overwhelmed
11 PLAYFUL
12 Weird

2003   **ULTIMATE GIRL RATING:** 🧩🧩

DIRECTOR: Dennie Gordon
BIRTHPLACE: Mainstream Hollywood
FILE UNDER: Father/Daughter Fantasy
RATED: PG

STARRING: Amanda Bynes, Colin Firth, Kelly Preston, Eileen Atkins, Anna Chancellor, Jonathan Pryce, Christina Cole, Oliver James

THE PROBLEM You don't know who your dad is, or you barely see him, or he's just not a big part of your life. You hear friends complain about their demanding or overly protective fathers and think they should get a real problem. What would it be like to suddenly discover that your real father is waiting to become your best friend?

The Reel Deal: This fun little film starring Amanda Bynes begins in San Francisco, where her character, Daphne Reynolds, is having her usual birthday crisis. Every year she thinks about the man who helped bring her into the world, some guy who lives far away and who her mom, Libby (Kelly Preston), doesn't really talk about. She's happy with her mom and their funky, San Francisco lifestyle, but would love to get to know her father. Finally, she gets more details about who he is from her mother and hops a plane to England to meet him.

Dad turns out to be Henry Dashwood (Colin Firth), a handsome politician from a prominent British family who met Daphne's mom on a Mideast sojourn in his youth. Daphne works her way onto his estate and shocks Henry with the news that he's a father. Apparently, Libby left him suddenly years ago and he had no idea that she was pregnant. Henry and Daphne get to know each other, but her wild, American spirit looks like a liability in his political campaign. She's also a major threat to his prim fiancée, Glynnis (Anna Chancellor), and her jealous daughter, Clarissa (Christina Cole). A cute guy (Oliver James), a great new dad, and fun in jolly old England make the mandatory Princess Diana makeover bearable for Daphne. But will it work?

Line That Says It All: "Why are you trying so hard to fit in when you are born to stand out?"

Girl to Watch: Amanda Bynes as the irrepressible Daphne.

Guy to Watch: Oliver James as Ian is pretty great. Older viewers will slurp up Colin Firth.

Scene Worth the Rewind: Dad and Daphne go shopping. The perfect fantasy montage for every teenage girl who's ever wondered what it would be like to have a dad who was like a friend...a really smoking-hot British friend. (Oh, sorry. Forgot we were talking about your father for a second.)

Fashion to Catch: Daphne gets to be gorgeous at the coming-out balls. For entertainment value, catch her dad trying on clothes from earlier days.

Watch This One With: The kids you babysit.

Movies with the Same Vibe: THE PRINCESS DIARIES, THE LIZZIE MCGUIRE MOVIE. Also check out *The Prince and Me* (2004), a contemporary Cinderella story starring Julia Stiles.

HOW THIS MOVIE HELPS

Chances are, you're not going to suddenly find out that your real father is a handsome, rich Brit who practically lives in a castle and is dying to get to know you better. Yet anyone can identify with a main character who wants equal parts approval from her family and the freedom to be herself. How do you manage to walk that formidable tightrope? It's different for everyone, but we'll agree with the title—it is what a girl wants.

What's Eating Gilbert Grape

MOOD CONTROL

1	2	3
4	5	6
7	8	9
10	11	12

▶ Press PLAY if you're feeling:

1 ADVENTUROUS
2 Ambitious
3 Artsy
4 Cynical
5 DEPRESSED
6 Heartbroken
7 Hopeful
8 Insecure
9 MISUNDERSTOOD
10 Overwhelmed
11 Playful
12 Weird

1993 **ULTIMATE GIRL RATING:** 🌸 🌸 🌸

DIRECTOR: Lasse Hallström,
BIRTHPLACE: Mainstream
Hollywood, Indie Heart
FILE UNDER:
Hidden Depp-th
RATED: PG-13

STARRING: Johnny Depp,
Leonardo DiCaprio, Juliette
Lewis, Mary Steenburgen,
Darlene Cates, Laura
Harrington, Mary Kate
Schellhardt, Kevin Tighe

THE PROBLEM

Everybody's family is kind of strange. We can all agree on that. But is your family strange in a way that makes it stick out like a sore thumb? Misery loves company. How cool would it be to have Johnny Depp and Leo DiCaprio in your support group? We thought so.

The Reel Deal: Gilbert Grape (Johnny Depp) lives in Endora, Iowa—population: not much—with his mother and three siblings. He works in a small grocery store, which is suddenly threatened by a large supermarket moving into town. Yet that's the only big news in a life that is depressing in a low-grade way that Gilbert hardly notices anymore. Every day is filled with taking care of people: his morbidly obese mother (Darlene Cates), who can't even leave the house anymore, and his developmentally disabled brother, Arnie (Leonardo DiCaprio), whose reckless enthusiasm for life gets him into one scrape after another. We later find out that Gilbert's mother was once quite beautiful and realize that life hasn't always been this way. In most movies, Gilbert would be some kind of rebel, fighting with everyone and trying hard to bust out of this town.

Yet his compassion for family and friends keeps him from questioning his world. He worries about the new gleaming supermarket, his Mom, Arnie, just about everyone but himself. Gilbert hums along in his funny little life, just keeping things going. Then one day an interesting girl passing through town takes a shine to him. Suddenly, Gilbert gets a glimpse of living a life beyond other people's needs.

Line That Says It All:
"Tell me what you want as fast as it comes to you."
"I want to be a good person."

Guy to Watch: Johnny Depp is the sweet, sensitive boy of our dreams, but Leo burns up the screen with acting genius.

Girl to Watch: Juliette Lewis as Becky, who seems smart, gentle, and perfect for Johnny.

Scene Worth the Rewind: When Gilbert's mom, Bonnie, finally leaves the house on a mission of love. It's heartbreaking and heartwarming.

Fun Factoid: How did they find an actress to play the very large and poignant Bonnie Grape? The casting director sought out a talk show to find some big women who might be right for the part. Darlene Cates was selected, despite her lack of acting experience. You'll see why; she's amazing in this powerful role.

Watch This One With: The Bush Twins, Chelsea Clinton, Madonna's kids.

Movies with the Same Vibe: EDWARD SCISSORHANDS, HAROLD AND MAUDE, GHOST WORLD. Also check out *Benny & Joon* (1993), another fun movie from the early Depp archives. In it, he plays a comic misfit who finds love with a pretty, mentally ill girl. She falls for Depp— how ill can she be?

HOW THIS MOVIE HELPS

Gilbert's family is sort of in a shambles, but they understand each other and stick together through some rough times. It's inspiring to watch Gilbert care about his strange family more than he cares about how they look to the outside world. It kind of reminds you that the world probably isn't judging your family that much; everybody is pretty busy trying to run their own messy lives. At the same time, GILBERT GRAPE reminds us that we just can't spend our whole lives taking care of those we love, especially at the risk of doing the right thing for our own future. If you find this a tough balancing act, you'll relate to Gilbert Grape.

White Oleander

2002   **ULTIMATE GIRL RATING:**

DIRECTOR: Peter Kosminsky   **STARRING:** Alison Lohman,
BIRTHPLACE: Michele Pfeiffer, Patrick
Mainstream Hollywood   Fugit, Renée Zellweger,
FILE UNDER: Mother Fearest   Robin Wright Penn
RATED: PG-13 (not your little
sister's PG-13)

THE PROBLEM

How do you get out from under the shadow of a larger-than-life parent? They need to believe that you're just like them to justify their own behavior. This worked well when you were little, when parents are our natural Gods, whether it's deserved or not. Yet when you get a normal perspective, you see them for what they really are: people with flaws. They are often as confused and wrong about things as other mere mortals. So now where do you go to worship?

The Reel Deal: Astrid Magnussen (Alison Lohman) grows up in sunny California, raised by her free-spirited single mother, Ingrid (Michelle Pfeiffer), from whom she inherits a spectacular beauty and artistic talent. She enjoys the privileges of a childhood where normal rules are suspended and interesting people abound. She also suffers hurt and confusion at the hands of a mother whose disinterest in the nuts and bolts of parenting is tantamount to neglect.

Things go from complicated to worse when one day Ingrid decides to kill a man she's been seeing for not putting her first. The murder makes no sense; it wasn't a serious relationship, and the crime is easily traceable back to Ingrid. Yet it gives us an idea of just how important loyalty is to her.

WHITE OLEANDER follows Astrid's dramatic journey through a series of foster homes, one more unpredictable than the next. Her odd anchor is the institution she returns to while waiting for further placement and the sweet fellow artist (played by Patrick Fugit of ALMOST FAMOUS) who works to win her trust. But even from prison, Ingrid exerts a strong pull over Astrid, playing all sorts of mind games to keep her from getting attached to anyone else. Astrid bonds with other women and radically changes her appearance, anything to try to break away from her mother. Her search for the strength and support to create her own life are at the heart of this wrenching film.

Line That Says It All: "I don't know how to express how being with someone so dangerous was the last time I felt safe."

Girl to Watch: Alison Lohman gives the performance of a lifetime. How often does an unknown get top billing over Michelle Pfeiffer and Renée Zellweger? She earns her title, and then some.

Guy to Watch: Patrick Fugit gives an affecting performance as Paul. His affection for Astrid seems all the more poignant given their awful circumstances.

How You Know It's a Movie: Everyone is *so* beautiful, and the scenery is amazing. Is this really a story of parental neglect and foster care trauma? Michelle Pfeiffer manages to make prison blues look like something out of the Tommy Hilfiger catalogue. What excuses some of the gloss is the fact that the dangerous deceptions of physical beauty are a core theme in this film: the white oleander of the title refers to the lovely, deadly flower that Ingrid uses to commit her crime.

Scene Worth the Rewind: The first long day that Astrid spends with her one truly kind foster mother is very touching. You see Astrid get a glimpse of a life that she could have had, and it borders on heartbreaking.

HOW THIS MOVIE HELPS

This film is very engaging. Whether or not it's an accurate depiction of the foster care system is a topic for another day. Yet it does make you think a lot about the price of loyalty, the family ties that bind and often chafe, and the way we judge people quickly before they have time to judge us. Your parents will probably seem really cool after spending an evening with Astrid's mom. Tell them that, and they'll probably spring for the rental.

Win a Date with Tad Hamilton!

MOOD CONTROL

1	2	3
4	5	6
7	8	9
10	11	12

▶ Press PLAY
if you're feeling:

1 Adventurous
2 Ambitious
3 Artsy
4 Cynical
5 Depressed
6 HEARTBROKEN
7 HOPEFUL
8 Insecure
9 Misunderstood
10 Overwhelmed
11 PLAYFUL
12 Weird

2004 ULTIMATE GIRL RATING: 🍿🍿🍿🍿

DIRECTOR: Robert Luketic
BIRTHPLACE: Mainstream Hollywood
FILE UNDER: Movie Stars in 3-D
RATED: PG-13

STARRING: Kate Bosworth, Topher Grace, Josh Duhamel, Nathan Lane, Sean Hayes, Gary Cole, Ginnifer Goodwin, Octavia Spencer, Amy Smart

THE PROBLEM

You have a little bit of an obsession with celebrities. Okay, maybe it's a *big* obsession. You wallpapered your bathroom with *People* magazine. You belong to five fan clubs. You lay awake at night worrying that two fictional characters who are all wrong for each another will get back together. You're so wrapped up in the comings and goings of imaginary people that you've neglected to pay much attention to the real life you're living in; you know, the one without a camera crew....

The Reel Deal: Rosalee Futch (Kate Bosworth) is a wholesome, quirky girl living in West Virginia with her dad (Gary Cole) and working at the Piggly Wiggly supermarket with her two best friends, store manager Pete (Topher Grace) and Cathy (Ginnifer Goodwin). The three friends grew up together and now spend their days working at the market and their nights tossing back beers and throwing darts. Pete has finally saved enough money to go to college and secretly plans to ask Rosalee to go away with him. One look at his face tells you that he has loved her forever.

Rosalee's romantic dreams, meanwhile, are fixated on a Hollywood icon, the dashing Tad Hamilton (Josh Duhamel). Tad's heroic movie characters convince Rosalee that he's her dream man, and when a contest to date him appears on the Internet, she enters with high hopes. Oddly enough, those hopes were not too high. Rosalee flies out to L.A. and has her date with the big man himself, an event that's portrayed as being every bit as weird and awkward as it would be in real life.

Tad finds Rosalee to be lovely and charming, but she really registers with him when she gently rebuffs his standard advances. Rosalee's strong sense of her own values is exactly what the free-wheeling movie star feels is missing from his own life, and he suddenly starts viewing her as the Fountain of Truth. His impulsive pursuit of Rosalee, and Pete's pained efforts to compete with such a suitor, forms the core of this sweet David-and-Goliath romantic comedy.

Line That Says It All: "Everyone is Tad Hamilton to somebody."

Girl to Watch: Kate Bosworth really pulls off the role of Rosalee. Gorgeous isn't hard for an already attractive actress, but she also had to come across as naïve yet smart, quirky yet universally appealing.

Guy to Watch: We have to send bouquets to both Topher Grace as Pete and Josh Duhamel as Tad, with the slight edge going to Josh.

Scene Worth the Rewind: Rosalee's arrival in Los Angeles is great, starting with the hilarious sight gags she spies from her airport limo. We love the whole dinner with Tad, the fact that it plays much like how that sort of evening would feel—fun one minute, artificial the next.

Watch This One With: Your celebrity-obsessed friends.

Movies with the Same Vibe: GET OVER IT, THE WEDDING SINGER.

HOW THIS MOVIE HELPS

WIN A DATE WITH TAD HAMILTON! might only fuel your celebrity fantasies, but it helps to remember that that girl is a movie star herself, and that this is a movie. Sorry to harsh your buzz. The next best thing might be to look around your own town for a casting call; surely there's a guy as dreamy as Tad to sigh over, another as caring as Pete to under-appreciate. So get out there and live dramatically.

Index

Acknowledgments

How do you write a movie guide that teens (and former teens) might really want to use? First of all, you talk to enough women of all ages to fill every seat in a multiplex. I can't imagine writing this book without the help of dozens and dozens of Ultimate Girls. They offered up lists of favorite movies, favorite moments, and smart thoughts on how big issues are addressed on the big screen. You spoke, I wrote, we made it together. Thank you.

A giant tub of buttered popcorn to the always-fun folks at Quirk Packaging who sent this one down the aisle: Sharyn Rosart, Lynne Yeamans, freelance editor Betsey Beier, and the ever-patient Sarah Scheffel. Jamie Bennett's clever art brought life to all these stories. Elizabeth Bracken at Simon & Schuster blessed this project with enthusiasm and great ideas. Finally, a jumbo box of Raisinettes to my sister Martha, a lover of movies filled with joy and adventure—movies a lot like her.

Meet the Author

Andrea Cornell Sarvady is the author of *The Modern Neurosis Handbook: A Guide to Coping*. She is also a die-hard movie buff, having learned at an early age that two hours in a theater watching the challenges of someone else's life sure beats two hours of stressing about your own. She has worked as a counselor for teens in both San Francisco and New York, where using movies to talk about feelings first occurred to her. Her favorite teen movie is *Harold and Maude*, mainly because she grew up just down the road from where the movie was made. Film courses exposed her to the meaning of camera angles and casting choices, but she never truly solved the mystery of why Johnny Depp always looks so tragic in films when, let's face it, he's a total babe.

Meet the Illustrator

Jamie Bennett has been an illustrator for more than twenty years. Her work has been featured in many notable publications, including *The New Yorker*, *Teen*, and *Lucky* magazines, and in several art shows. When she is not working for magazines, advertising agencies, or web sites, animation studios or book publishers, she likes to catch a movie. She lives in Toronto with her husband Alex, son Felix, and a husky named Hobo.

Printed in the United States
By Bookmasters